Innovative Behavioral Healthcare for Older Adults

Paula E. Hartman-Stein, Editor

Foreword by Tom Sawyer,
U.S. House of Representatives

Innovative Behavioral Healthcare for Older Adults

A Guidebook for Changing Times

Jossey-Bass Publishers • San Francisco

Substantial discounts on bulk quantities of Jossey-Bass books are available to corporations, professional associations, and other organizations. For details and discount information, contact the special sales department at Jossey-Bass Inc., Publishers (415) 433–1740; Fax (800) 605–2665.

For sales outside the United States, please contact your local Simon & Schuster International Office.

Jossey-Bass Web address: http://www.josseybass.com

 Manufactured in the United States of America on Lyons Falls Turin Book. This paper is acid-free and 100 percent totally chlorine-free.

Library of Congress Cataloging-in-Publication Data

Innovative behavioral healthcare for older adults : a guidebook for changing times / Paula E. Hartman-Stein, editor.
    p. cm.
    Includes index.
    ISBN 0-7879-0963-7
    1. Aged—Mental health services—United States.   I. Hartman-Stein, Paula E., date.
    RC451.4.A5154 1997
    362.2' 084' 60973—dc21   97-14981

FIRST EDITION
HB Printing   10 9 8 7 6 5 4 3 2 1

Contents

Foreword

This increase in the life span and in the numbers of
our senior citizens presents this Nation with
increased opportunities: the opportunity to draw
upon their skill and sagacity—and the opportunity
to provide the respect and recognition they have
earned. It is not enough for a great nation merely
to have added new years to life—our objective
must also be to add new life to those years.
—*President John F. Kennedy, special message to Congress on
the needs of the nation's senior citizens, February 21, 1963*[1]

It's become a journalistic commonplace: "In the next fifteen years,
as the baby boomers begin to retire . . ." Or words to that effect.

Throughout the mid-1990s, every editorial writer worth the
title has written about the enormous demographic shifts the nation
faces and their consequences for policy and practice. They are right
to arouse deep interest and concern. The aging of America will
shape all of our lives for the foreseeable future, in some ways we can
anticipate and in others we haven't yet clearly understood.

The elderly, once considered the remnant of an earlier generation, are already the fastest-growing fraction of the American pop-
ulace, years before the baby boomers' arrival at senior-citizen status.
Healthier and more vigorous today than most of their own elders,
they already bring a new set of life-planning presumptions whose
impact will last longer than those of any previous generation. And

the behavioral consequences of longer life will help define the character of those extended years.

Indeed, in traditional terms, the elderly are no longer a single generation at all. Rather, they include elders, living active, constructive postretirement lives, and the eldest, living out their end years at an older age and in larger numbers than ever before. This is not a bad thing in itself. In fact, it is a good thing. That is sometimes hard to remember in a time when we define eras by the crises they comprise.

Nonetheless, this demographic sea change will require Americans of every age, and in all of our capacities, to rethink the architecture of our lives and the public policy environment in which we make personal decisions. Nowhere is that need greater or more immediate than in the unstable territory of the broad healthcare landscape.

Much has already been done, of course, especially in meeting the altered needs of geriatric care. However, debate rages on in the financing, coverage, and delivery of healthcare for Americans of all ages. Issues of access, quality, and accountability are in conflict with questions of cost. And the most quarrelsome divisions of all have arisen at those points where these issues intersect with the widening importance of behavioral healthcare and mental health services in general.

The juncture between these life-span and healthcare issues is the fertile ground explored in this book, a widely useful treatment of the practices, programs, and policy that are evolving in geriatric behavioral care. Paula Hartman-Stein is both a scholar and a practitioner in this multidisciplinary setting. She and her collaborators focus needed attention on the many facets of caring for older adults, addressing the pressures and expectations that they and their families face in a time of transition. From best practices to model programs in an unfolding business to legal considerations, Hartman-Stein and a diverse team of professionals explore the clinical and organizational terrain underlying the headline issues of funding, eligibility, and need and transcending the partisan and generational divisions that too often characterize public discourse on healthcare and older populations.

Innovative Behavioral Healthcare for Older Adults: A Guidebook for Changing Times is an important and timely contribution to the work of practitioners and policymakers alike. It will broaden the perspective of all who are concerned about preventive care and about the integrated delivery of physical and behavioral healthcare as an affordable entitlement for larger, longer-lived future generations. This book will deepen the understanding of lay observers who write about these questions and shape public perceptions of this complex debate.

Perhaps most important of all, at a time when we are realizing the dream of adding new and productive years to all of our lives, we may actually achieve the objective of adding new life to those years. This work will help us reach that goal.

Washington, D.C.   TOM SAWYER
August 1997   U.S. House of Representatives

To the three most important men in my life: my father, a man of great generosity and gritty perseverance who exemplifies the best of the older generation; my husband, a baby boomer with a nurturing soul and a strong sense of fairness; and my son, a reason to make the future better

Preface

As the millennium approaches, a crisis for behavioral healthcare looms on the horizon. More and more individuals are reaching the age of Medicare eligibility, and the absolute number of older adults is also rising. With this change in demographics comes greater demand for such behavioral services as evaluation for cognitive and mood disturbance, psychotherapy, behavior-management consultation, and caregiver-support services. For example, the baby boomers view the need for psychological help as less of a stigma than earlier generations do. They are requesting counseling and other behavioral services not just for themselves but also for their aging parents, as when they seek information about their parents' functional and memory skills in order to ensure the best living arrangements for their parents. In the year 2011, the baby boomers themselves will begin reaching Medicare eligibility—right at the point when, according to economists' predictions, the Medicare system will become insolvent.

Individual consumers are not the only ones increasing the demand for behavioral expertise and services: so are institutions within the long-term care industry. For example, federal law is putting nursing homes under greater pressure to provide psychological intervention for the behavioral problems of residents with dementia, as opposed to using physical restraints or medication as their front line in treatment planning.

At the same time as the population of older adults is increasing, large numbers of mental health clinicians are becoming Medicare providers. Why the burgeoning interest in working with older adults? One critical reason is economic: clinicians who have not previously applied for membership on insurance panels, or who have fewer than five years' experience as licensed practitioners, rarely can become providers for managed-care programs, which means that many practitioners simply cannot earn a living in a private practice setting. Entrepreneurs have turned this limitation into an opportunity by forming companies that provide mental health services to long-term-care facilities, an arrangement that gives them access to groups of older adults as potential clients. In this field, traditional fee-for-service Medicare has become the final frontier of independent practice!

One result has been new problems. Although more frail older adults than ever before are receiving behavioral services for mental disorders, some observers have questioned the need for the care being delivered. The companies that hire therapists to work in nursing homes frequently place pressure on their clinicians to produce billable hours. Insurance carriers for Medicare are beginning to require documentation of treatment plans from providers, but in the recent past services that did not meet the requirement of medical necessity were easily rendered under fee-for-service Medicare. A controversial study conducted by the Department of Health and Human Services of 1993 records in nursing homes in five states suggested that $17 million of Medicare payments yearly were paid for unnecessary behavioral services.[1] Observers have also questioned the quality of these behavioral services, given that many of the clinicians who practice in nursing homes have little or no training or expertise in geriatric mental health.

One way of controlling the cost of Medicare's mental health services is to use the same methods that prevail in the private insurance sector: limit services, limit the number of providers, and "carve out" mental health from delivery of medical services. Service-limitation rules common in private sector health maintenance organizations (HMOs) include the disallowing of payment for cognitive evaluation, the authorizing of psychotherapy primarily for crisis management and stabilization, and the disallowing of any psy-

chotherapeutic services for individuals with a diagnosis of dementia. These service restrictions do not serve the individual older
adult well—nor, in the long run, do they save healthcare dollars.

The $64,000+ question is this: What changes are necessary in
the healthcare system so that the behavioral needs of elderly consumers can be reasonably met? This volume addresses solutions to
the problem of delivering behavioral services to older adults without losing sight of the need to maintain high-quality service while
reducing costs.

A Personal Perspective

For more than twelve years I worked as a hospital-based clinical
psychologist, specializing in health psychology with additional
training in geropsychology. In 1994 I left the hospital's employ to
found the Center for Healthy Aging, a multidisciplinary practice
whose mission is to help older adults and their families cope with
the transitions of aging. We provide not only neuropsychological
assessment and therapy services but also programs promoting the
concept of healthy, productive aging. My staff offers seminars on
such topics as memory enhancement, coping with grief, managing
chronic pain through massage therapy, preventing caregiver
burnout, and similar themes. We offer care-management services,
that is, education and support for sons and daughters who need
help selecting and overseeing community resources for their frail
parents. In addition, we provide consultation and training to continuing-care retirement communities and home-healthcare agencies.

Although the demand for these services is increasing, the
financial management of this service-based business is very difficult.
Changes in the healthcare-delivery system (for example, Medicare
beneficiaries joining HMOs), fluctuating regulations in the
Medicare system, and attitudes of older adults toward paying for
psychological care present real barriers. I am of necessity developing ways of practicing in a more cost-effective manner and plan-

ning for new methods of gaining access to pools of potential clients.

My motivation in editing this book was twofold. One motive was to learn cutting-edge methods of conducting business in the changing marketplace. The other, more important motive was to play a modest role in shaping the future of behavioral practice with older adults, emphasizing the need for quality care, integration of services, and cost-efficiency. To accomplish this ambitious, overwhelming task, I chose contributors for this volume who have varied backgrounds, who are pragmatic in approach, and who demonstrate careful, critical thinking about the future of practice.

Audience for This Book

Too many providers bemoan the changes in the healthcare marketplace without offering viable alternatives; this book is a proactive attempt to promote ideas and dialogue between clinicians and those with the power to institute changes in how behavioral care is delivered to older adults. Highlighting changes in methods of behavioral practice, as well as new roles for expert clinical geropsychologists in the context of an increasingly managed Medicare, the book is addressed to a varied audience: frontline practitioners, both experienced and novice; insurance executives who interpret Medicare regulations while managing and designing benefit structures; and legislators who are interested in revamping the Medicare regulations.

Overview of the Contents

The chapters in this volume are grouped to follow three areas of discussion. The first group, Chapters One through Three, focuses on the big picture, describing large-scale model programs that integrate psychosocial and physical care of older adults. The second group, Chapters Four through Seven, offers practical recommendations that clinicians can implement now. The third group, Chapters Eight through Ten, addresses issues for the future—such topics as therapies requiring less face-to-face contact with clients, new roles for clinicians in long-term care, changes in future marketing strategies, and legal issues involved in providing services to HMOs under Medicare.

Chapter One, by Nicholas A. Cummings, leads off the book by discussing the prevention of behavioral health problems and describing outreach programs to help two groups of vulnerable older adults: grieving spouses, and caregivers of people with Alzheimer's disease. With his usual eloquent style and candor, Cummings presents never-before-published outcome data that illustrate how prevention programs save future healthcare dollars.

In Chapter Two, a team from the Health Care Financing Administration—Stefan N. Miller, Nancy A. Miller, Elizabeth Mauser, and Kate O'Malley—describe the state-of-the-art Program of All-Inclusive Care for the Elderly (PACE), which integrates medical and behavioral care for frail older adults. By providing a wide range of social-support services, PACE helps older adults who meet the criteria for admission to nursing homes stay in community settings. The authors also present new data on the long-term cost benefits of this program.

In Chapter Three, James M. Georgoulakis compares the U.S. healthcare system with the Canadian healthcare system in terms of mental health services for older adults. He describes the underlying values and cultural underpinnings of the Canadian model, suggesting several lessons that the American system can learn from its northern neighbor.

The second section begins with Deborah W. Frazer's insightful contribution in Chapter Four, which deals with outcome measurements for tracking cognitive changes in older adults and evaluating the efficacy of psychotherapy with this group. Frazer points out that simplistic, global outcome measures, typically requested by traditional medical models and managed-care programs, offer no possibility of measuring therapeutic changes that are pertinent to adults in late life. She skillfully articulates the complexity of choosing outcome measures that capture quality-of-life goals, and she offers practical recommendations for clinicians and managed-care executives.

In Chapter Five, Peter A. Lichtenberg illustrates why managed-care programs need to include neuropsychological evaluation of older adults whose presenting problems have to do with memory and other cognitive functions. He describes the circumstances in which such evaluation is critical to planning for long-term care. He also presents pragmatic guidelines for a cost-conscious battery of tests that clinicians can use in the managed-care environment.

Chapter Six, by the psychology team of Thomas M. Meuser, Martha W. Clower, and Edgardo Padin-Rivera, emphasizes the cost-effectiveness and clinical efficacy of group psychotherapeutic treatment for older adults. The chapter highlights group interventions that treat such conditions as posttraumatic stress disorder, complicated grief, and other depressive disorders. The authors also describe innovative programs for demented older adults that enhance socialization and cognitive stimulation.

Forrest Scogin, in Chapter Seven, reviews the efficacy of a form of adjunctive, minimal-contact therapy known as *bibliotherapy* for depressed older adults. Scogin gives case examples showing how bibliotherapy can be used in treatment settings, and he speculates on when its use may be appropriate in a variety of managed-care systems, including capitation models of healthcare delivery. From an ethical perspective, he also cautions against its widespread use in the treatment of specific clinical problems.

The third section begins with Chapter Eight, by the long-term-care consultant team of Gael Gabrielle Smookler Jarrett, Stephen Jarrett Smookler, James J. Riemenschneider, and Thomas A. Riemenschneider. The authors outline ways for mental health professionals to position themselves in the environment of long-term care, which is increasingly subject to the practices of managed care. They describe a model collaborative effort being piloted in central Ohio, and they illustrate opportunities for behavioral providers to find new consulting and clinical niches.

In Chapter Nine, healthcare attorney David A. Weil II discusses issues of legal liability that mental health practitioners need to understand when they sign on to be providers in Medicare programs associated with HMOs. He highlights the practitioner's role in cost control, common potential liabilities in managed-care settings, and the obligations and risks of providers. He also gives practical recommendations on such issues as informed consent and denial of payment for claims.

In Chapter Ten, Marina Ergun and I describe present and future marketing opportunities in the specialized area of geriatric behavioral care. We present real-life examples of problems and pitfalls encountered in this ever-changing area of behavioral practice. We illustrate guidelines for marketing, and we describe innovative roles and services, outside traditional Medicare, that open up creative opportunities for clinicians.

Acknowledgments

The process of conceptualizing, writing, and editing this book has been a bit like planning for and delivering a baby. The project, which lasted ten months, was filled with lots of work, loss of sleep, growing pains, and moments of sheer joy. The big difference is that many people collaborated in this endeavor, making it not just bearable but also fun. Many thanks go first to the contributors, a varied group of experts who accepted suggestions well and were willing to revise their chapters several times to produce a cohesive volume. Not only did I appreciate their willingness to discuss and debate their viewpoints, I also enjoyed the friendships we strengthened or developed through working together.

Sincere thanks to Congressman Tom Sawyer for his thoughtful and poetic lead-in to the volume, highlighting the changing demography of this country.

I appreciate Nick Cummings's wit and reassuring wisdom, which helped to encourage me throughout this process as well as shape and clarify my thoughts at several difficult junctures.

Sincere words of heartfelt gratitude go out to Jim Georgoulakis, who finished his chapter even through a time of great personal tragedy and loss. Thank you so much, Jim.

This book would not be a reality without the invitation from Alan Rinzler, senior editor for Jossey-Bass. The initial idea was his, and for about one year he was incredibly persistent in his efforts to convince me to accept the challenge of what seemed an impossible task. Thanks, Alan, for your confidence and belief in this project.

I want to especially mention and thank Katie Levine, developmental editor at Jossey-Bass, whose role seemed to be that of literary midwife. She not only edited each page to make the book more readable but also encouraged, guided, and communicated with me every step of the way.

Thanks are in order to Carolyn Smith, my office manager, who was both personally supportive and instrumental in organizing various phases of the project.

The person who has most shaped my development as a psychologist and critical thinker about health reform is Jeanette Reuter, a mentor and close friend. She will find sprinklings of her influence throughout my writing.

Many of the guidelines presented in this volume come from direct experiences with older adult clients who have taught me about aging, coping with hardship, and recognizing what is important in life. Thanks go to my clients at the Center for Healthy Aging, as well as to the residents of Sumner on Merriman and Rockynol retirement communities.

Special thanks to my parents, Pauline and Ed Yurkovich, who have taught me firsthand about the value of working hard and sticking with a project. They are wonderful role models for keeping active and emotionally hardy as we age.

On the other end of the age spectrum, I want to thank my eight-year-old son, Eric, who was understanding of my long weekend work hours and took pride in his mom's writing.

Last, and most important, thanks to my husband, Rob. I am grateful for his support, encouragement, and love, which ultimately made this volume possible.

Akron, Ohio   PAULA E. HARTMAN-STEIN
September 1997

Innovative Behavioral Healthcare for Older Adults

Chapter One

Approaches to Preventive Care

Nicholas A. Cummings

For decades the conventional wisdom in healthcare held that older adults did not and would not avail themselves of mental health services. This seemed to be supported by the facts: in health plans where psychotherapy was a covered benefit, seldom did the use of the benefit by those over the age of sixty-five even approach .05 percent, whereas it would be several times that in the younger population. And if the senior patient did see a psychotherapist, he or she was unlikely to return after one or two visits. Now mental health treatment is one of the fastest-growing services in Medicare. What changed?

Meeting the Needs of Older Adults

During the era of the prevailing, and now outmoded, attitudes among behavioral health practitioners, no one bothered to ask if the mental health services offered were relevant to the needs of our senior patients. For this population, intensive long-term therapy might well exceed the life span of the patient.

Furthermore, the many issues bringing most patients to psychotherapy (marriage, divorce, parenting, career, job loss, relationships, and so on) are not the usual issues that plague one in later life (loneliness, retirement, widowhood, bereavement, alienation, chronic illness, disability of a spouse or oneself, terminal illness). Interestingly, issues revolving around one's own death are not paramount; rather, these seem to be the preoccupation of the middle and involutional years (forty-five to fifty-five), when one worries

1

that there is no longer sufficient time to accomplish things that need to be done. With older adults, feelings of being unwanted or no longer useful are intense. An almost universal and telltale complaint is the following: "When I am out in public, younger people just look right through me and never notice me."

When the issues of concern to the elderly, like feeling unwanted, are reflected in behavioral programs, that population's use exceeds even that of our younger patients. The erroneous belief that the elderly do not avail themselves of psychotherapy is forever dispelled in favor of the following truism: the elderly do not avail themselves of *traditional* (irrelevant) psychotherapeutic services.

In this chapter I describe a pioneering program, which was instrumental in this paradigm shift. My hope is to show that an extensive array of psychotherapeutic programs tailored to the elderly is not only effective in meeting the intense psychological problems of this population but is also cost-efficient and saves money in the long run by reducing the unnecessary use of medical services, to which the senior patient turns when feeling lonely, depressed, sad, or unwanted.

It would seem, from looking at the needs and fears of older adults, that the thrust should be that of preventive behavioral health services. These would address the tensions, stresses, and depressions resulting from the realities of this stage of life. Several such programs will be described, with the emphasis on a proven program that prevents the sudden and often debilitating increase of physical symptoms among surviving spouses after the death of one member of a long-term marriage.

A Model for Success

In 1988 the Humana Health Plan entered into a relationship with Medicare in which Humana was permitted to solicit an eligible population that agreed to receive healthcare exclusively through the Humana Health Plan. The inducement for Medicare recipients to do this was a much expanded benefits plan, including far more extensive mental health services than were otherwise extant. The setting was the East Coast of Florida, extending from just south of Miami, in Brower County, through Brevard County to the north and to West Palm Beach and environs. Although this geographic area was about one hundred miles from north to south, it was only a few miles wide.

This geographical "string bean" is immediately recognized as one of the nation's prime retirement zones, populated by senior citizens originally from such northeastern states as New York, New Jersey, Massachusetts, and Pennsylvania. (Although these demarcations are showing signs of changing, retirees from the Midwest are more likely to settle on the West, or Gulf, Coast of Florida, where in 1988 Humana did not have a Medicare contract.) Because of the density of retirees, within a few weeks Humana had a cohort of 140,000 Medicare patients who had assigned their eligibility to that health plan.

The Humana Health Plan entered into a subcontract with American Biodyne (now Merit Behavioral Care Systems) to provide the mental health/chemical dependency portion of the healthcare. Such an arrangement by a health plan with an independent behavioral healthcare company is known as a *carve-out*. In pricing its portion of the treatment costs, American Biodyne predicated its capitation rate on an aggressively increased annual penetration level, through outreach and provision of relevant services, to at least 5 percent or 6 percent of the total population. Surprisingly, the outreach and offered services were so successful in attracting these older adults that the penetration exceeded 10 percent. This initially placed a financial strain on the provider, but eventually the services proved remarkably cost-effective. The early financial crisis also increased the incentive for American Biodyne to appropriately tailor and streamline services to older adults.

Before the awarding of the Medicare contract to Humana, American Biodyne had created a series of staff-model behavioral care centers to service several hundred thousand employed subscribers who were carved out by Humana and other health plans. The 140,000 Medicare recipients were immediately absorbed into this system, which meant that the American Biodyne centers were within thirty minutes of one's home or office under normal driving conditions. Special transportation arrangements were made for the older adults who either did not drive or found driving difficult.

Although the programs for older adults were found in varying degrees of refinement throughout the system, the results described in this chapter are based on one American Biodyne center serving 22,000 older adults, where tracking systems and other information between Humana and American Biodyne were put in place so that the study could be conducted with accuracy and precision.

Two programs at this center will be described here: the program for bereavement outreach and counseling, which yielded impressive results; and the counseling program for spouses and families of patients with early-stage Alzheimer's dementia, a program that also included counseling for the early-Alzheimer's patients themselves.

The Bereavement Program

Bereavement is a major issue in later life. With a mortality rate of about 5 percent, these 140,000 older adults yielded nearly twenty widows or widowers per day. The center in which this study was conducted had to contend with an average of three per day, or more than twenty per week. Of all the patients seen in this center, from childhood through older adulthood, 8 percent of the total were recently widowed. Such a volume clearly called for aggressive and immediate outreach, with early intervention.

Creating a System of Outreach

The method in place, for financial and capitation reasons, to keep the health plan and subsequently the federal government informed of enrollees' deaths was much too slow to accommodate an early-intervention program. To speed this process, a form was created for immediate reporting, with the incentive of a promise of early reimbursement to the physician or hospital caring for the patient at the time of the patient's death. After glitches and resistances were overcome, this new system enabled the center to contact enrollees within two to three weeks of widowhood.

Once the center received the pertinent information, the surviving spouse was routinely assigned to one of the psychotherapists (an M.S.W. or a Ph.D. psychologist) for telephone outreach. The call followed a well-tested protocol and was sensitively conducted, ending with an offer to the patient to come to the center for help with his or her mourning. About 7 percent of the widowed enrollees had returned or were about to return to their states of origin to be with relatives and so were not available. Another 16 percent consistently expressed either reluctance or inability to come to the center, and a house call was offered. After the house call was made, this procedure yielded about half of those who had expressed initial reluctance. Throughout the year of the study, the outreach was successful in bringing about 85 percent of the surviving spouses into the Bereavement Program. This success rate reflects both the acute need of these patients for help and understanding and the compliance and respect for the doctor that is so characteristic of older Americans.

Screening: Depression Versus Mourning

Unlike mourning, which is nature's healing process, designed to enable a survivor to go on with life, depression can produce lasting, detrimental pain. In depression there are unresolved psychological issues in the relationship with the deceased, which lead to introjected rage. The repressed anger hides the true object of the unresolved hostility (the deceased spouse), and only a feeling of one's own worthlessness is expressed. Reactive depression prevents or drastically interferes with the work of mourning and results in protracted sadness, sometimes for many years after the death.

About one in five widowed patients predominantly demonstrates depression rather than mourning and is seen individually for the treatment of reactive depression. The four in five who clearly show mourning are referred to the Bereavement Program. The screening involves one individual session (occasionally two, in difficult cases) with the psychotherapist who will be conducting the Bereavement Program. The following two cases describe two very different survivors:

> Elaine, recently widowed at the age of sixty-nine from her seventy-six-year-old husband of forty-seven years, spent a great deal of her time crying and resisted being with concerned friends who were attempting to cheer her up. Throughout her marriage she had complained about her husband's fanatic interest in photography and how it had ruined many vacations because taking pictures interfered with having fun. Now she had taken up photography herself in an unconscious attempt (commonly seen) to keep her husband with her. In the evenings she was certain at times that she heard her husband's footsteps coming down the hall, only to be disappointed and plunge into sobbing. She was appropriately diagnosed as deep in bereavement and was referred to the Bereavement Counseling Program, where she did well.
>
> Arnold, a widower of seventy-two, was erroneously placed in the Bereavement Counseling Program, where his behavior became more apparent as that of depression. He was constantly self-deprecating and tearful, and instead of feeling the expected sadness at the loss, he berated himself for not having been nicer to his deceased wife before she died. His rage at himself clinically resembled a disguised rage at her, and the psychotherapist removed him from bereavement counseling and began individual psychotherapy for reactive depression. It became apparent that Arnold had severe unresolved issues with his wife, which had begun fifteen years before, when he became impotent after surgical removal of his prostate gland and later discovered that his wife was having an affair with his business partner. Arnold had repressed his rage at his deceased wife (not an uncommon defense mechanism after the death of the spouse) and had also hidden his own suicidal plan from

himself. Arnold was in what suicidologists call "automatic pilot," rushing toward suicide without conscious awareness. With appropriate referral for depression therapy rather than bereavement counseling, Arnold's life was spared.

How the Program Works

With five to eight mourners in each group (the number depends on the patient traffic), sessions are two hours each, with a total of fourteen sessions spaced as follows: four semiweekly sessions followed by six weekly sessions and then by four concluding sessions, held monthly. Accordingly, the program lasts six and one-half months. After completing the program, a patient can ask to repeat it, and about 15 percent of patients do. When a group member has already gone through the program, his or her participation enhances the experience for the other patients because the repeater assumes the role of quasi-cotherapist, which is also helpful to the repeating member. Women tend to outlive men, and so the groups are consistently made up of at least 75 percent women. This does not appear to deter men from participating: men seem to have even greater difficulty with widowhood than women do.

The program is psychoeducational in nature, imparting information about the process of mourning, encouraging patients to experience it, and providing relaxation and imagery techniques to help them over the most stressful period. A "buddy system" is established, with patients paired off for mutual support and accessibility, as needed. The patients do frequently call each other and talk by phone; some meet to talk in person. Both kinds of communication are encouraged.

In the not unusual event that a physician has prescribed antidepressant drugs or sleeping pills, the program recommends that patients discontinue them or at least use them only sparingly. Again, in keeping with our expectations of a generation that is conservative about medication and respectful of the doctor, most patients completely discontinue their medication, and the others reduce their intake to nearly zero.

Patients are also encouraged to read from a carefully selected group of titles. When a mourner does begin to show interest in reading these materials, it is a definite sign of progress in treatment. The overall objectives of the program are as follows:

- *Self-efficacy,* as conceived by Albert Bandura and his colleagues at Stanford University:[1] Self-confidence is increased by the performance of tasks that were part of a lifetime before ability was overwhelmed by feelings of bereavement. In the beginning, this step may involve basic grooming and eating. The tasks are gradually expanded until normal, prebereavement activities are resumed.

- Defeating *learned helplessness,* as described by Seligman:[2] Heretofore self-reliant persons are now plunged into learned helplessness by their overwhelming feelings, and by the destructive advice of well-meaning relatives and friends who either accept and encourage their helplessness or do the opposite and expect too much of them, thus convincing them that they are indeed helpless.

- Restoring a *sense of coherence* or meaning to actions and eventually to life, as described by Antonovsky:[3] Although the sessions cover specific materials, tasks, and information, there is ample opportunity for patients to participate, express feelings and attitudes, and seek help in addition to helping their fellow patients. Homework is assigned to each patient after each session, and it involves exercises in relaxation and imagery, permission to cry, visiting the grave of the deceased, doing assigned reading, and so forth. Grooming, proper eating, and other daily activities are consistently part of the homework. The encouragement of fellow patients is far more meaningful than the approval of the therapist, although the therapist's approval is also a necessary ingredient.

Bereavement and Use of Medical Services

It has long been observed that widowed persons manifest a sharp increase in physical symptoms, which necessitate frequent visits to the physician. This characteristic usually lasts one to two years following the death of the spouse, but it can sometimes persist beyond that time. It is not unusual for the surviving spouse to experience symptoms resembling those of the condition from which the deceased suffered, such as heart disease, cancer, and emphysema.

The medical care utilization of 323 patients who participated in the Bereavement Program was contrasted with that of a group of 278 widowed patients from an adjacent population of older adults whom American Biodyne had not yet brought into the program for bereavement outreach and intervention. Demographically, these 278 contrast-group members were identical to the 323 patients in the Bereavement Program. Twenty-six of the contrast group, however, had received psychotherapeutic services other than the formal Bereavement Program, and although this is a contaminant, if anything it should have militated against the dramatic results that were elicited.

The medical care utilization of each of the two groups was determined by way of a straightforward tabulation of all visits to physicians and emergency rooms; all outpatient procedures; use of all laboratory tests, X rays, and other imaging devices; and all prescriptions issued. For all patients there was a calculation for the 365 days immediately preceding the death of the spouse, for the first 365 days immediately following the death, and for the 365 days constituting the second year after the death. The results by averages for each group and each period are shown in Figure 1.1.

Both the Bereavement Program group and the contrast group reveal a somewhat low rate of medical care utilization for this age group in the year preceding the death of the spouse. This result probably reflects the surviving spouse's preoccupation with the dying spouse's illness, as well as the surviving spouse's attending to the needs of the terminally ill spouse, with a corresponding

Figure 1.1. Average Medical Care Utilization, in Dollars, for Two Widowed Groups Before and After the Spouse's Death.

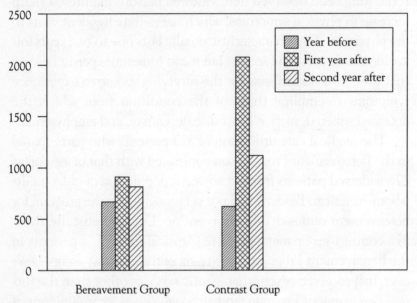

Note: Amounts are in 1982–1992 dollars.

subordination of his or her own medical needs. After the death of the spouse, the medical care utilization of the Bereavement Program group rises somewhat higher than would be expected of this age group, but then it declines in the second year after the death. The contrast group demonstrates a sharp increase in medical care utilization in the first year after the spouse's death, an increase more than twice that seen in the Bereavement Program group for the same period. Although average medical care utilization for the contrast group is considerably reduced in the second year, it remains 40 percent higher than in the Bereavement Program group.

The Bereavement Program was dramatically effective in preventing a surge in medical care utilization for an older adult population during the two years after the death of a spouse. The investment in behavioral care, focused on the needs of mourners and targeted to that population, is minuscule by comparison with the impressive savings in costs for medical services: the program's 14 sessions, doubled to account for the two-hour length and then divided by six (the average number of group participants), are the equivalent of 4.3 individual sessions for each patient treated; for the two years, the amount saved is $1,400 per patient. This amount, extrapolated to the general elderly population covered by this health plan alone, translates to several million dollars. Even more important, however, the program spares these widowed older adults two years of avoidable suffering from physical symptoms and ill health.

The Early-Alzheimer's Counseling Program

The other very successful program conducted by American Bio-dyne was focused on the caretakers of patients with early Alzheimer's dementia and on the patients themselves. It has been noted for some time that the hardship imposed on the caretakers of Alzheimer's patients results in an increased rate of illness among the spouses or adult children caring for a person with this dementia. The stress increases with both the length of the caretaking and the severity of the dementia, which is progressive and most often unpredictable. Some medical authorities suspect that the immune system of the caretaker is compromised by the constant and often mounting stress, and that this is reflected in a steady increase in the caretaker's use of medical services. It is not unusual for an Alzheimer's patient to live ten years after diagnosis, and some suffer for as long as twenty years. During this time, the caretaker is subjected to an ever-diminishing affectionate response from the patient, until the patient loses the ability even to recognize his or her spouse, daughter, or son. This feature of the dementia, which leaves the patient incapable of displaying the slightest bit of gratitude, places almost unbearable stress on the caretaker.

The early-Alzheimer's patient also experiences stress. Frequently disoriented when away from home, he or she soon experiences a characteristic "catastrophic emotional response" upon becoming disoriented in familiar surroundings. This response occurs before the dementia has damaged ego function; the patient is devastated by the experience and becomes frightened that it will recur. Reluctance to leave home, with a corresponding narrowing of life space, brings early stress and unhappiness both to the patient and to the nonafflicted spouse, who wishes to maintain the couple's previous lifestyle.

In a pilot project, the counseling of early-Alzheimer's patients and their caretakers reduced the use of medical facilities (in the form of visits to emergency rooms and reliance on clinics where appointments were not needed). The typical reaction of relatives and patients alike to the unpredictable, often baffling, but always frightening early symptoms of this dementia is to seek immediate medical help. The counseling program, by imparting information that anticipates the sporadic intrusion of brief episodes of disorientation into an otherwise normal life, and by teaching ways to handle such episodes, has brought about a dramatic reduction in the reliance on emergency services. Early-Alzheimer's patients who accepted counseling, and who carried two or three telephone numbers of loved ones whom they were to call if they suddenly found themselves "lost," did not need to be rushed to an emergency room when these frightening lapses occurred.

Ongoing counseling of caretakers on an as-needed basis (counseling that included initial training in meditation, relaxation, and imaging techniques) proved highly effective in reducing the caretakers' incidence of illness and its concomitant higher use of medical services. In this pilot study a hotline was also provided so that caretakers could seek advice in the face of the patients' more unpredictable symptoms. It was observed that the hotline also served as an emotional safety valve whenever stress became unbearable. These preliminary findings show promise that a program like this one would prove effective in the prevention of complications resulting from caretakers' stress and patients' distress, and that it would pay for itself in the savings accrued from reduction in the use of medical services. Here is one example of the benefits that counseling can bring:

> After her mother was widowed, Jane began to take her on an annual two-week holiday to Hawaii, in keeping with what had been her parents' custom. Last year, and for the first time, her mother was unhappy, agitated, and somewhat disoriented during the entire two weeks. This year, in their hotel room on the first morning in Hawaii, Jane's mother awakened completely disoriented. Her agitation increased until it was necessary to take her to the hospital emergency room, where she was quieted with haloperidol.
>
> Once Jane and her mother were back home, a diagnosis of early Alzheimer's was provisionally rendered, and mother and daughter were referred to the counseling program. Jane was advised to discontinue holidays far away from home, and to restrict her mother's environment as much as possible to familiar surroundings. Jane's mother was given information about her condition and what to expect, and both were able to anticipate and prepare for the day when Jane's mother would panic in familiar surroundings. The program enabled Jane to care for her mother with less stress and for a longer time than she would otherwise have been willing to do. When the day came that Jane's mother was incontinent, unable to walk, and unable to eat and do other routine things, Jane was able to find a suitable nursing home nearby, with a minimum of guilt and self-recrimination.

Other Preventive Services

Almost any of the techniques that reduce stress can also prevent unnecessary dependence on medical services in older adults. In offering these stress-reduction services, however, two factors must be borne in mind. First, this is a justly very proud generation, which survived the world's greatest war as well as the world's most severe economic depression. Furthermore, those among this generation who were chronic alcoholics or criminals, or who manifested other forms of self-destructive behavior, have long since done themselves in. These are now *the* survivors of a unique generation of survivors. They do not ask for help easily, and this trait should be understood and respected by therapists. Second, this generation is grounded in traditional values. On the one hand, this means that these patients respect their doctors, comply with advice, and perform all the exercises and homework that are assigned. On the other hand, these patients will shy away from anything that appears cultish or New Age. There are exceptions, but most will lose confidence in their doctors if recommendations appear faddish (for example, techniques for relaxation and using imagery might be welcomed along with meditation, but Transcendental Meditation (TM) could be seen as cultish.

Monitoring Medication

One of the most important services for older adults is to take an inventory of their medications and evaluate the appropriateness and interactions of the medications before concluding that the manifest symptoms of disorientation are actually due to dementia. These patients, being compliant and respectful, dutifully take every medication prescribed from every new physician, without remembering to tell the new physician about their current prescriptions. It is not uncommon, after medications have been reevaluated, to see the actual clearing of what had appeared to be dementia. Unfortunately, many physicians seem somewhat impatient with the elderly, perhaps believing that not much can be done for them. The patronizing but well-meaning reassurance "You are not as young as you used to be" is a prelude to dismissal. It is surprising that more physicians are not acquainted with the National Institute of Aging's list of the dozens of medications that are harmful to the elderly and that should not be prescribed, or that should be prescribed only with caution.

Accepting an Expanded Role

In treating older adults, the psychotherapist should be prepared to step out of his or her narrow psychotherapeutic role and do casework or perform other services, which may include helping an older adult overcome loneliness, learn how to date after widowhood, and adjust to the sudden increase in "togetherness" and in the unexpected that comes with retirement, as the following case illustrates:

> Ken, a sixty-five-year-old man, recently retired, was overwhelmed with anxiety and had been given every service from retirement counseling to stress management, all to no avail. Finally, someone who was willing to listen—and also to step outside the strict psychotherapist role—saw the problem.
>
> Ken and his wife, Elmira, had traveled to south Florida to spend a few days deciding whether they wanted to relocate there from Minnesota. They knew nothing of Florida other than its reputed mild winters. On their second day there, an aggressive salesman sold them a townhouse in a retirement community on south Florida's Atlantic coast.
>
> Once settled in, Ken and his wife became increasingly anxious until finally they were beside themselves. Their entire community of neighbors consisted of retirees from the Northeast, and all were of Jewish background, whereas Ken and Elmira were Lutherans. They were totally unable to fit into their new surroundings.
>
> The psychologist, discerning the inability of this older couple to make a quantum adjustment, contacted the builder of their townhouse, who also had a retirement community in Fort Meyers, on the Gulf Coast, where there were many retirees from Minnesota and from other parts of the Midwest. A trade was arranged, and almost immediately Ken's anxiety abated. The psychologist later received a letter from Fort Meyers, addressed with affection and gratitude "To my Doctor, the Expert Realtor."

The Economic Wisdom of Preventive Care

Ever since it was discovered, more than thirty-five years ago, that mental and behavioral health interventions save medical and surgical dollars, the most important argument for their inclusion in primary care is that they reduce inappropriate use of physical health services and further reduce the overall cost of providing healthcare. This *medical-cost offset*, as it is known in the literature, has been extensively reviewed over three generations of research

methodology, and this review has been accompanied by a delin-
eation of the circumstances and settings in which savings will or
will not be realized. The greatest impact occurs in organized settings with risk-sharing arrangements (such as capitation) and, even
more important, in settings where behavioral health interventions
are targeted to specific populations and are focused and innovative
in nature.

Research on medical-cost offsets has had a profound influence
on public policy in two different eras, thirty years apart. The early
studies persuaded the health insurance industry to include psychotherapy as a prepaid benefit, whereas previously it had been mil-
itantly excluded. The second and more recent impact was the
decision by the Health Care Financing Administration (HCFA) to
open Medicaid to full behavioral health benefits through contracted arrangements with managed-care and health maintenance
organizations.

Curiously, HCFA has been reluctant to alter its regulations so
that behavioral interventions geared toward prevention, and similar benefits, can be extended to recipients of Medicare as well. In
large measure this is because the Medicare program is in severe economic difficulty, and it requires a great deal of courage to extend
benefits when a system is financially ailing. This is penny-wise and
pound-foolish, however, inasmuch as thirty-five years of research
have demonstrated that an extensive behavioral health benefit will
result in a net savings. Recent research indicates that the potential
savings brought about by the provision of preventive behavioral
interventions may be even greater than the medical-cost offset in
the general population . What may appear to a timid bureaucrat as
a bold stroke may actually be a matter of dollars and sense.

Suggested Reading

Cummings, N. A. "Does Managed Mental Health Care Offset Costs Related to
    Medical Treatment?" In A. Lazarus (ed.), *Controversies in Managed
    Mental Health Care*. Washington, D.C.: American Psychiatric Press,
    1966, pp. 213–227.

Cummings, N. A. "The Successful Application of Medical Offset in Program Planning and Clinical Delivery." *Managed Care Quarterly*, 1994, 2(2), 1–6.

Cummings, N. A., Dörken, H., Pallak, M. S., and Henke, C. J. "The Impact of Psychological Intervention on Health Care Costs and Utilization: The Hawaii Medicaid Project." In Foundation for Behavioral Health (ed.), *Medicaid, Managed Behavioral Health and Implications for the Public Policy*. Vol. 2: *Healthcare and Utilization*. South San Francisco, Calif.: Foundation for Behavioral Health, 1993.

Chapter Two

PACE

Innovative Care for
the Frail Older Adult

Stefan N. Miller, Nancy A. Miller,
Elizabeth Mauser, Kate O'Malley

This chapter is a discussion of the Program of All-Inclusive Care for the Elderly (PACE) and its impact on the behavioral healthcare of its enrollees. PACE is a healthcare-delivery model designed to foster the health of frail elderly persons who maintain community living arrangements and who also meet state eligibility requirements for admission to a nursing home. In the material that follows, we provide background about On Lok Senior Health Services (the prototype PACE provider) and about the congressionally authorized PACE demonstration. Key features of the PACE model are highlighted in this chapter. They include the use of interdisciplinary teams and the integration of primary care with center-based and in-home services. The chapter describes adaptations that the PACE sites have made in order to care more appropriately for enrollees with dementia and other mental health problems. Factors that affect both enrollment and disenrollment decisions are also discussed, particularly as these factors concern enrollees with mental health problems. The chapter also presents two typical case studies, which represent both the melding of services within the

Note: The opinions expressed in this chapter are those of the authors and do not necessarily reflect the views of the Health Care Financing Administration or On Lok Senior Health Services.

interdisciplinary team and the preliminary findings from the independent evaluation of the PACE demonstration.

Each of the four authors is intimately involved with the PACE program and has visited numerous PACE sites at various times since June, 1990. Three are researchers with the United States Department of Health and Human Services, Health Care Financing Administration (HCFA). As an agency, HCFA has been formally associated with the PACE model of care since 1983, and the authors employed at HCFA are responsible for managing and evaluating the national PACE demonstration. They have worked with PACE policymakers and program directors across the country. The fourth author is the director of On Lok Senior Health Services, today the largest PACE provider in the nation, where she has been employed for seventeen years in a variety of positions. She is a strong proponent of the PACE model because she has witnessed its success.

The apparent success of PACE has generated interest from many quarters. PACE is designed to foster the health of frail, elderly persons who maintain community living arrangements and who meet state nursing home eligibility requirements. Like their counterparts in nursing homes, PACE enrollees are a particularly vulnerable group of elderly. On the average, PACE enrollees have eight diagnosed medical conditions, the most common being diseases of the eye, hypertension, arthritis, dementia, and cardiovascular disease. Approximately 42 percent of all enrollees are experiencing some form of dementia (rates for individual sites range from 13 percent to 75 percent).

At the time of this writing, eleven PACE sites are operating in nine states and have enrolled more than three thousand persons, the vast majority of whom are eligible for both Medicare and Medicaid. Forty-eight additional organizations are in various stages of developing PACE sites.

The PACE Model

In PACE, a voluntary program, enrollees agree to receive all acute- and long-term healthcare services (including inpatient, outpatient, and in-home care) through the PACE site, which is paid a monthly capitation (an agreed-upon fee) by Medicare and Medicaid. PACE is one of several federal demonstrations operated under the auspices of HCFA. It maintains frail elderly individuals (aged fifty-five or older) in the community by applying a model of care that at times may be somewhat unorthodox but is highly enrollee-focused. By saying that the model may be unorthodox, we mean that PACE sites are not bound by the conventional understanding of what are considered to be "covered services" for the purposes of payment. Medical and nonmedical services, as well as products not ordinarily paid for by health insurance, are considered for use if it is believed that the enrollee will benefit.

The PACE model of care began with community concern for the elderly of San Francisco's Chinatown, North Beach, and Polk Gulch neighborhoods in September 1971. Frail elderly people, who met eligibility requirements for nursing-home levels of care, were being displaced to nursing homes in distant communities where California's Medicaid nursing home beds were available. A community organization called On Lok Guey (the name, translated from Chinese, means "happy, peaceful abode") was formed to find ways of keeping these frail elderly people in their communities. After ten years of developing and integrating community-based services under federal and state grants, On Lok Guey (later shortened to On Lok) established an association with HCFA in 1983, as a result of the passage of Public Law 98–21. This law authorized the Secretary of Health and Human Services to waive certain Medicare and Medicaid requirements so that the model of care developed and refined by On Lok could be used in a federal demonstration program with government funding. Subsequent legislation, Public Law 99–509 (the Omnibus Reconciliation Act of 1986), authorized the national replication of On Lok's model of care.

Interdisciplinary Teams

The core of the PACE model is its approach to communication, which is based on care coordination, care management, and the use of an interdisciplinary team responsible for overseeing all enrollee- and care-related matters. This team and the results it yields are certainly not a convention "invented" by the PACE founders, nor are they limited solely to the PACE experience, but the typical healthcare organization has not adopted this principle of communication as its primary tenet. Effective communication among caregivers is especially important as it applies to the PACE population, given the following enrollee descriptors:

- 68 percent are over the age of seventy-five, and 29 percent are older than eighty-four
- At least 20 percent have some level of demonstrable expressive and receptive communication disorder
- Roughly 14 percent exhibit some degree of verbal disruption, physical aggression, and regressive behavior

The interdisciplinary team consists of all the personnel who influence an enrollee's PACE experience—for example, a physician, a nurse, a dietitian, a homemaker aide, a PACE van driver, a member of the Adult Day Health Center (ADHC) staff, a social worker, and a member of the rehabilitation and recreational therapy staff. In addition, the team process in PACE programs includes the medical records staff, speech therapists, chaplains, and even families. Psychologists and psychiatrists are also interdisciplinary team members when they provide contract services to select enrollees referred by the care staff. Each team member is expected and encouraged to contribute in an active manner, in ways that will advance the care enrollees are receiving.

Interdisciplinary communication is accomplished through formal daily morning meetings, intake/assessment meetings, and frequent informal contact among team members. As part of the intake/assessment meetings, the interdisciplinary team reviews all applicants for acceptance into the PACE program. These meetings typically occur after one or two home visits have been conducted with applicants who meet the PACE site's initial screening requirements, and after the PACE applicant has made two or more visits to the ADHC.

PACE staff considering a prospective enrollee are commonly concerned about the applicant's cognitive insufficiency. Although all sites enroll applicants with dementia and other mental health problems, it is a factor that needs to be considered, especially in cases of individuals with very severe cognitive disabilities, because agitation is a common feature and could cause disruption in the setting of a day center.

Meetings are generally free-flowing discussions where a multitude of information is shared by those staff who are working closely with the enrollee. Between the time an enrollee is picked up at home by a PACE van and transported back home, a variety of healthcare providers have furnished care or interacted with the enrollee. Information gleaned from these one-to-one encounters serves as the basis for discussions at the morning meetings and for modifying individual care plans. Observations made by every member of the team (professional and associate-level personnel) are valued and given consideration.

Assessment and Treatment Plans

Although we are beginning to see variations in the frequency with which teams review enrollees' care plans, the most common assessment model requires each member of the team to complete a healthcare assessment every three or four months for each PACE enrollee. The team meets once or twice a week to discuss selected enrollees and reevaluate (and, as necessary, modify) the care plan of everyone who has received a health assessment. It is interesting to note that the two variables that appear to affect initial care plans the most are the enrollee's mental status and the enrollee's current living situation, which includes the extent of family or caregiver support.

Although PACE sites utilize social workers and nurses in primary-care roles in the management of enrollees with behavioral problems, sites generally contract with psychologists to provide specialized services as they are needed. The majority of PACE enrollees who are being furnished mental healthcare are diagnosed with depression, dementia, anxiety, or some combination of these conditions. Of the sites reporting mental healthcare utilization data for calendar year 1996, the Beth Abraham site in The Bronx, New York, reported 479 enrollee visits (irrespective of the type of care provider), mainly for depression and dementia.

Role of Psychologists

Psychologists' involvement is a relatively new part of the PACE program. This component of PACE was developed by Community Care for the Elderly (CCE), Milwaukee, in conjunction with Dr. Robert Hirschman, director of neuropsychology at Lakeview Neurorehabilitation Center Midwest, in Waterford, Wisconsin. Hirschman was at the time (and still is) a consultant to CCE, providing neuropsychology and behavior intervention assessment and treatment services. The authors discussed the development and operation of the CCE program with Dr. Hirschman.

CCE is one PACE site that uses doctoral candidates under the supervision of a psychologist. In calendar year 1996, doctoral students from the Wisconsin School of Professional Psychology and the Mt. Sinai Samaritan Medical Center (the teaching affiliate of the University of Wisconsin's medical school) were introduced to the PACE model at CCE, where they fulfilled practicum and internship requirements through their involvement in the care of thirty-two enrollees. Some initially expressed resistance to the PACE model, but after learning more about it and interacting with the interdisciplinary team for a short while, they readily accepted it. This program is still operating, with students, staff, and enrollees all pleased with the experience and the outcomes.

Role of Physicians

As in other healthcare models, the ultimate responsibility for treatment rests with the PACE professional staff, especially its physicians. By contrast with what occurs in other healthcare models, however, PACE physicians practice shared decision making as members of the interdisciplinary teams and are not automatically considered "team leaders." A physician does play an important and undeniable leadership role in directing an enrollee's medical care, but care-management decisions are complex for this population. The complexity is compounded by the enrollee's mental status, housing, access to transportation, lack of family involvement and/or conflicting family needs, and nursing needs. Because some physicians are not prepared or willing to manage care in this type of environment, PACE sites have found that it is extremely important to be prudent in hiring physicians or contracting for their services.

Adult Day Health Centers

In the eyes of observers, PACE is defined as much by the extensive use of Adult Day Health Centers (ADHCs) as by the use of interdisciplinary teams. The ADHC is the actual physical site where all those associated with the PACE program—enrollees, healthcare providers, and administrative personnel—are able to interact. A variety of services are provided at the ADHC, and for many enrollees it represents an opportunity to engage in recreational and social activities that would otherwise be unattainable. Moreover, healthcare providers are able to monitor enrollees while delivering a variety of health-related services at the ADHC. Average frequency of attendance varies, from six days a week to less than once a week, with attendance based on the enrollee's physical and mental status, as determined by the interdisciplinary team and as agreed to by the enrollee and his or her family and/or caregiver.

For enrollees with dementia or behavioral problems, most sites have developed some sort of specific ADHC programming, and because the busy setting of an ADHC sometimes makes it difficult to manage enrollees who have behavioral problems, sites may also opt to develop behavior-specific settings. Structurally, this arrangement may take the form of a special unit within an existing ADHC (for example, a quiet or low-stimulation room), or an entire ADHC may be designed specifically for enrollees with dementia.

Eau Claire, one of the ADHCs of the Palmetto (South Carolina) SeniorCare site, exemplifies a dementia-specific center. A prerequisite for the enrollee's attendance at this ADHC is dementia as his or her primary diagnosis. Team dynamics and care-planning strategies directly reflect the unique needs of this ADHC's enrollees. For example, the input of all the disciplines involved in the care-planning process is more critical because team members must collectively gather information that the enrollee is unable to communicate. This concept is evidenced by the inclusion and active participation in daily and intake/assessment meetings of staff not normally involved in direct patient care—van drivers, medical records staff, and environmental staff. The typical service package is also distinct for enrollees at the Eau Claire ADHC because care plans are likely to be rich in less tangible services (team discussion, monitoring, assessment, family contact, education, respite) and lighter with respect to more concrete services (inpatient care, rehabilitative therapy).

Eau Claire enrollees generally attend this ADHC more frequently (often five times a week) than the Palmetto SeniorCare site's other enrollees. Their more frequent attendance facilitates the staff's observation of their behavior, provides a daily routine that is important in minimizing behavioral problems, and serves as respite for family members and other caregivers. Respite care is also provided more liberally at Eau Claire and includes overnight stays at the program's apartments or at a nursing home.

PACE sites have learned that the decision-making process needs to reflect issues specific to enrollees with dementia. Because slight changes in an enrollee's behavior can signal underlying health, medication, or family problems, staff members who are making decisions about an enrollee's care place significant weight on supplemental information gained through observation. Apart from small changes in behavior, the typical manifestations of dementia—memory loss, disorientation with respect to time and place, confusion, delusion, paranoia, wandering, and combativeness—also influence decision making. For example, such problems as delusion, paranoia, and confusion may require substantial redirection and one-to-one attention, changes that in turn may affect staffing decisions, as well as the structure of the ADHC. Issues around quality of life for the enrollee and the family or other caregivers carry a lot of weight in team decision making, particularly where diagnostic testing, assessment, and medical intervention are concerned.

Capitation Payment

Integrating acute and long-term care involves coordinating and integrating service delivery and financing. Integration of financing involves the pooling of funding from Medicare and Medicaid into a single funding stream. Current managed-care models attempt to integrate services by using capitation models of payment for providers, an arrangement that gives managed-care organizations flexibility in tailoring benefits to the distinct needs of each beneficiary.

Integration of funding sources alone does not ensure integration of services, however. Today various managed-care plans coordinate the delivery of acute and long-term care to differing degrees. A key goal of PACE is to reduce fragmentation of services and effectively integrate acute and long-term care into a single, seamless system. Some plans simply facilitate transitions between settings; PACE interdisciplinary team members can work together to manage medical and social services across acute-care and long-term-care settings.

All PACE sites are paid a monthly capitation by Medicare and/or Medicaid. The Medicare capitation rate is determined on the basis of the "average adjusted per capita cost" (AAPCC) method, developed in accordance with the 1982 Tax Equity and Fiscal Responsibility Act to pay risk-based health maintenance organizations (HMOs) serving Medicare enrollees. By contrast with Medicare, however, no single method exists for the development of a Medicaid capitation rate. Each state's Medicaid agency develops its own capitation rate, which reflects its own environment with respect to the need for long-term care, the existing benefits and service-delivery system, and the existing policy for apportioning services. Some states simply base the Medicaid rate on 95 percent of the average cost for care in a nursing home. Others have developed a blended rate that also draws on home- and community-based waiver costs and on costs for home healthcare or assisted living. Medicaid capitation generally accounts for two-thirds of a PACE site's total capitation.

A risk-sharing provision is contained in the federal demonstration project and protects sites from losses above a certain level for the first three years of operation, after which PACE providers assume full financial responsibility. Losses at several sites have been compensated by HCFA and by the sites' respective state Medicaid agencies, but the compensation amounts have been relatively small. Several of the earlier demonstration sites that received grant support also used this funding to offset early losses.

Housing

As originally designed, PACE is not intended to provide housing, because all enrollees at the time of their enrollment are required to be living in the community (that is, not in an institution). As sites continue to grow and care for their enrollees, however, it has become evident that enrollees—especially those living alone in houses or traditional apartments, as well as those experiencing emotional or behavioral problems—are not always able to manage their living environments effectively. Eventually, because of cognitive problems or other reasons, some of these enrollees will require short- or long-term institutionalization.

A PACE enrollee's placement in an institution results in a certain loss of independence for the enrollee, but it also brings the potential for an increase in the PACE site's costs because PACE sites are required to pay for their enrollees' hospitalization, care in a skilled nursing facility, and medical care in long-term-care settings. Like many other healthcare programs these days, the PACE sites are reacting to enrollees' needs, requirements in the general marketplace, and cost increases. As a result, they began to realize that housing can be integral to successful programming. The majority of the demonstration sites are now actively engaged in supporting housing arrangements for enrollees. In fact, some sites will consider building an additional ADHC only if it can be situated in a multiunit housing structure; sources of financing range from Department of Housing and Urban Development Section 202 funding to community grants and partnerships between PACE sites and developers.

In developing housing for participants, several sites have constructed housing units specifically for participants with dementia. For example, in one of its housing units, the Milwaukee PACE site has included a floor devoted exclusively to enrollees with dementia. This floor also includes a special ADHC for participants with dementia, an arrangement that enables intense supervision of participants in a safe, low-stimulation setting.

Service-Delivery Enhancements

In their care of enrollees with dementia and other mental health problems, the PACE sites use a variety of clinical activities:

- Use of outcome-oriented, standardized problem lists that incorporate psychosocial issues
- Creation of low-stimulus environments, with entire ADHCs or portions of these centers specifically designed to care for enrollees with dementia

• Provision of housing designed for enrollees with dementia

Individual sites differ on a number of variables, such as enrollee-related demographics, the availability of professional healthcare personnel in the community, and the community's patterns of healthcare practice. In the effort to maintain necessary levels of care, sites have modified staffing to be more responsive to enrollees with dementia and other psychosocial problems. For example, one site experimented by adding a pharmacist to the interdisciplinary team because polypharmacy, and medications in general, can exacerbate the behavioral problems associated with dementia.

Outcome-Oriented Care Planning

Over time, as previously noted, PACE sites have evolved in their care planning from a discipline-specific orientation, in which discipline-specific problems guide the care-planning process, to an outcome-oriented approach, in which enrollees' problems and their outcomes guide the care-planning process. In the outcome-oriented approach, the team identifies a measurable goal or outcome associated with each problem and assigns to that problem only those disciplines that will contribute directly to the attainment of the goal. Although sites are about equally split between the use the discipline-specific approach and the outcome-oriented approach, several sites that have been using the discipline-specific approach are engaging in efforts to make care planning more integrated and more in line with the outcome-oriented approach.

Among sites that have evolved toward the outcome-oriented approach, some have developed standardized interdisciplinary team lists of problems, objectives, and treatments. These lists are used as guidelines in documenting and implementing care plans. Other sites have developed more customized lists of problems, objectives, and treatments for individual enrollees. At the sites using standardized problem lists, several problems may be related to psychosocial issues. For example, On Lok's set of twenty-one problems includes depression (moderate to severe), behavior management, cognitive deficit, inadequate interpersonal skills, and social isolation. At Elder Service Plan, in Boston, thirteen functional areas are addressed, including cognitive function and mood or behavior. For each problem there are guidelines for care planning by the interdisciplinary team and guidelines for determining appropriate goals and assigning the disciplines that will be accountable for developing and monitoring interventions. The following two case studies illustrate how PACE manages the care of participants with dementia and/or behavioral problems:

An Elderly Man with Progressive Dementia and Depression

Mr. Jones enrolled at a PACE site in February 1995 at the age of seventy. Before enrolling, he had received his healthcare from a large HMO. In early 1994 he was diagnosed as having Alzheimer's disease, which seemed to be progressing rapidly; by the end of 1994 he needed help and supervision in getting dressed, bathing, and performing other routine activities.

Divorced for many years, he had no children and lived in an apartment with a friend who was devoted to his care but who was away from home during the day. She was finding it quite difficult to provide the level of oversight he needed to meet his daily needs, and for his safety she was thinking seriously about placing him in a nursing home.

During the initial PACE assessment, Mr. Jones was clearly impaired in his orientation, memory, intellectual processes, and judgment. He could not remember simple phrases or do simple calculations. He knew his name but not the name of the city or the date. PACE staff also remarked on how withdrawn he was, requiring a lot of coaching to interact. Functionally, he was physically capable of managing activities like dressing, bathing, and toileting, but he required continuous prompting. He walked without assistance, but the PACE interdisciplinary team did not think it was safe for him to walk alone in the community. Given his cognitive limits, he was assessed as being unable to manage his finances or his medications. After the team's complete assessment of his medical, functional, and social needs (and the needs of his family caregiver), the team proposed center attendance five times a week and in-home personal care twice daily, to alleviate caregiver burnout.

He adjusted well to the center and to the medication prescribed for his depression. He became much more interactive, would initiate conversations, and participated in a small-group program with others who had Alzheimer's disease. His participation allowed him to receive personal attention and interact with others in a low-stimulation setting. At home, his ability to manage dressing and other daily activities improved, and his caregiver reported that he was easier to manage. Except for a urinary tract infection and several falls, which necessitated an adjustment in his medication, he remained relatively stable for about two years.

In the spring of 1996 the staff noted that his energy was declining. He was requiring more help with daily activities, and he was less interested in eating and in social interaction. He now required help to walk upstairs, but he was still able to stay at home. Medical evaluation did not reveal any treatable health problems, and the team concluded that his dementia was progressing.

As Mr. Jones deteriorated, his friend recounted previous discussions with him about his healthcare wishes. She remembered clearly his statements that he would not wish to have his life prolonged if he were no longer able to enjoy it. She raised the issue of quality of life and expressed her concerns to the social worker and the physician. She also was concerned about the heaviness of his physical care and how unlikely it was that he would get any better.

In June 1996 Mr. Jones developed a fever, and his physician began an evaluation as to its cause. During this evaluation, Mr. Jones became less and less responsive. With the involvement and direction of his friend, the team developed a plan for comfort care. After a few days, Mr. Jones died peacefully at home.

An Elderly Man with an Organic Delusional Disorder

Mr. Fish is an eighty-year-old man who suffered a brain injury twenty years ago in a car accident. Before the injury he had been healthy, working in construction and living in the community. Since the injury he has been severely disabled by a psychiatric illness arising from the damage to his brain.

His disorder is characterized by his inability to care for himself, his poor judgment and reasoning, and his belief that people are trying to hurt him and "mess him up." In the twenty years since the accident, he has had at least six psychiatric hospital admissions against his will and has been evicted from several residential hotels for disruptive behavior, urinating in the hallways, and yelling at other occupants. At one time he lived with his son, but his behavior was so disruptive that he could no longer be managed there.

At the time of his referral to the PACE site he was living in a psychiatric board-and-care facility but was again facing eviction for not taking his medication and for engaging in disruptive, combative behavior. The PACE site was contacted by a community service agency, and Mr. Fish was assessed by the PACE team in January 1995. It was noted at the time that he was "disheveled, unshaven, and smelled of urine." The team felt that the keys to his management would be his compliance with his medication regimen, the team's ability to develop a trusting and therapeutic relationship with him, and the coordination of ADHC services and care in his home. Given the long-standing nature of his condition, it was unlikely that his delusional disorder could be cured. If he was not well managed, however, he would face a continuous and probably escalating cycle of hospitalization, discharge to community care, and rehospitalization.

One month after his assessment, his son helped him move to private senior housing managed by the PACE site. The team recommended that he attend the center three times a week, have personal care services and daily showers, have medications administered to him, and have personal care provided in his home for help with dressing, grooming, and toileting. In addition, with both clinic and center services available in the senior housing building, his health status could be closely assessed and evaluated for changes.

In the two years since his enrollment, Mr. Fish has not had any hospital admissions. His behavior has been manageable, and he does not present a danger to himself or others. He receives his medications as needed, and his team works continuously and consistently with him on personal hygiene. He has had some relatively minor problems: multiple urinary-tract infections (but his urinary incontinence has improved), an episode of bleeding in his intestines (which was evaluated and resolved with minor surgery), and a cataract (extraction yielded positive results).

In November 1995, staff noted that his chronic mental health problem is stable and that he had made friends in the center (he "watches out for his lunch-table companions"). He is cooperative with staff and with the other residents, and the team expects him to remain in his current living situation indefinitely.

These two men are typical PACE enrollees. In both instances, the team approach to care management created the capacity to provide continuous assessment, intervention, and reassessment. The teams were able to respond quickly to changing needs, and they had the flexibility to adjust treatment plans as new information arose.

The integration of medical care, ADHC services, and in-home assistance creates a twenty-four-hour support system for frail elderly people in a community setting. A decision to use specialized mental health professionals (psychiatrists and psychologists), who are not generally part of the full-time permanent interdisciplinary team, depends on a variety of factors, among them the needs of the enrollee, the availability of the mental health professionals, and the needs of the staff.

Enrollment, Nonenrollment, and Disenrollment

A special study, covering January 1995 through June 1996, of the decision to enroll in PACE found that minority groups and people with low levels of income and education were disproportionately represented among PACE applicants. The only demographic characteristic significantly associated with the probability of enrollment was home ownership, with applicants who owned their own homes less likely to enroll. The role played by health status in the enrollment decision was not a simple one: those least likely to enroll were either applicants reporting at least good health, on the one hand, or, on the other, applicants who needed particularly intensive care (as defined by their use of a hospital during the previous six months) or whose condition was terminal (as defined by the likelihood of their dying within three months of applying to PACE). Although enrollees and nonenrollees did not differ in the number of the daily activities (such as bathing, dressing, and walking) in which they were experiencing limitations, PACE enrollees were more likely to need assistance with the instrumental activities of daily living (such as preparing meals, managing money, and taking medications).

A number of variables, as cited by PACE staff, influenced the acceptance of an enrollee into the program. The most common factors included the applicant's sociability, the safety of transporting the applicant, the applicant's level of family support, the level of the applicant's cognitive sufficiency, and the degree of the applicant's disruptive behavior. Some PACE staff believe that a more sociable person is better equipped to attend and participate in the ADHC. Family support is critical because enrollees return to their homes in the evening, and care must be provided during those hours.

PACE disenrollment rates have been low by comparison with disenrollment rates found in Medicare's risk-based HMO program. In 1994, of 2,231 enrollees across ten sites (including On Lok), about 5 percent (111) disenrolled. In terms of age, gender, marital status, education, annual income, and functional status, there were no significant differences between disenrollees and those who continued in PACE, but the disenrollees did have a higher frequency of poor performance on the Mental Status Questionnaire (MSQ)[1] than the continuing enrollees did: more than 40 percent of the PACE disenrollees scored eight or more errors on the MSQ, as compared with 26 percent of the continuing enrollees. Those who disenrolled were also more likely to have been enrolled for six months or less than were those who were still enrolled at the end of 1994.

Evaluation Design and Interim Findings

The evaluation of PACE is designed to address how this model of care compares with the current Medicare and Medicaid programs. From the perspective of PACE site staff, numerous different mechanisms in this model of care enable the sites to achieve positive patient outcomes. These mechanisms include flexibility and freedom to make timely and creative decisions, ongoing contact with enrollees, integration and consolidation of acute and long-term care, and interdisciplinary coordination.

Preliminary quantitative analyses from the PACE evaluation (being carried out under an HCFA contract with Abt Associates of Cambridge, Massachusetts) examine the effects of PACE on use of health services, on health and functional status, on quality of

life, and on satisfaction with services. The information for these
analyses comes from a survey of PACE applicants that began in
January 1995. Those who entered PACE form the treatment group;
those who applied to PACE, met the eligibility criteria, but decided
not to join are the comparison group.

PACE applicants are interviewed before making their decisions
about enrollment in PACE, and they are reinterviewed every six
months. It is important to note that all the evaluation results
reported here are preliminary and are based on the first six-month
follow-up of the treatment and comparison groups. Additional
analyses will be conducted with larger samples and longer follow-
up periods, but the initial findings are very favorable for the PACE
model of care.

Use of Supportive Services

A number of supportive services help enrollees with the activities
of daily living, as already described. These services include home
visits from a nurse, formal (paid) care received at home, informal
(unpaid) care from friends and relatives, and ADHC services. After
controlling for demographic differences (including any differences
in health and functional status) between PACE enrollees and the
comparison group at the time they were applying to PACE, we
found that PACE enrollees, during the first six-month follow-up,
were significantly more likely to take advantage of the ADHC services. They were also significantly less likely to receive home visits
from a nurse. It appears that ADHC attendance is substituting for
these visits. There were no significant differences in receipt of formal and informal care between PACE enrollees and the comparison group.

Use of Medical Services

To determine the use of medical services by PACE enrollees, the
use of hospitals, nursing homes, and ambulatory-care visits was

examined. Preliminary results from the first six-month follow-up show that PACE enrollees were significantly less likely to use the services of hospitals and nursing homes but were more likely to use ambulatory-care visits. In fact, 20 percent of the PACE enrollees were hospitalized during the first six-month period, by contrast with 37 percent of the comparison group, with an average of 2.4 inpatient nights for the PACE enrollees and 5.8 for the comparison group. The results so far suggest that PACE has been successful in reducing the use of institutional services.

Health Status and Quality of Life

The goals of PACE include maintaining or improving the health status, physical functioning, and quality of life of PACE enrollees. In view of the capitation method of payment, there is an incentive for PACE sites to reduce the provision of such costly services as hospital care, and so it is important to examine whether PACE has an impact on the health and functional status of enrollees, as well as on their satisfaction with care.

The PACE model emphasizes both preventive services and coordination of care, which should have an impact not only on health but also on the quality of the enrollees' lives. Results from the preliminary evaluation suggest that PACE is associated with improved health status, higher quality of life, and higher satisfaction with overall arrangements for care, but not with functional status. Through its coordinated approach to providing acute and long-term care, as well as its emphasis on preventive and rehabilitative care, PACE has been successful in reducing the use of institutional services while improving the health status, quality of life, and satisfaction with care of the PACE enrollees.

Subgroup Analyses

The impact of PACE on enrollee outcomes was also examined for subgroups of PACE enrollees. Specifically, the impact of PACE was examined for two groups of enrollees who had, at the time they applied to the program, different levels of limitation in their ability to carry out the activities of daily living. One of the groups had two or fewer limitations; the other had three or more. PACE had a greater impact on the group that had the larger number of functional limitations. Perhaps because of the more regular monitoring of the PACE enrollees, those with three or more functional limitations had an even lower number of stays in hospitals and nursing homes, by contrast with the comparison group, than did those with two or fewer functional limitations. Moreover, the enrollees who had three or more functional limitations at the time of application to PACE had perceived higher levels of health and satisfaction with life at the six-month follow-up.

Discussion

With a significant segment of PACE enrollees suffering from dementia and other mental health disorders, these positive interim findings suggest that acute and long-term health and social services, when effectively integrated, can improve the quality of life and satisfaction of the frail elderly who are suffering from significant mental impairment. The key features of the PACE model of care, as well as the adaptations of the PACE model that individual sites are beginning to make in order to serve these enrollees more appropriately, provide examples of ways to improve assessment, care planning, and monitoring of care for this vulnerable population of the elderly.

The higher rates of disenrollment among those enrollees with dementia, as against the low disenrollment rates overall, suggest that PACE, although it is responsive to enrollees' and their families' health-related needs, should continue refining the model for this population. The recent ability of the sites to expand to new dementia-specific ADHCs, the addition of housing, and related changes in service delivery offer the promise of continued enhancement to this apparently successful model for the frail elderly.

At the time of this writing, On Lok, the National PACE Association (the nonprofit membership organization representing the interests of the PACE demonstration sites as well as other PACE-related entities), and others are seeking support from members of Congress to make PACE a permanent part of the Medicare and Medicaid programs. PACE legislation is contained in the President's budget bill and has been introduced in the House of Representatives (H.R. 1464) and the Senate (S. 720). This is the first time an integrated service network for long-term care has been considered for this kind of status.

Suggested Reading

Branch, L. G., Coulam, R. F., and Zimmerman, Y. A. *Cross-Site Analysis of the PACE Demonstration: Calendar Year 1992*. Washington, D.C.: Health Care Financing Administration, Apr. 1994.

Burstein, N. R., White, A. J., and Kidder, D. *Evaluation of the Program of All-Inclusive Care for the Elderly (PACE) Demonstration: The Impact of PACE on Participant Outcomes*. Washington, D.C.: Health Care Financing Administration, Nov. 1996.

Coulam, R. F., and others. *Growth and Development of the PACE Sites: Calendar Year 1993*. Washington, D.C.: Health Care Financing Administration, Sept. 1994.

Irvin, C. V., Dorsey, T. C., and Lamkin, N. *Evaluation of the Program of All-Inclusive Care for the Elderly (PACE) Demonstration: Determinants of Enrollment Among Applicants to the PACE Program*. Washington, D.C.: Health Care Financing Administration, Feb. 1997.

Zimmerman, Y. A., and others. *Evaluation of the Program of All-Inclusive Care for the Elderly (PACE) Demonstration*. Washington, D.C.: Health Care Financing Administration, May 1996.

Chapter Three

Integrating Mental and Physical Health Services

What the United States Can Learn from Canada

James M. Georgoulakis

Providing affordable healthcare to all their citizens is one of the most difficult challenges facing the industrialized nations of the world today. The similarities among Australia, Canada, France, Germany, Great Britain, Japan, the Netherlands, Sweden, and the United States are striking. All these nations are concerned with the management of medical technology, efficiency in the delivery of healthcare, the quality of healthcare, and the provision of universal healthcare while containing costs. For example, Great Britain is spending 6 percent of its gross national product (GNP) on healthcare; Japan, about 7 percent; Canada, approximately 10 percent; and the United States, more than 16 percent, with 18 percent projected for the year 2000. Moreover, if demographers are correct about the demographics of aging, and if healthcare systems remain the same, costs will begin to increase at an accelerating rate in the next few years.

In an attempt to address some of the concerns raised by healthcare researchers, this chapter will focus on three major areas:

- Problems concerning the types and delivery of behavioral healthcare for older adults

- The most important similarities, differences, and challenges facing the U.S. and Canadian healthcare systems in the provision of services to older adults
- Lessons the United States can learn from the Canadian healthcare experience

It goes without saying that any comparative discussion of the Canadian and U.S. healthcare systems will reflect the experiences of the individual conducting the comparisons. And my comparison will not be an exception. I hope that my experiences in healthcare in the United States and Canada will enable me to provide a more balanced view. So far in my healthcare career it has been my good fortune to serve in the United States Army as a mental health professional for twenty years. During that time I have had the opportunity to provide direct mental health services and to conduct some of the largest ambulatory healthcare projects ever initiated by the United States Army's Medical Department. I have also served as a healthcare consultant to the Health Care Financing Administration, the American Psychological Association, Harvard University's School of Public Health, and Med-National, Inc., among other organizations. For the past four years I have been a consultant as well to Alberta (Canada) Health and to the Canadian Institute of Health Information. I believe these experiences, along with my current academic position, have provided me with a unique opportunity to observe developments in both public and private healthcare on both sides of the U.S.–Canada border. It is through these experiences that I offer the following observations and comments.

How People Use Healthcare Services

Universally, individuals use the healthcare system throughout their lives. As medical technology improves, and as definitions change with respect to what is considered the beginning or the end of life (definitions, for example, about when an individual should be removed from life supports), the use of healthcare services occurs at both earlier and later stages of life than ever before.

While medical technology is altering the definition of life and extending the life span, what is remaining fairly constant is when we use the healthcare system. Both the use and the cost of healthcare parallel the life cycle. As we age, not only do we use more healthcare, the healthcare is more costly. For the most part, children, teenagers, and twenty-somethings generally do not use the healthcare system to any great extent, with the exception of women during their reproductive years, who use the system more than men. As we move through our thirties, forties, and fifties, we use more healthcare. The costs of healthcare have rapidly increased by the time an individual reaches his or her sixties, and they remain at that higher level until the individual dies. In the United States, it has been estimated that more than half of all the costs associated with healthcare will occur in the last six months of an individual's life.[1] Moreover, with an individual's advancing age, the frequency of hospitalization increases. It has been estimated that by the time individuals are in their late seventies, their rate of hospital use will be five times higher than what was their prior lifetime average rate of use. To put this another way, if an individual averaged one hospitalization per year before reaching his seventies, by his late seventies this individual will average five hospitalizations per year for each remaining year of his seventies. If the individual survives into his late eighties, his hospital use will increase to twelve times more than his prior lifetime average. Moreover, these hospital stays will be longer and more complicated.

The fastest-growing segment of the industrialized world's population consists of individuals over the age of sixty-five. Within this segment in the United States, the fastest-growing age group is people over eighty. The baby boomers, defined as individuals born between the years 1947 and 1966, add to the future strain on the U.S. healthcare system. This group of individuals, estimated at more than seventy-seven million, has underused healthcare services up to this point. As this large group ages, its members will not only require more healthcare but will also utilize many different types of healthcare services. To put this point simply, not only will national healthcare costs rise, some types of healthcare services, including mental health services, will be taxed beyond their present limits.

Older Adults and Behavioral Health Services

Common physical illnesses occurring in older adults include such conditions as arthritis, congestive heart failure and other cardiac disturbances, Parkinson's disease, and strokes. Documentation of these conditions and their increasing frequency with age has been facilitated by the use of the nomenclature developed by the World Health Organization and published in the various volumes of the *International Classification of Diseases* (ICD) series.[2] With respect to issues and types of mental disorders among older adults, however, the research is not as clear. For the most part, funds have not been as readily available to conduct large-scale psychiatric epidemiological studies among older populations. In addition, mental health records have not been as readily accessible to researchers for review as medical records have been. Unlike physical illnesses, most mental health disorders lack objective, easily measured markers. Instead, mental disorders are diagnosed on the basis of symptoms reported by patients and observed by clinicians.[3] In the area of mental health, the United States and a limited number of other countries have relied on the American Psychiatric Association's *Diagnostic and Statistical Manual of Mental Disorders* (DSM)[4] rather than on the ICD. Because these two classification systems differ on types of mental disorders, epidemiological comparison of mental disorders among various countries is not as clear as it could be (although with ICD-10 and the recently published DSM-IV, these differences are minimized). Fortunately for international comparisons, however, Canada and the United States employ both ICD and DSM nomenclature.

Canada and the United States:
Similarities and Differences

Although Canada has a much smaller population than the United States and occupies a larger land mass, there are many demographic, economic, linguistic, and cultural similarities between the two countries.

As in the United States, an ever-increasing segment of the Canadian population is elderly. The largest population centers in Canada lie relatively close to large populations in the United States. Both are predominantly English-speaking countries, and although Canada is officially bilingual, the English-speaking community has dominated the national economy. Even in the province of Quebec, where 80 percent of the population speaks French, the English-speaking population has been economically dominant until recently. Both countries have been greatly influenced by the English with regard to government and social values (the French, however, have exerted great influence in the province of Quebec, especially in the organization of mental health services).

There are also differences between the two countries. As already mentioned, Canada spends almost 10 percent of its GNP on healthcare. This is more than any other country in the world except the United States (where almost 16 percent of GNP is spent on healthcare).

Another difference has to do with the prevalence of psychiatric disorders in older adults. In recent years, gerontologists have begun to emphasize the mental health aspects of aging. This is extremely important because within twenty years, one-third of the U.S. population will be over the age of fifty-five, and almost one-fifth of the population will be over sixty-five. (If Sigmund Freud is credited with inventing psychotherapy for emotional and mental health problems, Woody Allen and Hollywood have popularized the notion for baby boomers that an analyst is needed by everyone.)

Research conducted by epidemiologists and gerontologists in both Canada and the United States has indicated that the aged in both countries experience similar types of psychiatric disorders in terms of both frequency and diagnostic category. Moreover, gerontologists and epidemiologists in both countries acknowledge that social and cultural factors, combined with fragmentation of services, hinder more accurate studies of the elderly. This discussion of mental health disorders in older adults will be limited to depression; delirium; dementia; and paranoid ideation, alcoholism, and anxiety disorders.

Depression

The research on depression in older adults presents an excellent illustration of the concerns addressed in this chapter. Depression, as the most common mental health disorder, has stimulated the most research in geriatric mental health. In Canada, depression is estimated to affect around 10 percent of the elderly. This figure may be low because private nursing homes in Canada care for large numbers of the mentally ill elderly, and nearly all these nursing homes have limited expertise in mental health. Studies of the nursing homes have indicated that at least 80 percent of their residents suffer from some form of mental disorder. The two most widely cited disorders were dementia and depression.

In the United States, estimates from a number of research studies,[5] including the Epidemiological Catchment Area Program,[6] indicate lower rates of depression in the elderly. Similar to Canadian surveys of nursing homes,[7] U.S. studies,[8] including the National Nursing Home Surveys, have indicated that nearly 70 percent of all residents of U.S. nursing homes had a chronic mental disorder contributing to social dependency, functional impairment, and the need for institutional care.[9] Despite these surveys, it is still entirely possible that both countries may have greatly underestimated the incidence of clinical depression among older adults. For example, a study on older adults indicated that primary-care physicians detected depression in only 51 percent of patients with depressive and dementive disorders.[10] In addition, a number of studies have indicated that older adults report as many depressive symptoms as younger individuals, yet they rarely receive the diagnosis of depression.[11] Several factors contribute to the underestimation of depression. First, clinicians assume that the depressive symptoms reported by older adults are due to their physical problems rather than to psychological problems. Second, healthcare providers are reluctant to give mental health diagnoses to older adults. Third, clinicians are more comfortable focusing on the physical problems of the elderly. Fourth, some clinicians believe that the depressive symptoms presented by older adults may not fit the current DSM criteria. Fifth, the American Psychiatric Association states that it is "often difficult to determine whether cognitive symptoms are better accounted for by dementia or by a major depressive episode."[12]

Delirium

Delirium is a much clearer diagnosis to document in the elderly population. In clinical terms, "delirium is defined as a disturbance of consciousness that is accompanied by a change in the thinking processes that cannot be accounted for by a preexisting or evolving dementia or other medical condition."[13] This disturbance develops over a short period of time, usually hours to days, and tends to fluctuate during the day. The individual's ability to focus, sustain, or shift attention is impaired. The person is easily distracted and is difficult to engage in a conversation. Researchers report that about 30 to 50 percent of the hospitalized elderly exhibit some form of delirium.[14] In the United States it is estimated that approximately 10 per cent of individuals who are hospitalized for a general medical condition exhibit signs of delirium on admission, with the possibility of an additional 10 to 15 percent developing delirium while in the hospital.[15]

Dementia

In both Canada and the United States, it is clear that dementia increases with age, especially after the age of seventy-five. Some researchers have estimated that as many as 50 percent of individuals over the age of eighty-five may have some type of dementia. Similarly, in both countries moderate to severe dementia is estimated to affect 3 to 5 percent of the population over the age of sixty-five.

Paranoid Ideation, Alcoholism, and Anxiety Disorders

In both countries, the diagnosis of paranoid ideation occurs in about 4 percent of the older population.[16] According to a number of sources, alcohol abuse among the elderly is becoming a growing concern.[17] The incidence of anxiety disorders among the elderly should also be mentioned. A recent and growing body of research indicates that anxiety disorders, including simple phobias, may be far more prevalent in older adults then previously believed. For example, simple phobias may be more likely than other anxiety disorders to have an onset after the age of sixty.[18] Some elderly people experience an anxiety disorder for the first time in late life, whereas others continue to suffer from preexisting anxiety disorders. Regardless of the course of an anxiety disorder, the prevalence of these disorders in older adults merits additional research.

Culturally Defined Goals in Healthcare

Discussions of healthcare reform in the United States have generated a number of articles about the Canadian healthcare system. It is not the intent of this chapter to provide a discourse on the Canadian healthcare system, but a number of factual points will be made:

- Canada does *not* have a national healthcare system per se; what Canada does have is a national insurance program (for the sake of convenience, however, I will continue to refer to "the Canadian healthcare system").
- Canada provides broader insurance protection than the United States.
- The life expectancy of men and women living in Canada is slightly longer than for men and women living in the United States.[19]

- Infant mortality is lower in Canada than in the United States.[20]
- Canada has a lower administration cost than the United States does for healthcare services.[21]
- Canada rations medical care according to need.
- Government (both federal and provincial) exercises control over specialized facilities and technology.
- Surveys of Canadian citizens indicate that although they are satisfied with the healthcare they receive, they recognize that improvement is needed.
- Canada, like the United States, believes it has too many hospitals and has taken a number of initiatives, at both the federal and the provincial level, to reduce the number of hospitals.
- According to the World Bank, both Canada and the United States have a high doctor-to-patient ratio.[22]
- Canada and the United States both offer physician-provided healthcare predominantly on a fee-for-service basis.
- The Canadian healthcare system, like the U.S. system, is considered too costly and in need of improvement.
- Canada, like the United States, is embarking at both the federal and the provincial level on plans to contain healthcare costs.
- As the noted Canadian demographer David Foote says, "If the cost of healthcare is a problem in the mid-1990's, demographics tell us that, as the saying goes, we ain't seen nothin' yet."[23]

In order to appreciate the Canadian healthcare system, it is important to know that it is anchored in the following culturally defined goals:

- Universal entitlement to healthcare
- Immediate access to healthcare

- Portability of benefits
- Limited healthcare costs
- Access to high-technology medicine

Although the United States has no formal policy, former U.S. Surgeon General C. Everett Koop[24] has stated that Americans hold three fundamental desires with respect to healthcare:

- Immediate access
- Limited costs
- Access to high-technology medicine

At this time a fourth desire, that of portability, may be appearing, advanced by the first Clinton administration. If the concept of universal coverage is also accepted in the United States as a fundamental desire, then the goals for the two countries are very similar.

Integrating Mental Health and Behavioral Health Services

In this discussion of the similarities and differences of the U.S. and Canadian systems, a comment of the American literary critic Leslie Fiedler comes to mind: "Canadians like to emphasize our differences and Americans our resemblances."[25] I want to articulate the best of both systems and try to keep in mind what Bachrach meant when she wrote, "Americans should not attempt to replicate Canadian solutions, for this would be a virtually impossible task, given the basic differences in philosophy that divide the two countries."[26]

The mental health history of each country is replete with parallels. History notes that in the last century both countries had the political option of government-financed healthcare. Canada opted for government financing, and the United States did not. This has resulted in a fragmentation of the U.S. healthcare system. In the United States, private foundations play a critical role in financing medical education and research. Employers, unions, and insurance companies are involved in financing the services. Federal, state, and local government are also involved. As a result of this fragmented funding system, the United States has difficulties in coordinating healthcare. Canada, with its single-source and provincial funding arrangements, clearly has the advantage in coordinating health services. This greater coordination is also facilitated by the differences in population between the two countries (nearly 270 million in the United States versus 30 million in Canada). Moreover, because it has been estimated that over $250 billion of the $1.1 trillion U.S. healthcare bill is related to administration costs,[27] the value of a single-payer system, in terms of a reduction in administration costs, should not be minimized. The savings in administration costs from a single-payer system can be used to provide direct care.

Historically, because Canadian physicians function in the British tradition of continuity of care, rather than in the context of case management, the integration of behavioral and physical healthcare has been facilitated. In keeping with European medical traditions, where ownership of hospitals and treatment facilities is in the hands of a single source (government), the integration of care can be legislated. Again, the United States, with its fragmented ownership of facilities (federal, state, county, and city government; private, for-profit organizations; not-for-profit organizations), finds the integration of care more difficult.

Much of the baby-boomer population in both countries will be more demanding that mental health services be integrated with physical health services. In Canada, where culturally there is less stigma attached to mental health services, this should prove easier. The general acceptance of mental health services in Canada is further facilitated by federal policies that highlight public participation in the development of mental health and healthcare programs. As pointed out by Bachrach, "Canada has a bottom line in mental health service delivery that is absent in the United States. All Canadians, irrespective of age, gender, ethnicity, socioeconomic status, or degree of physical impairment of psychopathology, have a basic and fundamental entitlement to healthcare, including mental healthcare."[28]

Allied health professions, such as occupational therapy, have a long tradition of being part of mental health services, thus facilitating the integration of physical and behavioral health services. In addition, Canada has a long tradition of incorporating both mental health services and medical (physical) services into psychiatric treatment plans. Inclusion of allied health professions is a more recent development in the United States. Canada's healthcare system was built through political consensus on types of care (it includes behavioral and physical health), and that consensus is reflected in an integrated federal healthcare policy.

A major contrast between the two countries' philosophies of care is Canada's lack of distinction between the entitlements of behavioral and physical health services. A basic underlying principle is that every Canadian citizen has a fundamental right to mental healthcare. This is reinforced by the fact that Canadians do not have to contend with individual limits on total expenditures per year, or with a fixed number of psychotherapy sessions per year, or with a fixed number of days of inpatient treatment. This lack of financial distinction between behavioral and physical health services strongly facilitates integration of the services.

Despite the mental health parity law passed in 1996, U.S. mental health services are a long way from achieving parity with physical health services. The law does not actually mandate that mental health services be provided. It only stipulates that if a company offers mental health services, they must be provided with the same limitations that apply to physical health. This law does not mandate companies without mental health programs to institute them, nor does the law apply to self-insured companies. U.S. laws do mandate that an individual have access to mental healthcare. Unfortunately, this mandate is limited to crisis-intervention services provided in a hospital emergency room.

All Canadians enter their healthcare system through the family physician or general practitioner. This "common referral pathway" is conducive to the integration of behavioral and physical medicine. (It has been said, in a tongue-in-cheek manner, that general practitioners, or GPs, practice so much psychiatry that Canada has introduced a new specialty of psychiatry, referred to as "GP psychiatry.")

In summary, although the two countries have similar mental health histories, they have developed different strengths. Canada, which has never differentiated between behavioral and physical healthcare, has developed a more coordinated system of healthcare delivery. This has proven especially beneficial to older adults. From the perspective of the older adult, Canada's single-payer system has led not only to lower administration costs but also to less complicated filing of claims.

A major strength of the U.S. healthcare system is that nowhere else in the world is there such a large number of highly trained mental health professionals. This highly skilled cadre includes practitioners who are specialists in the delivery of services to older adults. Another strength of the U.S. healthcare system is its commitment to research. The research being conducted in the United States to understand the relationship between mental and physical health in older adults will result in improved services for the older population. Yet another (and more ironic) strength of the U.S. healthcare system is that both political parties are now concerned about the cost of providing services to older Americans, and it may be this concern with costs that leads to the development of an integrated behavioral and physical healthcare system for all older adults in the United States.

Contemporary Funding Issues

A discussion of Canadian and U.S. mental health services would be incomplete without mention of contemporary funding issues. In the early 1970s, the United States initiated the comprehensive Community Health Center Program. Under this program, community health centers were funded primarily by grants from the National Institute of Mental Health (NIMH), with some state and limited local general-fund contributions. The grants were designed as "seed money" to start and run the community health centers until more permanent sources of funding could be obtained. Unfortunately, the communities, and to a large extent the states, were never sure of where or how they could obtain the necessary funds to continue the community health centers. Toward the end of the 1970s, NIMH funding gradually declined, and the search for funds shifted to other sources, including state and local government and private donors. The cost, in time and resources, of acquiring and administering these various funds was extremely high.[29] Moreover, government agencies, under pressure from special-interest groups, were forced from time to time to shift funding priorities. Today funding issues are at the boiling point. Virtually all the states are mandated to have a balanced budget on an annual or biannual basis. As healthcare costs increase, states will be faced with raising taxes, reducing healthcare benefits, curtailing other state programs (including education), or choosing some combination of these or other alternatives. In the near term, as the result of the congressionally mandated balanced budget, the federal government will not have the funds to assist the states in paying for medical care. Current projections by the Congressional Budget Office and the Office of Management and Budget indicate that by the year 2002 or 2003 the entire federal budget will be needed to pay for Social Security and healthcare benefits alone.[30] This would leave no money for national defense, education, or any other program. Clearly, this will not be allowed to occur.

Canada, by contrast, has remained fervently committed to fully government-budgeted mental health services: a single funding entity. To this end, provincial governments provide all mental health services, either directly or under contracts or grants. Funds are administered by mental health service divisions within each province's Ministry of Health, under the direction of a politically appointed deputy minister who reports to the minister of health. (The minister of health in each province is appointed by the provincial minister.) Throughout Canada, this system ensures that virtually all payments for physician and hospital mental health services are made by the Ministry of Health. The Canadian federal government assists and participates in the funding of mental health services, with certain requirements attached. Specifically, to receive federal funding, the provincial Ministries of Health must conform to the five national mandated principles: public administration, portability of benefits, comprehensiveness of service, universality of coverage, and accessibility.

Adherence to these principles (combined with a single-payer system) and the effort to become more efficient in the delivery of services have enabled Canada to attain a significant lead in coverage and efficiency over the United States. For approximately 75 percent of per capita costs in the United States, virtually 100 percent of Canadian residents now have coverage for all inpatient and outpatient mental and physical health services, physician services, services in residential settings, home-care services, and medications, as well as for other healthcare services. In terms of integrating physical healthcare, mental healthcare, and community healthcare services into a comprehensive funding framework, the completed and ongoing research at the Canadian Institute of Health Information has clearly moved Canada ahead of the United States.

Canada, almost since its inception as a country, has had a history of providing care for defined populations (that is, individuals residing in the provinces). The U.S. healthcare system, with the exception of the military and the recent introduction of health maintenance organizations, has focused on providing care for individuals. This has contributed to the development of a coordinated system in Canada and a fragmented system in the United States. It may be time for the United States to further explore the concept of providing care for defined populations in an integrated manner.

Historically, Canadians have relied on government to manage healthcare services. The United States has depended on the free market to solve problems. The use of such free-market concepts as supply and demand may be appropriate in purchasing goods and services, but healthcare services do not conform to traditional economic principles. The hope that adherence to the traditional free-market philosophy will solve U.S. healthcare concerns may be a faint hope at best.

Canada should not be looked to as a healthcare utopia; it does have a number of healthcare problems. Moreover, the question should not be which country has the better healthcare system. The more important issue is what the United States can learn and apply, not just from Canada but from itself and other countries as well. U.S. Senator Phil Gramm (R. Texas), chairman of the U.S. Senate Health Care Subcommittee, has remarked that today's solvency crises in Medicare are occurring at a time when the number of retirees receiving Medicare benefits is growing at a modest rate of 200,000 per year. Fifteen years from now the number of Americans who are sixty-five and older will be growing by 1,600,000 per year and will remain at that level for the next twenty years.[31] At the current rate of growth in Medicare costs and the current rate of decline in the ratio of workers to retirees, *Medicare poses the greatest internal financial crisis ever faced by the U.S. government* (emphasis mine).

The dramatic increase in the number of older Americans requiring healthcare services may also tax the nation beyond its healthcare resources. On the basis of demographics alone, the United States can be judged to have a short time in which to develop an integrated, affordable system of behavioral and physical healthcare for older adults. In light of this looming crisis, perhaps the words of Sir Winston Churchill can provide a measure of hope. In Churchill's words, "you can count on Americans to do the right thing, once they have exhausted all other alternatives."

Chapter Four

Quality Psychotherapy

Measures for Tracking Change

Deborah W. Frazer

In the olden days, determination of good clinical work was a matter to be determined by the therapist, the client, and the therapist's conscience. In an agency setting, there might be a clinical supervisor or an administrator who would occasionally ask questions about the therapy. Colleagues from other disciplines might quietly ask, "What do you talk about in there all that time? Does it really do any good?" In private practice, patient and referral-source satisfaction provided an evaluation mechanism by ensuring a healthy caseload to those who satisfied their patients. And yet we knew in our hearts that patient satisfaction alone was not synonymous with good or appropriate care.

What, exactly, *is* good and appropriate psychotherapeutic care for older adults? Strangely enough, many experienced clinicians are having to fundamentally rethink our methods of evaluation and self-evaluation in this era of managed care. Increasingly we are being asked to apply scientific principles to the therapeutic process. This worries us. Are we sacrificing the "art" of therapy, the spiritual or existential dimensions, and the healing powers of relationship for consistency, standardization, and cost-benefit analysis? How do we objectively measure such outcomes as internal peace, renewed hope, or a sense of legacy?

Treating a Diverse Community

Psychotherapy with older adults has always presented therapists with complex challenges. When geriatrics began to be recognized as a specialty, it seemed to promise the predictable developmental stages and problems of pediatrics. However, geropsychologists quickly learned that the over-sixty-five crowd is a very diverse group indeed. Whereas toddlers and teenagers share a great deal of behavior that is based on age or developmental stage, older adults are far more heterogeneous.

At first, we divided the elderly into the "young" old (sixty-five to seventy-four), the "middle" old (seventy-five to eighty-four), and the "old" old (over eighty-five), as a way to think about the diversity among older adults. Then we began to recognize that chronological age is not nearly as important as physical health in predicting issues and outcomes for the elderly. Gender, socioeconomic status, religion, and cultural background also contribute to variability. Managed care, with its emphasis on cost containment and assumption of financial risk, has been devising ways to stratify risk by assessing and categorizing older adults into "successful" agers (low risk), "typical" agers (moderate risk), and "accelerated" agers (high risk). In the future, we will no doubt continue to see models that more finely capture the diversity of this age group and use these analyses to determine interventions and predict outcomes.

For the therapist, diversity is represented in the types of problems and issues that clients bring to sessions. Some issues are typical for any adult psychotherapy practice: depression, anxiety, interpersonal difficulties, chronic mental illness, substance abuse. Some issues are more prevalent in late life: cognitive impairment or dementia, significant and multiple losses, functional and sensory changes or impairments. Some issues are related to physical illness, medication, or surgical procedures: depression in Parkinson's disease, left-hemisphere strokes, or end-stage cardiovascular disease; anxiety in chronic obstructive pulmonary disease (COPD); cognitive impairment related to antihypertensive medication or cardiac bypass surgery. The therapist is certainly challenged by the complexities of the elderly population and their range of issues.

To work with this diverse set of older individuals and issues, a wide range of therapeutic modalities has been developed. Again, some modalities are precisely those used in any adult practice: cognitive-behavioral, psychodynamic, interpersonal, and behavioral therapies all have demonstrated feasibility, utility, and efficacy with cognitively intact older adults. Other modalities and approaches have developed specifically in response to older adults' needs: reminiscence therapy, validation therapy, environmental modification, and support for caregivers are a few examples. In addition, some traditional modalities have been modified or adapted for use with the cognitively and sensorially impaired. There is, unfortunately, considerably less empirical validation of the therapeutic approaches used with frail and/or cognitively impaired elderly.

Variations in Outcome Measurement by Goal of Treatment

With this diversity of population, issues, and therapeutic modalities, how do we conceptualize an approach to outcome measurement? Measurement of the outcome of treatment is really trying to answer the question "Did application of this treatment achieve the goal?" On the surface, this is a relatively straightforward question, but changes in the underlying philosophy of healthcare render it more complex.

In the acute-care medical model, which currently governs Medicare fee-for-service reimbursement and many private sector managed-care companies, the goal of treatment is the amelioration of disease and disability. This model developed from the acute-care medical model, which flourished in the postantibiotic era. Modern medicine optimistically pursued the development of a chemical and surgical armamentarium to conquer diseases. Does the client suffer from depressive illness? Prescribe one pill daily (and/or provide one session weekly) for four to six weeks, and recheck the Geriatric Depression Scale score: diagnose and measure the illness, apply the treatment, and assess the extent of the "cure." Only services that are "medically necessary" are reimbursed—which usually means services that will cure or ameliorate an identified disease. It is a straightforward, clean-but-narrow model, and it is perfectly appropriate in some cases.

In the behavioral medicine model developed over the last two decades, the goal of treatment was broadened to include prevention of disease and disability. This model recognized that the best approach to COPD was not to give drugs or oxygen therapy to a seventy-five-year-old but to provide smoking-prevention and smoking-cessation programs to thirty-five-year-olds. In the behavioral health arena, we saw the rise of stress-management programs, medication-compliance programs, wellness programs, and brief psychotherapies oriented to solving everyday problems *before* a clinical depression or a panic attack developed. These approaches are primarily supported by managed-care organizations (MCOs) that assume financial risk for all treatment for a specified population. Unlike the fee-for-service arrangement of indemnity insurance, some MCOs recognized that they could increase profits by preventively maintaining the health of the "capitated" population. Under this model, outcome measurement may assess the treatment effects of acute care; in addition, however, outcomes are defined epidemiologically as well as clinically. Can COPD or clinical depression be prevented in an entire defined population by encouraging lifestyle or behavioral changes through prevention programs? Prevalence and incidence rates became critical measures for a population's health and, therefore, for the profitability of MCOs in the private sector.

Managed care has added a new feature to outcome measurement in healthcare: customer satisfaction. As healthcare becomes "industrialized," competition is fostered in the marketplace. Remember patients, clients, consumers, and nursing home residents? Now "customers," whether they are individuals choosing an insurance plan or employers choosing plan options for their employees, are subjected to marketing from various plans. To enroll and retain customers, MCOs need to measure satisfaction and develop a process for remedying situations that produce dissatisfaction. Satisfaction-related outcomes are generally not measured in traditional indemnity-based insurance plans. Measures of customer satisfaction are also a point of leverage that patients have when MCOs manage only costs, not care.

Adapting Models for Geriatric Care

Traditional medical models and managed-care models alike are challenged by geriatric healthcare. As geriatrics developed as a field, it began to define the goals of healthcare, and therefore the measurement of outcomes, in entirely new ways. Geriatrics is defined by chronic, not acute, illness and by comorbid, not single, conditions. The goal is not necessarily a cure and not necessarily prevention. In fact, the goal may not even be to preserve life (heretofore a medical given), but rather to balance the preservation of life with a higher quality of life. End-of-life care in particular has moved increasingly to a "palliative care" model, where treatment of acute conditions may be forgone entirely in pursuit of the goal of a peaceful, pain-free, and meaningful or dignified death. Thus geriatric medicine has broadened the goals: from cure to prevention to quality of life. The new challenge becomes the definition and measurement of quality of life.

As managed-care organizations develop more experience in the care of the frail elderly, they will continue to struggle with the definition of the goals of care. Full capitation, or assumption of full risk, offers many opportunities as well as dangers. Capitated acute care can include the goals of curing disease, preventing disease, and enhancing quality of life. But capitated long-term care offers even greater opportunities, especially the reintegration of medical, mental, and social approaches to care. Using a "biopsychosocial" or "holistic" model of care, integrated long-term-care systems can provide interdisciplinary team services, recognizing the inextricable links among medical, mental, and social issues. It is to be hoped that we will see an end to the practice of "carving out" behavioral care and completely ignoring such social issues as family support and problems of a legal, financial, transportational, and residential nature.

But integrated care will also require integrated outcome measurement. For example, we will recognize that an intervention in the biological, the psychological, or the social domain can have repercussions in one or both of the other domains. Assessing, tracking, and analyzing these complex pathways are measurement challenges, to be sure, and yet for the first time we may be closer to measuring the complexity of real-life outcomes.

Comparing Models of Care

How might these different models of healthcare—the traditional medical model, managed care, and integrated care—suggest different goals in a specific case? Let us imagine the case of Mr. B., an elderly man:

> Mr. B. Lives at home with his wife. Ten years ago he developed diabetes. Always a hearty eater who relished his food and drink, Mr. B. reacted poorly to his diagnosis, prognosis, and plan of care. He refused to change his eating and exercise habits, stating that he preferred to die "fat and happy." Over time, diabetic complications began to set in: problems with vision, peripheral numbness and tingling, lingering foot infections. Different medications were tried, and brief exhortations were made about diet and exercise. Mr. B.'s foot infections became more severe, and he was finally told that his leg would need to be amputated below the knee. Mr. B., who had alternated between despair and rage over his deteriorating condition, lapsed into a profound depression. Between her husband's depression and the prospect of caring for an amputee, Mrs. B. became overwhelmed. She began to consider placing her husband in a nursing home. At this point, Mr. B.'s physician started Mr. B. on antidepressant medication and referred him to a psychologist for therapy.

If Mr. B. goes to a traditional psychologist under traditional Medicare reimbursement, the psychologist must diagnose the illness (depression) to establish medical necessity. The treatment goal will be to lessen or even cure the depression. In addition, the psychologist may attempt to increase Mr. B.'s motivation to control his blood-sugar levels. The service pattern will probably be weekly outpatient psychotherapy sessions lasting forty-five to fifty minutes. The outcome will be measured by a decrease in Mr. B.'s depressive symptomatology (reported or observed) and by a reported increase in Mr. B.'s motivation to improve control of his blood-sugar levels.

If Mr. B. goes to a behavioral health "carve out" psychologist, the goals, service delivery, and outcome measurement will be similar, with the exception that the service will probably be limited to a defined number of sessions.

If, Mr. B. goes to a behavioral health provider working as part of an interdisciplinary health team, the goals (and therefore measurement of the outcome) will be much broader: to support Mr. B. and his wife in ways that will maximize Mr. B.'s independent functioning and mental well-being in an optimal environment. The provider may combine traditional psychotherapy with monitoring of Mr. B.'s glucose testing, arranging for Mr. B. to meet with a diabetes educator, setting up family sessions, arranging individual support for Mr. B.'s wife, and arranging transportation for Mr. B. to a diabetes-support group. In the beginning, sessions may be short and held every day; as goals are achieved, they may taper off. Sessions may also be provided in Mr. B.'s home. The outcome will be measured by a decrease in Mr. B.'s depression and an increase in his motivation to control his blood-sugar levels, but it will also be measured in terms of Mr. B.'s (and his wife's) perceived well-being, their satisfaction with services, the length of time that Mr. B. will remain able to live at home, and the costs and use of all services.

At its best, capitated integrated healthcare will allow behavioral health providers to reach beyond the narrow goals and outcomes of the traditional medical model. Roles for the individual therapist may expand to include elements of case management, medical monitoring, family counseling, and environmental consulting. Outcome measurement broadens as the goals of integrated healthcare become broader. In the case of Mr. B., behavioral health is recognized as having effects at the biological level (Mr. B.'s diabetes), the psychological level (his depression), and the social level (where Mr. B. lives). The relief of depressive symptoms is only one of multiple foci for behavioral intervention.

Outcome Measurement in an Integrated Care System

Four principles underlie outcome measurement in integrated care. First, the outcome measurement recognizes that individuals are multifaceted and exist in a physical and psychosocial environment. Second, outcomes can be specified and measured across a continuum, from the most "proximal" or biological dimensions to the most "distal" or social dimensions. Third, the outcomes to be measured include both objective factors and subjective perceptions. Fourth, measurement of outcomes is included for both the client and family members.

Each individual provider in the integrated care system brings a unique perspective, set of goals, and potential suggestions for measuring outcomes. What the behavioral healthcare provider brings is specific expertise in issues of cognition, affect, and behavior. Each of these three areas has an extensive array of measures for adults in general and older adults in particular[1].

Assessing Cognition

Change in cognition would most likely be targeted as a goal if the identified problems and interventions addressed the following conditions:

- Delirium
- Reversible dementia
- Alzheimer's disease being treated with chemical agents

- Cognitive impairment associated with mood or anxiety disorders, or with substance abuse or misuse
- Remediation of cerebral insults
- Mild cognitive disorders due to "disuse"

In each case, selection of the assessment instrument would be based on a combination of factors related to the time and/or resources available for assessment and to the need for fine-grained analysis. In many of these problems, it should be noted, intervention will be medical, not psychological, but the psychologist may be asked to measure cognitive outcomes because of his or her expertise in this area.

In all cognitive assessment, it is critical to be sensitive to issues that may affect performance on a test. Education level, cultural and ethnic influences, and generational or cohort effects can all compromise measurement. Of course, as with any other kind of assessment, accommodations should be made to an individual's sensory impairments, level of fatigue, and speed of processing and response. The majority of my own assessment experience has been with clients who require adaptations of standard instruments or procedures: very old and medically frail people, elderly schizophrenics, and immigrants. When working with individuals like these, I am rarely confident that a single assessment session accurately captures cognitive capacities; I much prefer a repeated-measures approach, where the first of several assessments functions as a personal baseline against which future assessments are measured. I find that the information gathered from repeat testings—individual advances and declines in specific areas—is far more valuable than comparison of an individual's data to a hypothetical "norm." For example, it has never been helpful to me or my client to know that a seventy-five-year-old schizophrenic does not have "normal" cognition; it is far more helpful to know whether his lifelong abnormal function is getting worse. Various "corrections" have been published for education and age, and recently tests have become available for assessing cognitive function in ethnic-minority elders. These help to address the "error variance" if the psychologist has only one opportunity for assessment, but my own strong suggestion for best practice is to follow someone over time and assess intraindividual variability.

It is particularly important to attend to and measure patient and family reports of functional difficulties if time allows only for cognitive screening. It is never wise to base decisions about treatment or its outcome on a single source of data, particularly if that data source is a screening instrument. In today's cost-and-time-conscious climate, however, behavioral healthcare providers will be pressured to pick one simple measure, set precise values predictive of risk, qualify an individual for service, and measure the outcome. This kind of pressure assumes a scientific level of measurement that has not yet been achieved. Providers must resist this pressure, insist on multiple data sources, and insist on the need, in selected cases, to gather more extensive data.

A recent document will give practitioners the basis for insisting on adequate assessments. The Agency for Health Care Policy and Research (AHCPR) has issued a clinical-practice guideline for recognition and initial assessment of Alzheimer's disease and related dementias[2]. The AHCPR recognizes the need to combine a clinical interview with functional and mental-status assessment, and it recommends both direct and informant-based assessment. The flowchart included with this document specifies that further evaluation is needed when results of either the functional assessment or the mental status are abnormal.

Of the brief mental status instruments, the Mini-Mental State Exam (MMSE) is my personal favorite (there is a new "3 MS" version, which I have not tried). The MMSE is widely used and relatively quick. It has demonstrated reliability, validity, and fairly good range, and it is sensitive to change. Because it is so widely used, it is often possible to obtain prior MMSE scores from previous providers or sites. It can be administered by other professionals, although there is often minor disagreement on scoring. (For example, if an individual says that today is April 30 and it is actually April 29, does he really have to lose the point?) A major difficulty at the upper end of the MMSE is its lack of sensitivity to impairment. A well-educated and/or well-compensated individual can score in the 27–30 range and still show significant cognitive impairment on more detailed assessments. Conversely, it is not a useful instrument with severe dementia.

My own experience with the MMSE is that it is extremely valuable as a thumbnail sketch of a client. When supervisees are presenting cases to me in clinical supervision, the first thing I ask for is an MMSE score. It gives me a ballpark range of cognitive function. When I am discussing a case over the phone with the attending psychiatrist, the MMSE score orients both of us at the outset of the discussion. We use a particular MMSE score (about 15) as a rough guide to whether psychotherapy has become "friendly visiting" because of the client's potential inability to maintain within-session gains over time. We groan when asked to do competency evaluations on clients with scores in the low 20s because we know the call will be difficult. We know that scores under 10 generally mean that talking therapy is out of the question—yet there are always exceptions. There is sadness in watching an annual MMSE go from 27 to 24 to 20 to 17; little numbers capture an entire person slipping away. And there is always the excitement of watching an MMSE go *up* in poststroke recovery, successfully treated delirium, or, what is most gratifying, successfully treated depression with cognitive impairment.

The danger is in thinking that the MMSE score is a direct and accurate window into a person's brain. Too many times I have been shocked by a disconnection between the MMSE score and my clinical experience—discovering, for example, that the woman with whom I was having such terrific therapy sessions (including insight) scored only in the mid-teens, or that a man who scored in the 20s seemed to understand everything and yet later remembered nothing. The brain and its diseases are complex, and a simple score derived in ten minutes cannot fully capture either the brain's limits or its potential.

Beyond using cognitive screening instruments like the MMSE, the psychologist may want to assess specific areas of cognitive

function. The specific capacities to be assessed will be determined
by the goal of the intervention, but they may include measurement
of one or more of the following domains:

- Attention and concentration
- Learning and memory
- Reasoning and executive function
- Expressive and receptive language
- Visual-spatial abilities
- Visual-motor functioning

As mentioned earlier, these tests are reviewed in two very useful
documents prepared by the National Center for Cost Containment,[3] and Costa, Williams, and Somerfield also review instruments and short batteries.[4] (For additional review material, see
Chapter Five of this volume.)

Assessing Affect

The most prevalent affective disorders in the elderly are depression
and anxiety. Measurement of these conditions is difficult because
many of the physical symptoms (fatigue, restlessness, loss of weight
and/or appetite) are also indicative of medical conditions or reactions to medication. There is a further confounding of affective
symptoms with cognitive symptoms (for example, the dementia
syndrome of depression). Like the measurement of cognitive capacities, the measurement of affect should comprise more than one
data source. In addition, some capacity for assessing qualitatively as
well as quantitatively adds valuable clinical information.

The Geriatric Depression Scale

Perhaps the most widely used tool for assessing self-reported depression is the Geriatric Depression Scale (GDS), especially in its short form of fifteen questions. This scale is not only brief but also easily administered, still useful with individuals who show cognitive impairment, less confounded with medical issues than other scales are, and sensitive to change. Other popular scales are the Hamilton Rating Scale for Depression, the Zung Self-Rating Depression Scale, and the Beck Depression Inventory, all developed for younger populations. The Center for Epidemiological Studies' Depression Screening Measure (CES-D) is a brief, twenty-item scale with strong psychometric properties and research in diverse populations. It was designed as an epidemiological instrument, but it works as a brief screen for depressive symptoms over the past week. Newer scales developed for the elderly are the Geriatric Depression Rating Scale, the Cornell Scale for Depression in Dementia, and the Dementia Mood Assessment Scale.

My personal experience with the GDS is somewhat more mixed than with the MMSE. By comparison with the fifteen-item version, the longer version of the GDS is stronger psychometrically but redundant and unnecessarily time-consuming. The Clinical Research Center group at the Philadelphia Geriatric Center has established that the GDS's reliability and validity hold up with some cognitive impairment, and my clinical experience is consonant with that finding. Several researchers have pointed out, however, that cognitively impaired persons may underreport depression, and that informant reports and clinical interviews are necessary to a full assessment of depression. My own concern about the GDS really has to do with a question involved in any self-report depression measure: To what extent are we getting a "response set," influenced by gender and by ethnic, personality, and situational variables, rather than an accurate measurement of some affective "truth"?

Let me give some examples. We know that women in general endorse depressive symptoms more than men do. Are women truly more depressed, or do they simply discuss their feelings more readily? We know that certain ethnic groups in general are more emotionally expressive than others. Does this mean that they experience depression more or report it more? I always take particular note of a GDS score of 30 (endorsement of every single item). A GDS score of 30 raises a personality-disorder flag for me, but I don't know of actual research on this subject; I suspect that this is a person who is never going to be happy with anything, but who may actually be functioning fairly well.

Then there are situational variables. I have suspected on occasion that self-reports of depression are elevated because my clients (who are no dummies) realize that for our sessions (which they enjoy) to continue, "problems" are required. I worry that they offer me a nice high GDS score to keep me engaged with them. These are only clinical musings, but I suspect that they may speak to some underlying problems with self-report instruments. An alternative to a GDS self-report might be a depression-symptom checklist based on the criteria for depression listed in the fourth edition of the *Diagnostic and Statistical Manual of Mental Disorders* (DSM-IV).[5] As someone who works with the frail elderly, this would be less acceptable to me because the vegetative signs of depression are so terribly confounded with medical and medication problems. On the whole, I find the GDS useful and sensitive to change, especially if I balance it with my clinical judgment.

My main difficulty with using depression measures to track outcomes is that they don't capture a *single* yet clinically critical change. Two cases immediately come to mind. The first involves a man who over a five-month period was dying of brain cancer. I was originally called in because he was so angry and abusive to the staff. Over the course of our sessions, we identified his underlying depression, and his sadness came to the fore. Although I wasn't tracking it then, his GDS score would have gone up. Two weeks before his death, he was sobbing and sobbing, saying, "I missed the whole point—the whole point is people!" He continued to actively mourn his lifelong lack of interpersonal relationships, and he felt he wasn't ready to die because he had only just now "understood." Three days before his death, having completed his mourning, he announced that it was all right; he was ready to die. The next day he went into a coma, and two days later he died. I have never been so moved during therapy. I feel that this man and I gave each other precious gifts of understanding. He did enormous work, and he achieved both understanding and peace. If I had been tracking his GDS score, he would have looked worse. If a managed-care company had been using a GDS score to determine whether therapy was working and should be continued, we would have been denied authorization for treatment.

The second case that comes to mind was one that I was supervising. The woman was in chronic pain, very old and very frail. Everything hurt, she was miserable, and her misery showed up in her endorsement of nine out of nine DSM-IV symptoms of depression. On the item about death, she had thoughts of death, wished to die, had a plan for dying (to waste away), and had made an "attempt" to die in that she was indeed slowly losing weight. The young therapist saw her over several months, in two weekly sessions of twenty to thirty minutes. The pain continued, the depression continued, and she still endorsed nine out of nine symptoms. But on the item about death, although she still had thoughts of death and wished to die, she no longer wanted to take her own life. Something had changed through that therapeutic relationship, and she had begun to treasure what life she still had. She decided that she would "let nature take its course," and she did in fact die several months later, of natural causes. The change that happened for this woman in therapy would not have been picked up as significant on either the GDS or a symptom checklist, and certainly not on the Global Assessment of Functioning scale required by many managed-care companies. Her change would have seemed very minor on a scaled score, yet it was the difference between internal war and peace. How do we measure that?

Measuring Anxiety

Depression is the most common disorder that we treat in the elderly, but anxiety, alone or in combination with depression, is also prevalent. Scales specific to anxiety are not in wide use with the elderly, and measurement of anxiety symptoms is generally done with broader measures of psychopathology, such as the Symptom Checklist-90-Revised (SCL-90) or its short form, the Brief Symptom Inventory (BSI). The SCL-90 has been used widely as a sensitive measure of change. It provides an overall estimate of distress and nine subscales. The test takes about fifteen to twenty minutes to complete, whereas the BSI takes about ten minutes. The psychometric properties are acceptable, and geriatric norms are available on the BSI. In addition to measures of depression and anxiety, the SCL-90 and the BSI yield scores on seven additional domains: somatization, obsessive-compulsivity, interpersonal sensitivity, hostility, phobia anxiety, paranoid ideation, and psychoticism. For a brief but broad measure of pathological symptoms, these instruments are probably the strongest.

Other Measurements

In addition to measuring outcomes related to pathology, providers may want to look at broader psychosocial outcomes. The oldest instruments for measuring these are the Life Satisfaction Index (A and B); the Life Satisfaction Instrument—Z, Satisfaction with Life Scale; the Philadelphia Geriatric Center Morale Scale—Revised; and the Life Satisfaction in the Elderly Scale. These scales have been used extensively for research purposes, but they have received less clinical use. Because we clinicians have been operating under a strict medical model, with "medical necessity" determined by a disease state, the tracking of outcomes related to quality of life has been discouraged. I am hopeful that greater sophistication about behavioral healthcare for the elderly will increase awareness of the importance of these "quality of life" instruments. Even greater challenges will come from the hospice and palliative-care movements. How will we identify and track "outcomes" at the point where psychotherapy blends with spirituality? A few instruments—such as the Life Purpose Questionnaire and the Purpose in Life Test—attempt measurement in the more existential realm.

The specific concerns of caregivers have spawned a group of "caregiver burden" instruments: the Caregiver Burden Screen, the Burden Interview, and the Caregiving Hassles Scale. These instruments, as well as several others designed for such specific therapeutic issues as abuse, marital satisfaction, and retirement, are unlikely to serve widely in tracking outcomes, because they are so narrowly concerned with single therapeutic issues. I am currently working with an outcomes specialist to determine whether therapeutic work on specific issues might best be tracked through the old method of goal-attainment scaling. In that system, the therapist and the client work toward highly individualized goals, and measurement is in terms of the percentage of gain toward the goals. That method also may prove useful for tracking progress in palliative care and other less medically defined therapeutic situations.

Assessing Behavior

Assessment of behavior generally falls into two categories: functional behavior, such as the activities of daily living (the ADLs) and the instrumental activities of daily living; and dysfunctional behavior that is problematic to the client or to caregivers. An old, quick, reliable favorite of mine for assessing six basic ADLs is the Physical Self-Maintenance Scale (PSMS). Its partner instrument, the Instrumental Activities of Daily Living (IADL) Scale, measures competence in eight more complex behavioral areas. Costa, Williams, and Somerfield, after a meta-analysis of functional and mental tests, recommend the use of the Functional Activities Questionnaire (FAQ).[6] This test is informant-based and rates ten complex, higher-order functional activities. I haven't used the FAQ, but the quantitative data presented in the guideline are impressive. Hartman-Stein has recently developed an inventory of functional competence to be administered to caregivers: the Behavioral Competence Inventory (BCI).[7]

Three comprehensive functional "batteries" assess individuals on multiple domains, including functional behaviors, resources, and mental and physical health: the Older American's Resources and Services Questionnaire (OARS), the Multilevel Assessment Instrument (MAI), and the Comprehensive Assessment and Referral Evaluation (CARE). Developed primarily for community-residing individuals, they have the multiple domain structure of the Minimum Data Set (MDS) in use in nursing homes. All are quite long and represent a significant commitment for planning and tracking comprehensive care.

Numerous scales are available to rate dysfunctional or problematic behaviors. Among them are the Neuropsychiatric Inventory (NPI), the Revised Memory and Behavior Problems Checklist (RMBPC), the TRIMS Behavior Problem Checklist (BPC), the Disruptive Behavior Scale (DBS), the Nursing Home Behavior Problem Scale (NHBPS), and the Cohen-Mansfield Agitation Inventory (CMAI). Personally, I prefer to use instruments that are integrated into my clinical work. For problem behaviors, I like to choose one or two behaviors to focus on and then get the caregivers to track specific behavioral incidents. In nursing homes this has become common because of Omnibus Budget Reconciliation Act (OBRA) mandates for documenting behavioral problems among residents who are on psychoactive medications, but in my experience the behavior-tracking forms that often are developed by pharmaceutical companies tend toward simple recordings of frequency. Recently I have been working on modifying behavior-monitoring forms to increase their clinical utility by adding components of behavioral analysis (antecedents or triggers, consequences, time of day, and so forth). I have found that the pharmaceutical companies are very willing to modify or customize their forms. The real trick is to develop a form that is complex enough to be useful for behavioral analysis and outcome measurement and yet simple enough to be used by direct-care providers. Staff in nursing homes are now willing to use these tracking forms, recognizing them as a regulatory "must," but caregivers in assisted-living or home-healthcare settings may need to be persuaded (and shown) that such forms are useful. I think that if informants can reliably record behavior on the monitoring forms, these forms are the best way to track specific disruptive or difficult behaviors.

As mentioned earlier, the psychologist will have to weigh the characteristics, strengths, and weaknesses of each of these measures against the demands of the situation when it comes to selecting a specific measure or set of measures. Consider the amount of time available for assessment, the need for a narrow rather than broad focus, and the client's cognitive level now and over the expected period of service. Consult the reviews and manuals for psychometric properties, and select the most reliable and valid measures possible. Test out a few measures before making a commitment.

Integrated Healthcare Outcome Measures

Ideally, psychologists work as part of an integrated-care team. As such, they should be cognizant of measures in use to broadly assess the impact of illness on an individual's life. Two of the most widely used instruments for evaluating health outcomes are the Sickness Impact Profile and the SF-36. The former has 136 items and takes approximately thirty minutes to complete, as either a structured interview or a patient-completed instrument. It is scored in three dimensions and on twelve categories ranging from self-care to instrumental activities to social and emotional behavior and to such biological functions as sleep. It is well validated but quite long for routine use. The SF-36 is a newer instrument, developed as part of the Medical Outcomes Study approach.[8] It has 36 items and takes approximately fifteen minutes to complete. It is designed to be completed by the patient. It measures three major health attributes (functional status, well-being, and overall health) and eight health concepts, including physical and social functioning, role limitations, mental health, energy/fatigue, pain, and general perceived health. The psychometric properties in this instrument are strong, and its brevity is appealing. I do worry that the 6-point Likert-scale format is much too difficult for someone with cognitive impairment.

Both instruments add the helpful dimension of subjective perception of health status and its impact on quality of life. I was delighted to discover the significant extent to which both instruments accord weight to the social and psychological outcomes of illness. They begin to address the geriatric concerns of balancing quality of life against attempts to cure disease. Other measures that will be important to measurement of outcomes in integrated healthcare are objective health-status measures, measures of satisfaction with the living environment, measures of social and informal support and of satisfaction with them, and measures of healthcare use and the costs of care. As managed-care organizations seek to limit healthcare use, it will be imperative that data be carefully collected to measure use and costs of healthcare against broad measures of healthcare outcomes.

Measurement Challenges

I've found that clinicians, even scientist-practitioner clinicians, have always been a little suspect of research-generated "truths." We always know the one client who doesn't fit the model at all. And we know, from firsthand experience, when these research-oriented measures don't work right. How do we caution the managed-care organizations that are now going to rely on "objective" data?

First, a great many of the instruments discussed in this chapter use self-ratings, and we must watch out for self-ratings performed by cognitively impaired people. Cognitive impairment is more subtle than an MMSE score would lead one to believe. Even mild impairment may interfere with reliable and valid ratings. Moreover, factors related to social desirability, particularly in this noncomplaining cohort, can affect validity. Further threats to validity come from the fact that clients and caregivers often are aware of the potential impact of their ratings. For example, every admissions staff person in a nursing home knows that "problematic" behaviors are terribly underreported when families are attempting to place someone. The reliability and the validity of an instrument are usually determined under research conditions, not when Mom's placement is being determined. Users of these instruments must also be aware of how the financial and service structures could affect reporting, and they should make adjustments as necessary.

Second, we must realize that although it is advisable to use multiple data sources, we are then confronted with data conflicts. Mom reports no depression in Dad, but the adult son reports that Dad is constantly complaining. Mom does all her self-care at home, but she collapses into dependence at the Day Center. These are clinically interesting and challenging events, but how do we report "objectively" on Mom's or Dad's capacities? When service use is being determined by rating scales, we need to develop conventions for addressing conflicting data in a way that doesn't deny care when it is needed.

Third, we must not be simplistic about cause and effect. As already mentioned, the impact of an intervention in one domain may be measured in the outcomes of a completely different domain. We are only at the beginning of understanding the complex causal pathways involved in comprehensive care of the elderly. Measurement of outcomes needs to proceed experimentally and cautiously, not be used prematurely to deny care or cut costs.

Let's return to our initial concerns. What, exactly, *is* good and appropriate psychotherapeutic care for older adults? Are we being asked to sacrifice it in the name of cost-benefit analysis? At the moment, I feel humble about our ability to answer the first question. I feel a new appreciation for the Boulder model of psychologist as both scientist and practitioner in which we were trained and a renewed closeness to my scientific colleagues. Only when scientists and clinicians work together to answer the first question convincingly (especially where frail elders are concerned) will we have the ability to demonstrate the benefits of quality behavioral care. When we can scientifically demonstrate the benefits of good care through careful measurement of positive outcomes, the cost of our interventions will be worth it.

Suggested Reading

U.S. Department of Veterans Affairs & University HealthSystem Consortium. *Dementia Identification and Assessment: Guidelines for Primary Care Practitioners*. Washington, D.C.: U.S. Department of Veterans Affairs, 1997.

Chapter Five

Cost-Effective
Geriatric Neuropsychology

Peter A. Lichtenberg

Clinical neuropsychology, a subspecialty of clinical psychology that has rapidly expanded since the early 1970s, is the application of brain-behavior knowledge to patients. Well before the advent of modern brain imaging—for example, computerized tomography (or CAT scanning), magnetic-resonance imaging (MRI), and positron emission tomography (or PET scanning)—neuropsychologists had demonstrated that brain dysfunction could be detected by a series of carefully constructed paper-and-pencil tasks. The tasks were created to formally assess such cognitive functions as attention, language, memory, visual-spatial skills, mental flexibility, and psychomotor skills. Currently neuropsychologists complete a doctorate in psychology and then spend one to two years in postdoctoral training, obtaining advanced supervised experience in neuropsychology. Born from half a century of detailed work on how the aging process affects cognitive functioning, geriatric neuropsychology is the clinical application of aging and cognition knowledge, along with the integration of what is known about brain-behavior relationships.

Neuropsychology's Roles in Recent History

Psychologists trained to work with older adults brought the use of geriatric neuropsychological techniques forward in the 1980s. In the early 1980s Albert wrote her seminal paper on geriatric neuropsychology.[1] The greatest challenges, she pointed out, were in the separation between normal age-related changes and early dementia. To accomplish this separation, she wrote, the application of several known neuropsychological tests would have to be expanded to the aged population—that is, normal performance by healthy older adults would have to be defined on a variety of tests known to be sensitive to brain damage in younger adults. Only by amassing good normative data, Albert argued, could a single patient's score be evaluated for impairment. She also argued that cutoff scores would need to be developed in order to demonstrate that cognitively impaired elders differ in reliable ways from cognitively intact elders.

Later in the 1980s, geriatric neuropsychology received recognition from the work group of the National Institute of Neurological Communicative Disorders and Stroke and Alzheimer's Disease and Related Disorders Association (NINCDS-ADRDA) in its clinical criteria for the diagnosis of Alzheimer's disease. The work group stated that for a diagnosis of probable Alzheimer's disease, dementia must be confirmed by neuropsychological tests. As a result of the development of these criteria, geriatric neuropsychology was included in the core elements of the diagnostic workups for most Alzheimer's disease centers.

The best way to describe the practice of geriatric neuropsychology is to discuss the roles played by neuropsychologists. The role of interpreter is one important dimension of the neuropsychologist's practice. Many patients undergo careful medical and radiological examinations that reveal brain damage. This information is usually conveyed to other healthcare providers in highly technical language, and it is useful for the psychologist familiar with older adults to integrate and summarize these findings so that the behavioral manifestations of the brain damage can be understood. Thus another important role for the neuropsychological practitioner is that of educator: brain damage often causes certain predictable behavioral disturbances (confusion, withdrawal, paranoid beliefs) that mystify families and many healthcare professionals, and neuropsychological practitioners can help educate others about which behaviors are under a patient's direct control and which are due to brain dysfunction.

But the two most important roles for the neuropsychological practitioner working with older adults are the roles of diagnostician and interventionist. As will be discussed in more detail, assessment of cognition in older adults may be the most accurate and cost-effective way of detecting dementia. In addition, the use of the results of cognitive testing for practical treatment recommendations makes neuropsychological testing an incredibly valuable service.

Today's healthcare market is beginning to limit the availability of geriatric neuropsychological practice. Many if not most managed-care plans do not cover neuropsychological assessment services. This limitation, coupled with primary-care healthcare providers' comparative lack of sophistication about dementia, leads to below-par diagnostic and treatment services for dementia. The purpose of this chapter is to educate healthcare administrators and clinical colleagues from other disciplines about the value of including geriatric neuropsychological services in the managed-care arena.

Clinical practice in this era of tightly controlled managed care requires that three conditions be satisfied:

1. The practice of neuropsychology must demonstrate added value to the healthcare of the consumer.

2. The practice of neuropsychology must be cost-conscious and competitive with other practices.

3. The practice of neuropsychology must specify a set of easily followed standards of care.

Geriatric neuropsychology is in danger of being left out of the managed-care arena because it has failed so far to demonstrate its compliance with these three conditions in a convincing fashion.

This chapter will argue for the inclusion of neuropsychological assessment for older adults in managed-care plans, define the added value of this inclusion, address issues of cost, and lay out a standard of care. Specifically, I will argue that neuropsychological practice has the added value of detecting dementia earlier and better than any primary-care or specialty-care service can, and therefore of helping patients and healthcare providers plan appropriate care. The specific training that psychologists receive in assessment is unique; without that training, physicians and other healthcare providers are very limited in their ability to detect dementia.

Shortcomings of Assessment in Primary Care

Primary-care physicians often fail to detect dementia in their older patients. The doctor-patient relationship, which underlies primary-care practice, is based on the assumption that patients will report their problems to physicians and that, largely on the basis of those reports, the doctor will determine appropriate differential diagnoses and use his or her expertise to identify the correct disease and provide treatment for it.

This model is useless in the detection of dementia in older adults. Rarely will dementia patients tell their physicians that they are experiencing problems with memory. In fact, most dementia patients go to great lengths to conceal their deficits. It is not that dementia patients are purposely concealing information from their doctors; dementia patients often truly lack awareness of their condition. In the absence, then, of the patient's complaints of cognitive problems, the physician does not even consider evaluating the patient for dementia.

A second reason for physicians' failure to uncover many dementias is overestimation of the physician's ability to "sense or suspect" dementia through an interview. Primary-care physicians hold the strong belief that they can uncover cognitive problems through their examination of a patient—that is, the belief that talking to and observing an older patient will be enough, given the physician's keen clinical skills, for the physician to suspect dementia. But casual observation of a patient with early dementia rarely uncovers anything. In fact, the type of conversation encouraged in an examination by a physician is highly structured, provides many nonverbal cues, and taps most strongly into social skills. Maintenance of excellent social skills happens to be a hallmark strength of most patients with early dementia, and so the physician is likely to conclude the interview entirely convinced that the patient is functioning at full capacity.

Finally, primary-care physicians lack the ability to uncover dementia because they are untrained in administering and interpreting psychometric instruments (paper-and-pencil tests) that tap into cognitive functioning. The Mini-Mental State Exam (MMSE), for example, which is the most widely used cognitive test in the United States, is typically administered and interpreted in an improper fashion by primary-care physicians. Physicians rarely give the entire MMSE, thereby rendering it impossible to score. Typically, a physician will pick and choose the items to be administered, basing this choice on instinct during the exam. Unless the whole test is given and scored, it cannot be accurately interpreted. Even when the entire MMSE is given, physicians have neither the knowledge of statistics nor the normative data to interpret it correctly. Accommodations, for example, may not be made for educational level, even though education may account for a lower score. A background in statistics is needed in order to evaluate the quality of the normative data that are available and to determine the range of normal scores for a given patient.

Physicians in primary care have consistently left such psychosocial problems as depression and alcohol abuse undetected in older adults. This failure is a particularly critical one because depression and alcohol abuse are much more prevalent in those older adults who frequently see their physicians. Indeed, among hospitalized elderly patients, rates of depression and alcohol abuse can be two to five times greater than among nonhospitalized older adults. Symptoms of depression and alcohol abuse, like the symptoms of dementia, are not likely to be discovered in the typical doctor-patient interview.

The presentation of depression and alcohol abuse in older adults, by contrast with their presentation in younger adults, is most frequently one of negative symptomatology—that is, the classic florid symptoms of these disorders are not apparent. In assessing a patient for depression, for example, a physician may ask whether the patient has been having trouble eating or sleeping, or whether the patient has been feeling guilty (all symptoms of possible depression), but the physician may fail to ask whether the patient has been listless, withdrawn, and feeling downhearted. The two most common features of depressive disorders in older adults are lack of energy and social withdrawal.

A similar pattern exists in the assessment of alcohol abuse. Physicians may look for overt liver disease, and for the possibility of delirium tremens, but alcohol's interaction with an older person's physiology is different from its interaction with a younger person's, and so the physician will often miss detecting the alcohol abuse. Older people who have drinking problems often drink less than their younger counterparts do. They don't need to consume as much alcohol as they did in the past to obtain the same heightened blood-alcohol levels. As a result, overt symptoms of alcohol abuse may not be present, and certain direct questions about alcohol use, such as asking about the quantity of alcohol consumed, may not be useful. General symptoms (such as overall poor health, unexplained confusion, falls, burns, or accidents) may be the best tips that the older patient is abusing alcohol.

Added Value in Using Geriatric Neuropsychology

The added value of geriatric neuropsychology lies in the detection of dementia, depression, and alcohol abuse and in the use of neuropsychological evaluation data to guide treatment and other relevant healthcare decisions. Assessments of dementia are guided by three main questions:

1. Is there evidence of impairment?
2. What are the areas of cognitive strength and weakness?
3. What practical recommendations can be made on the basis of the results of testing?

In order to answer question 1, three conditions must be present. First, the assessment must be administered and scored in a complete and accurate fashion. Second, an appropriate normative database must be identified. Third, the examiner must have experience in this type of test interpretation. The answers to questions 2 and 3 depend heavily on the accuracy of the answer to question 1.

Evidence for Added Value in Detecting Dementia

Psychometric testing, rooted in quantitative data, is the best way to detect dementia, and psychologists proficient in geriatric neuropsychology are the persons best qualified to perform these assessments.

What is a psychometric test? In an evaluation for dementia, a psychometric test is a test of a general or specific area of cognition. The test relies on standardized administration and scoring. Tests like the MMSE and the Mattis Dementia Rating Scale are general approaches to the assessment of cognitive impairment. Specific procedures are detailed for administration of the test, and specific scoring criteria are outlined as well. Tests like the Fuld Object Memory Exam or the Boston Naming Test are geared more specifically to the assessment of memory and particular aspects of language. These also have standardized procedures and scoring rules.

What does it mean to say that psychometric testing is rooted in quantitative data? Quite simply, it means that the tests are accurately administered, and that their scores are calculated and used. Cognitive assessments, like most medical tests, use a deficit model in assessing cognition. A particular patient's scores are compared with normal performance—that is, I compare the MMSE scores of my patient with those of nondemented older adults. How will these nondemented older adults do on our tests, and what affects their performance? Test scores are affected by a number of variables that have nothing to do with the experience of dementia. Scores in normal, healthy older adults are affected by such factors as educational and cultural background (particularly familiarity with traditional English) and age.

Psychologists with training and experience in the neuropsychology of older adults are uniquely qualified to interpret the test scores. First, psychologists understand the assessment process, and they know the importance of following standardized procedures. Second, the field of geriatric neuropsychology has produced the best normative data available. Third, trained psychologists apply normative data properly. When medical personnel use normative data, they are often unaware of the strengths and weaknesses of the data, and so they misapply it. The failure to use normative data that include persons of comparable age and education can lead to faulty test interpretation. For example, in work with urban older adults' performance on the Boston Naming Test, use of improper norms can misclassify 80 percent of normal scores: the urban adults typically have less than a high school education, whereas other normative data have been gathered on individuals with an average of fifteen years of education, a difference that is enough to account for the differences in performance between the two groups.

Primary-care medical personnel who use psychometric testing instruments in the assessment of dementia commonly fail to understand the tests. Psychologists trained in working with older adults understand the relationship between a test score and an interpretation of cognition. Psychologists, with their background in scientific methodology, understand the separation between theory and method, and they do not confuse the two. Primary-care medical personnel do not typically have training in scientific methodology, and so they often confound methods with theory.

Let me illustrate this important principle by using the Logical Memory subtests from the Wechsler Memory Scale—Revised. These subtests are two stories that are read by the examiner and recounted by the patient to the best of his or her ability, once immediately after each story is read and then again thirty minutes later. The subtests are intended to assess memory functioning for verbal, contextual information. Primary-care medical personnel typically equate a low score on this exam with impairment in memory functioning. By contrast, a psychologist trained in geriatric practice understands that although the test was developed on the basis of our *concept* of memory functioning (that is, our theory), scores can be influenced by many *components* of the test properties themselves (that is, our testing methods). We call it a memory test, but that does not mean that the score always actually measures memory in the patient. Our methods are not always as elegant as our theories. On this test, for example, someone with a subtle language disorder might score horribly, and yet he could score perfectly well on other memory tests that were less reliant on language, and he could have an essentially normal memory.

The use of psychometric instruments that derive quantitative scores in dementia assessment is supported by conceptual reasoning and by empirical data. Conceptually, the cognitive assessment is a performance-based approach, not a self-report approach. A parallel exists with many medical conditions. If we want to see how well the heart can function, a stress test is given—that is, the performance of the heart is assessed. If we want to know how well a patient is performing cognitively, we can administer a cognitive assessment.

Therein lies one of the real strengths of cognitive assessment: performance-based approaches get away from the possibility of a patient's faulty self-report (and, in dementia, the probability of faulty self-report). Performance on an assessment instrument can then be properly interpreted so that we can see if cognitive deficits actually exist.

The use of psychometric instruments that derive cognitive scores in dementia assessments is overwhelmingly supported by empirical data. Instead of reviewing these data here, I will simply review the diversity of the samples. In some, patients were originally involved as subjects in longitudinal studies of normal aging.

As time went on, their dementia became apparent. Their early assessment scores were compared against the scores of those who did not go on to develop dementia, and evidence was provided for preclinical signs of dementia—that is, those who went on to develop dementia showed poorer memory functioning before the obvious onset of dementing illness, by comparison with those who never developed dementia. In other studies, patients were registered from Alzheimer's centers, and particularly those patients with early dementia were compared with a control group of healthy older adults who were similar on such variables as age and education. In these studies, cognitive assessments were able to distinguish the groups between 96 percent and 98 percent of the time—that is, the cognitive assessments were able to clearly distinguish those with early dementia from those with no dementia. What is even more impressive, many of these cases were then confirmed on autopsy. The research evidence also clearly supports the use of performance-based cognitive assessments in detecting dementia.

Improving Accuracy

Geriatric neuropsychological evaluations clearly add value in the detection of dementing disorders. Both conceptually and empirically, support is provided by the use of cognitive assessments. The importance of understanding the strengths and weaknesses of the assessments and of knowing how to interpret the scores has been emphasized. Primary-care medical personnel are not commonly trained to provide accurate assessment and interpretation of cognitive assessment data. Still, given that primary-care practitioners may be called on to administer cognitive-screening exams, there are several steps that they can take to improve the accuracy of their clinical decision making:

1. Use performance-based cognitive tests (for example, the MMSE) in addition to clinical interviews.

2. Administer the tests completely, and then accurately score them. To improve the accuracy of scoring, the patient's

responses should be taken down verbatim, and scoring should be done after all tests have been administered.

3. Develop a notebook of normative data containing information about subjects' age and educational background.

4. Compare the patient's individual score with a normative database that approximates the patient's age and education.

5. Remember that relying on a single test is guaranteed to make the physician miss dementia in up to one-third of those who enter the office already suffering from dementia.

The assessment of depression and alcohol abuse, by contrast, can be performed accurately by primary-care medical personnel. Typically, improvement in detection of these problems is greatly aided by self-report or observer-rated scales. Depression scales for older adults, such as the Geriatric Depression Scale (GDS), tap into the psychological aspects of depression, as well as into the negative symptomatology discussed previously. Use of the CAGE, a four-item alcohol-abuse questionnaire, or of some other brief alcoholism-screening test, can quickly and accurately identify older adults who are abusing alcohol.

Depression and alcohol problems are not among those that require performance-based assessment. Interview techniques based on assessment of symptomatology can be accurate. But the GDS and the CAGE, though widely available, are not used enough in primary-care practice. The co-occurrence, in various combinations, of cognitive disorders with depression, dementia, and alcohol abuse is common. The psychologist trained in treating older adults is in the best position to determine the effects of these psychosocial problems on cognitive functioning.

Influence of Mental Health Problems on Medical Outcomes

In managed medical care, each procedure or service must add value not only to the assessment of problems but also to medical outcomes. Medical outcomes equal costs. The more problematic the case, the more costly it is in terms of office visits, use of the emergency room, and hospital admissions. We are learning more and more that mental health problems, particularly cognitive and depressive disorders, affect patients' medical outcomes. Cognitive functioning—or, more specifically, the presence of cognitive disorders—is predictive of an older patient's inability to manage his or her own medications, cook safely, manage money and perform other financial tasks, and maintain his or her ability to live independently.

Cognition

The following example of my and my colleagues' research on independent living illustrates the necessity of understanding cognitive abilities in older medical patients. In a study of 372 older medical rehabilitation patients who had lived alone before being admitted to the hospital, rates of physical recovery were compared in two groups: those who returned to living alone, and those who were discharged to a family caregiver's house or to a nursing home. There were no differences between the groups in self-care skills or even in the ability to ambulate, nor were there any differences in severity of medical condition or on such demographic variables as age and education. The only significant differences between the two groups were in the domain of cognitive performance, and cognitive assessments were the most powerful determinant of whether a patient was discharged to live alone or discharged to a family caretaker or a nursing home. Why was this the case? Our interpretation of these data was that the central factor in a patient's actual ability to carry out the requisite tasks of living alone was the integrity of the patient's brain. The patient's level of performance on cognitive tests was used to assess brain functioning, and this performance-based measure was closely linked to actual discharge data.

The link between these data and costs is highlighted by a recent study on emergency care.[2] The most costly emergency care, and the highest rates of mortality and medical morbidity, were found in older adults who were living alone and who also had a cognitive disorder. In many instances, there had been a failure to adequately assess cognitive functioning in these patients and to integrate assessment results into planning for discharge and treatment. Failure of this kind needlessly costs the healthcare industry money because emergency care is one of the most expensive types of care to provide.

Depression

There is a growing awareness that depression, the most treatable of all mental health disorders, has profound effects on medical outcomes. Depressed older patients do not respond as well to such medical interventions as rehabilitation. They have higher rates of cardiac dysfunction, as well as higher rates of mortality, and they use more healthcare services than nondepressed older adults do. Depression treatment, whether it is carried out through medication, psychotherapy, or a combination of the two, has proven to be effective and safe. Treatment can be adapted to hospital settings, outpatient settings, and even home settings. The clear cost benefits of treating depression cannot be denied.

The detection of dementia has been emphasized as one important function of performing cognitive evaluation of older adults, but there are also many functional questions that can be specifically answered by psychologists:

Can the patient independently manage her own medication?

Can the patient manage his finances independently?

Can the patient safely live alone?

Can the patient make competent decisions about healthcare?

Can the patient compensate for her cognitive deficits?

Can the patient drive safely?

Can the patient benefit from intensive rehabilitation or educational interventions?

The Importance of Brief Test Batteries

Geriatric neuropsychology has its roots in traditional neuropsychology, as exemplified by the Halstead Reitan Test Battery (HRB) approach. The HRB takes many hours to complete, and it typically costs between $800 and $1,200, several times the cost of a CAT scan or an MRI brain scan. The neuropsychological data are performance-based and can guide treatment decisions better than brain scans can. Clearly, however, brief batteries must become the norm, so that instead of a full day of testing, a two- or three-hour test battery can be adopted.

There is growing awareness of the need for brief psychometric cognitive evaluations, especially in healthcare settings. First, there are the issues of cost and reimbursement. Many managed-care plans place limits on the length of the cognitive testing for which they will pay. Second, time limits are a factor: inpatient stays are shorter, and so there is competition for the time needed to perform cognitive evaluations, particularly if one is competing with speech therapists, occupational therapists, and physical therapists. Third, there is the issue of fatigue and rapport: older adults in healthcare settings tire easily, and rapport can be affected dramatically by lengthy testing (that is, testing that takes four to eight hours). Fourth, there is now empirical support for the use of brief test batteries. Much of the rest of this section describes four established brief batteries.

Washington University (St. Louis) Battery[3]

One of the first brief test batteries constructed to document the cognitive effects of dementia was part of a longitudinal study of Alzheimer's disease. In their test battery, which lasted from ninety minutes to two hours, the authors used portions of a number of established psychometric instruments, all of them paper-and-pencil examinations with specific instructions for administration and scoring.

The initial sample comprised forty-three individuals with mild Alzheimer's disease and forty-three control subjects enrolled in the

Washington University Memory and Aging Project. The subjects were matched on age (mean age was seventy-one years) and on education level (mean education was 12.5 years). Follow-up data, collected over two and one-half years, were obtained for twenty-two of the Alzheimer's subjects and thirty-nine of the control subjects.

There were noteworthy findings from both the cross-sectional data and the longitudinal data. One was that almost all the individual tests initially differentiated the two groups, including those tests that were not expected to measure cerebral deterioration. Examination of the longitudinal data from this study indicated that, overall, the Alzheimer's subjects deteriorated over the follow-up period, but there was no change in the normal controls. Although the Washington University battery was created for use in research, it could easily be used in a clinical setting. The tests in the battery are diverse enough to tap into multiple domains of cognitive functioning, and yet they can accurately detect dementia. The benefits of using this battery would be improved diagnostic accuracy, improved treatment planning, and lower costs.

The Iowa Battery[4]

A comprehensive neuropsychological assessment of normal and demented adults between the ages of sixty and eighty-eight, conducted in Iowa, led to the development of a brief (thirty to forty-five minutes) testing battery capable of identifying demented individuals. The original battery consisted of eight tests: four memory tests, one auditory-attention task, one verbal-fluency task, and two visual-spatial tasks. The sample consisted of fifty-three normal control subjects and fifty-three dementia subjects matched for age, education, and sex.

The means and standard deviations for all tests were significantly higher in the normal subjects than they were in the demented subjects. Certain tests, however, were far better at detecting dementia (for example, the test of orientation alone detected dementia in 57 percent of the demented subjects, but the test of facial recognition detected only 32 percent).

Stepwise linear discriminant-function analyses were used to determine which were the most effective and parsimonious groups of tests that would detect dementia, and one group of three tests—the Temporal Orientation Test, the Controlled Oral Word Association Test, and the Benton Visual Retention Test—was able to accurately classify 85 percent of cases. The authors then cross-validated their findings in a new sample of fifty-three normal and fifty-three demented individuals. In this second sample, overall, correct classification for this group of three tests was 89 percent, a rate that provided strong support for the original findings.

The findings from this study are most relevant to primary-care physicians' offices where cognitive screening may be taking place in cases of suspected dementia. The simple lesson to learn here is that the use of only a single measure will lead to poor detection of dementia; in this study, the highest rate of detection through the use of a single test was only 57 percent. Several brief tests, each tapping into a slightly different domain of cognitive functioning from the others, should be used. Primary-care physicians can improve their detection of dementia by using the three tests found most sensitive to dementia in this research.

The CERAD Battery[5]

In 1989, the sixteen Alzheimer's Centers designated by the National Institutes of Health worked together to produce the Consortium to Establish a Registry for Alzheimer's Disease (CERAD) neuropsychological battery. The aim of the project was to produce a brief (thirty to forty minutes) test battery that would characterize the primary manifestations of Alzheimer's disease. Therefore, tests were chosen to represent aspects of memory, language, and praxis. They included a verbal-fluency test (animal naming), the fifteen-item Boston Naming test, the full Mini-Mental State Exam, a word-list memory task created by the consortium, four line drawings, and a word-list recognition task created by the consortium.

The authors of a paper describing the project reported the results found with 350 subjects who had Alzheimer's disease and 275 control subjects. Test-retest reliability correlations, over a one-month period, ranged from .52 to .78. The tests readily distinguished the normal controls from the Alzheimer's patients. The authors interpreted these data as providing solid support for the CERAD battery.

Subjects matched for sex, age, and education were used in the next investigation of the CERAD battery's utility, in which 196 subjects were placed into one of four groups: a control group, a mildly demented group, a moderately demented group, and a severely demented group. The average age of the subjects was seventy-one, and the average length of education was fourteen years. Stepwise linear discriminant-function analysis was used to determine how accurately the CERAD battery classified the subjects. The CERAD battery accurately classified 96 percent of the normal controls, the moderately demented subjects, and the severely demented subjects, and 86 percent of the mildly demented subjects. The best predictor of accurate classification was the delayed-recall score from the word-list memory task: the proportion of words retained in memory was 85.6 percent for the normal controls, 35.8 percent for the mildly impaired group, and 16 percent for the moderately and severely impaired groups. The worst predictors were the number of intrusion errors on the word-list memory task, the word-list recognition task, and the recognition memory score. The authors concluded that the CERAD battery may be useful in aiding in the early detection of dementia.

The data on the CERAD battery underscore the helpfulness of using psychologists in dementia evaluations. In this case, psychologists created and were easily able to interpret a very brief examination that accurately detected dementia. The utility of the

CERAD battery in answering specific questions (for example, about a patient's ability to live alone) has not been well tested, however.

The NSRP Test Battery[6]

The Normative Studies Research Project (NSRP) test battery takes from one and one-quarter to two hours. Memory testing is emphasized, and it includes tests that tap into the domains of language, visual-spatial skills, and executive functioning, as well as a test of reading. Among a sample of 236 urban older adults, 60 percent of whom were African American, 74 were cognitively intact and fully independent in the activities of daily living (ADLs), 89 were cognitively impaired and had deficiencies in at least three ADLs, and the remaining 73 were either cognitively intact but had ADL deficiencies or were cognitively impaired but had few ADL limitations.

The sample was given a total of five tests. In view of the high degree of correlation among them, however, only the Dementia Rating Scale (DRS) was used to distinguish cognitively unimpaired patients from mildly impaired patients. The DRS was relatively better at classifying cognitively unimpaired patients than it was in classifying cognitively impaired patients. There was relatively good discrimination between the cognitively unimpaired and the impaired older urban medical patients, which clearly indicates the usefulness of the NSRP test battery. Its important benefit is to demonstrate that even in minority populations, psychological tests can accurately detect dementia when the proper normative data are used. These data give credibility to the use of cognitive tests with a broad range of patient populations.

Summary of the Brief Batteries

Across a heterogeneous group of participants, four brief testing batteries proved accurate in detecting dementia. The studies just summarized provide clear guidance on the clinical utility of brief cognitive test batteries in work with older adults. The data on differentiating demented from nondemented elderly patients point to the importance of emphasizing memory assessment in the cognitive evaluation. Indeed, tests of memory function were key in each of the brief batteries reviewed here. Tasks involving attention, language, visual-spatial functioning, and executive functioning, as well as general tests of cognitive functioning, were all clinically useful in the identification of demented individuals. Reading tests, by contrast, are relatively poor at discriminating between demented and nondemented individuals, although they can be used as crude estimates of an individual's premorbid level of intellectual functioning. The data on brief batteries provides support for the notion that cognitive assessment of older adults can be completed in a timely, cost-effective fashion, with no sacrifice of diagnostic accuracy.

Guidelines for a Cost-Conscious Test Battery

The use of a brief (two to three hours) test battery should become routine practice in the managed-care environment. Without sacrificing diagnostic accuracy, a brief battery is cost-competitive with brain scans and provides the added value of guiding treatment, as discussed earlier. What exactly should go into such a battery? Should there be one standard battery across the nation? Because there are so many reliable and validated assessment instruments, and because the choice of instruments may be determined by such patient characteristics as education level or cultural background, there should not be one fixed battery for all assessments. Instead, there should be agreement about the types of tests to be used. As already mentioned, an emphasis on memory testing is paramount in cognitive assessment, and such testing should typically consist of at least two types of memory tasks (for example, story recall and word-list recall and recognition). Tests that tap into confrontational naming, language comprehension, visual-spatial processing, abstract reasoning, mental flexibility, and psychomotor functioning should also be included. Reading tests, which can estimate the patient's premorbid level of functioning, are also required. Finally, screening measures for the detection of depression and alcohol abuse are also necessary.

Practice Must Specify Standards of Care

Standards of care define the training needed to perform a certain practice and outline the elements of standard practice. Providers of geriatric neuropsychology services must be trained in several aspects. I will not undertake a comprehensive review of them here, but they include a general knowledge of aging; an understanding of normal aging and cognition; the ability to perform cognitive assessments with older adults and interpret test results with respect to dementia; knowledge of and ability to treat mental health disorders in older adults; and knowledge of how assessment results can be used in the diagnosis and treatment.

There are a number of routes a psychologist can take to receive training in these areas. The three most likely ones are a focus on geropsychology, a focus on neuropsychology, and/or a focus on rehabilitation psychology. Each of these areas can train psychologists in the skills necessary for carrying out the tasks just described. Training in geropsychology will probably emphasize cognitive assessment and mental health treatment, but it may not expose trainees to older adult medical patients. Training in clinical neuropsychology will clearly teach thorough assessment skills and will emphasize brain-behavior relationships in dementia, but it may not emphasize treatment planning; in fact, it may even stress that mental health treatment should be performed by someone other than the assessing psychologist. Training in rehabilitation psychology will probably emphasize medical patients, cognitive assessment, use of assessment results in treatment planning, and brief psychotherapeutic treatment, but it may not emphasize knowledge of normal aging. A person with a background in any of these areas could capably perform the roles of a geriatric neuropsychologist in managed care.

In the fee-for-service healthcare paradigm, assessment and treatment are too often performed by separate professionals or groups of professionals. This arrangement is not useful in the managed-care model, particularly with older adults. As much as possible with older adults, assessment and treatment should be conducted by the same provider. Older adults are often uncomfortable, in my experience, about seeing new practitioners to have the treatment recommendations implemented. When I diagnose an older patient in a primary-care setting as having a depressive disorder, my patient is often relieved that I can offer follow-up treatment. Geriatric neuropsychologists will have to remain broad in their practice and offer services ranging, for example, from cognitive assessment to the treatment of anxiety and pain.

Collaborating with Primary-Care Physicians

Collaboration between primary-care medical personnel and geriatric neuropsychologists must be strengthened if appropriate services are to be rendered in the managed-care environment. Psychologists must insist that medical personnel use some type of formal screening process to determine the presence or absence of cognitive dysfunction, depression, and other mental health problems. As stated earlier, many self-report and objective-rater instruments can be used to assess mental health problems; it is in the realm of cognitive screening that new practice must be established.

In order to ensure that only necessary psychology referrals were being obtained, my research group established a decision tree for physicians to use in an inpatient medical rehabilitation setting, but it is easily adaptable to outpatient settings as well (see Exhibit 5.1). The issues that led to the decision tree's creation were diverse. We had demonstrated that problems of cognitive decline, which were of critical importance to some patients' discharge planning, were routinely being missed in physicians' histories and physical examinations, and this situation had led to several last-minute referrals and to delays in patients' being discharged. (It was being discovered that patients who had expressed the goal of returning to

Exhibit 5.1. Decision Tree for Neuropsychology Referral: Cognitive Issues.

Temporal Orientation Test Score

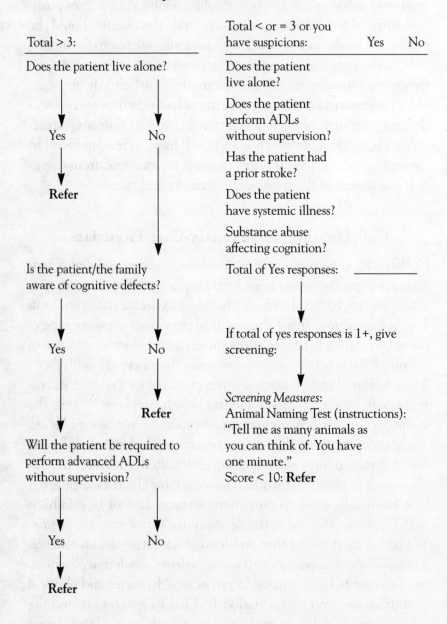

Total > 3:

Does the patient live alone?

Yes   No

Refer

Is the patient/the family aware of cognitive defects?

Yes   No

Refer

Will the patient be required to perform advanced ADLs without supervision?

Yes   No

Refer

Total < or = 3 or you have suspicions: Yes   No

Does the patient live alone?

Does the patient perform ADLs without supervision?

Has the patient had a prior stroke?

Does the patient have systemic illness?

Substance abuse affecting cognition?

Total of Yes responses: _____

If total of yes responses is 1+, give screening:

Screening Measures:
Animal Naming Test (instructions):
"Tell me as many animals as you can think of. You have one minute."
Score < 10: **Refer**

living alone were unable to do so because of previously unrecognized dementia.) As a result of these trends, physicians were persuaded to use simple, brief, standardized instruments and quantitative scoring to help detect cognitive problems. A set of questions helped guide the decision-making process, and these questions ultimately led to the decision tree.

The decision tree assesses three components: the patient's basic cognition, the patient's and family's awareness of cognitive problems, and the level of the patient's independence. Basic cognition is assessed by the five-item Temporal Orientation Test. Benton and his colleagues provided normative data regarding the test and, in their sample of 162 older adults between the ages of sixty-five and eighty-five, no more than 6 percent of the cognitively unimpaired older adults scored in the impaired range on the test.[7] The decision tree includes another simple test to use as a screen for cognition, the Animal Naming task (which is also included in the CERAD battery. Together, these two tests take fewer than five minutes to administer and score. We decided that it would be easier for physicians making referrals to use a single cutoff score on each test.

If the patient fails one of the screening exams, his or her living situation is assessed, and patients living alone are referred for evaluation. If the patient does not live alone, the patient's and the family's awareness of a cognitive impairment is assessed before consultation is sought. If both the patient and the family are well aware of the problem, a cognitive evaluation may not be called for; often, however, patients and families are not aware of the problem. Finally, the level of caregiver support is assessed. If the patient is expected to perform instrumental activities of daily living (ADLs) unsupervised once he or she has returned home, the patient is referred for evaluation. This decision tree helps cut out referrals of cognitively unimpaired patients. It also eliminates referrals of patients who have moderate to severe cognitive impairment but will be receiving twenty-four-hour care upon discharge.

Geriatric neuropsychology has earned its way into being a core service under managed care. Geriatric neuropsychological assessment is highly accurate, and it leads to crucial treatment planning. It can also be cost-effective and may even save money, if we consider what can happen when treatment decisions are not based on neuropsychological assessment data. The standards for the type of expertise needed to perform geriatric neuropsychology can be plainly stated. On scientific and clinical grounds, the case for geriatric neuropsychology is a strong one. Its inclusion in managed care may depend on the advocacy and political skills of neuropsychology professionals.

Suggested Reading

Beresford, T. P., and others. "Alcoholism and Aging in the General Hospital." *Psychosomatics*, 1988, *29*, 61–72.

Brink, T., and others. "Screening Tests for Geriatric Depression." *Clinical Gerontologist*, 1982, *1*, 37–41.

Bush, B., and others. "Screening for Alcohol Abuse Using the CAGE Questionnaire." *The American Journal of Medicine*, 1987, *82*, 231–235.

Christensen, H., Hadzi-Pavlovic, D., and Jacomb, P. "The Psychometric Differentiation of Dementia from Normal Aging: A Meta-Analysis." *Psychological Assessment*, 1991, *3*, 147–55.

La Rue, A. *Aging and Neuropsychological Assessment*. New York: Plenum Press, 1992.

Lichtenberg, P. A. "*A Guide to Psychological Practice in Geriatric Long Term Care*." Binghamton, N.Y.: Haworth Press, 1994.

Rapp, S. R., Parisi, S. A., Walsh, D. A., and Wallace, C. E. "Detecting Depression in Elderly Medical Inpatients." *Journal of Consulting and Clinical Psychology*, 1988, *56*, 509–513.

Welsh, K., and others. "Detection of Abnormal Memory Decline in Mild Cases of AD Using CERAD Neuropsychological Measures." *Archives of Neurology*, 1991, *48*, 278–281.

Chapter Six

Group Psychotherapy

Ideas for the
Managed-Care Environment

Thomas M. Meuser, Martha W. Clower,
Edgardo Padin-Rivera

Group therapies are undergoing a resurgence in the present managed-care environment. Although cost reduction has been a primary impetus for this renewed interest, in our experience the clinical efficacy and flexibility of group psychotherapy are what consistently stand out. Many of our clients who benefit from individual counseling benefit even more when they are placed in the interpersonal microcosm that is group therapy, but they often do so at half the economic cost. When people with similar behavioral health problems and/or diagnoses are treated in a group setting, the interpersonal learning and support of psychotherapy are maximized while expensive professional time is kept to a minimum. For instance, we have found that group interventions lasting ten to twenty sessions can often restore a patient to a reasonable level of functioning, and that this progress can then be maintained through informal peer-support meetings.

Professionals committed to serving the behavioral health needs of older adults have begun to look beyond ageist stereotypes and to recognize the resilience of older people in mastering the hurdles of daily life and the aging process. When psychological problems arise, older persons' years of life experience and reflective self-understanding often hold the keys for healing. This chapter focuses on how to use these keys to rekindle latent strengths and empower older clients to attain personal goals of well-being, with an emphasis on group psychotherapy as a treatment of choice.

Recognizing the Needs of Older Clients

For time-limited group interventions to be effective, they must be tailored to the specific psychological and developmental needs of the population being served. We believe that the therapeutic factors at work in group treatment are uniquely suited to the psychological needs of older adults. Cost containment is an important issue in managed care, but maximizing successful outcomes for individual patients is still the bottom line. An understanding and appreciation of the normal aging process is critical for the group therapist who seeks the best outcomes for his or her older adult clients. In this chapter, we summarize aspects of normal aging, and we offer suggestions for addressing older persons' needs in therapy.

Many kinds of group activities (for example, support groups, Alcoholics Anonymous meetings, and stress-reduction training groups) have therapeutic benefits. Under current models of reimbursement, however, only certain interventions qualify as reimbursable forms of group psychotherapy. According to the Health Care Financing Administration (HCFA) guidelines for Medicare, psychotherapy is treatment of mental illness and/or behavioral problems by a trained professional that establishes a professional contract with the patient through definitive therapeutic communication and accomplishes one or more of the following goals:

- Attempts to alleviate emotional distress
- Attempts to reverse or change maladaptive behavioral patterns
- Encourages personality growth and development

Group interventions that are mainly social, recreational, diversional, or oriented toward cognitive stimulation do not meet these criteria and are unlikely to be reimbursed under managed care. Under these criteria, a meaningful treatment structure, a successful outcome, and payment for services are all closely linked.

Developing reimbursable group interventions, we believe, requires a dual focus on symptom amelioration and restoration of the client to a reasonable level of psychosocial functioning. Irvin Yalom, a noted authority on group work, emphasizes the power of group therapy to foster insight and promote improved coping through the here-and-now experience of group interaction.[1] Regardless of their psychiatric diagnoses, group members support, challenge, and learn from one another, thereby healing and growing as individuals. It is the job of the group therapist to structure group interactions so as to maximize growth opportunities and highlight such occurrences for group discussion. To be effective in group work with older adults, these *structuring* and *highlighting* tasks must be guided by an awareness of the aging process.

Treating the Whole Person

The normal aging process can be understood in terms of both thematic and functional changes. Important themes in later life include multiple losses and grief, changes in social roles and personal identity, constriction of social networks and interpersonal involvement, life review and reminiscence, concern about death, an increased emphasis on spiritual faith, and adjustment to widowhood, among other themes. Although such themes often do define the experiences of older adults, it is also important to remember that the full range of personal, relational, sexual, and emotional concerns present at younger ages do not simply disappear but are also alive and well in older age. A combined aging and "whole person" focus, one that encompasses such themes as well as individual differences, has enriched our clinical work with older adults. We believe that this broad focus is essential to working effectively as a therapist with older people. For example, simply to see an older woman who has lost her spouse as a widow in need of grief-related support ignores the larger context of her life, where vital keys for healing may reside.

From a functional perspective, older age often brings a decrease in physical stamina and endurance, reduced heart and lung capacity, reduced muscle and bone mass, and a lessening in the speed of mental processing and memory retrieval, but these changes do not always limit the activities in which a given older adult may engage. The majority of older people readily maintain sufficient functional ability to accomplish meaningful tasks of daily living. Although it is not viewed as a part of normal aging per se, physical illness of one form or another is still a fact of life for many older adults. Growing older brings more opportunities for illness and/or injury, which can limit functional ability. Like the themes of older age, some functional changes are inevitable as we grow older, yet their impact on and meaning for individuals can vary quite a bit. The older "couch potato" of today could just as well be the senior Olympian of tomorrow; a lot depends on individual expectations and motivations, which the astute therapist can help mold. Group psychotherapy is an ideal intervention for fostering expectations of success in coping with the troublesome themes, functional changes, and psychological disorders of older age.

Therapeutic Factors in Group Therapy

In his now classic book, *The Theory and Practice of Group Psychotherapy*,[2] Yalom details various therapeutic factors that make group therapy such a helpful intervention. *Universality*, the understanding that others share similar troubles, is particularly important for older adults, who may fear being labeled crazy or senile. Normalizing one's experiences through *identification* with others in the group allows for a sense of personal control and mastery to develop: "If he can manage retirement that well, maybe I can, too." *Cohesiveness* and *interpersonal altruism* among group members foster needed social support, as well as a sense of shared responsibility. These factors are particularly important for older clients, who may feel isolated or may lack meaningful social roles; helping others can restore a sense of meaning and purpose to the individual. Finally, the group setting allows for emotional issues to be worked through so that *catharsis* and healthy adjustment can take place. We believe that there are at least seven keys to maximizing these group-therapeutic factors for older clients.

First, *maintain clear expectations for success and personal responsibility*. This is often more difficult in practice than it sounds. Many therapists, ourselves included, often fail to recognize or question subtle ageist stereotypes that shape the beliefs and expectations underlying our clinical work (for example, that older people are fragile and easily harmed; that they need to be cared for and guided by the therapist; that they are incapable of intensive personal exploration and emotional expression; that their ability to learn and grow in therapy is limited). Many older people have similar beliefs about themselves. Recognizing and correcting such biases is a critical challenge for therapist and client alike. We believe that it is incumbent on therapists or therapy teams, before starting a group intervention, to examine their beliefs about aging so that they can avoid contaminating the group process with limiting expectations. From beginning to end in each group intervention, we make it a point to express realistic, positive expectations for individual responsibility and success. We suggest and even predict how group members are likely to experience growth over time, and we incorporate time to review and reinforce such growth into the group structure. The older adult who enters therapy expecting to be "fixed" by the therapist soon learns to view the final "repair" as coming from within, as it almost always does.

Second, *help group members set clear, concrete, attainable goals*. Discussing individual goals early in the group process goes a long way toward building a sense of cohesiveness, mutual support, and interpersonal accountability. Defining the goals of therapy can be a challenge for any client, young or old. Many clients start with general expectations for growth that are difficult to quantify (for example, "to communicate better" or "not to get so angry"). It is up to the therapist and other group members to help each client define specific behaviors to change. For example, the general goal of "not to get so angry" may translate into "stop and recognize when and why I'm angry, and tell my reactions honestly to my wife." A written, concrete goal provides the individual with a map for change, as well as giving group members a way to evaluate progress and provide assistance to each other over time.

Third, *structure group interventions to maximize peer support and accountability.* The real power of group therapy lies in the social microcosm that it represents. Unlike the members of a psychoeducational group, who behave in tune with established student-teacher boundaries, clients in group therapy must play multiple supporting, teaching, and learning roles in order to experience the benefits of this form of intervention. These roles can be difficult for anyone, but they can be particularly challenging for older adults, who may not be accustomed to sharing personal details and emotional reactions with others. A helpful first step in building a sense of safety and community is to allow group members opportunities for getting acquainted and feeling comfortable at the person-to-person level. This step can be taken early in the group process, through life-review and autobiographical exercises. It is often helpful for the therapist to model appropriate personal sharing through selective self-disclosure. By telling about herself or himself, the therapist models the openness and shared responsibility necessary for successful group work.

Fourth, *be cognizant of normal age-related changes.* Memory-formation and memory-retrieval processes become somewhat slower and less efficient as we age. Fatigue can limit sustained concentration for certain older adults, particularly those with chronic illness. Hearing and visual impairments are common. The group therapist can respond to these realities in a number of ways. Voice amplification, as well as large typefaces on handouts, will often work well when sensory deficits are a problem. Parsimony and repetition are helpful in dealing with the cognitive changes that come with age. The effective group therapist gets to the point without unnecessary explanation, repeats important ideas to maximize comprehension and recall, and builds in brief rest breaks to counter the effects of fatigue. Asking members to repeat important points is also a useful tool, both for checking on comprehension and for fostering interpersonal learning.

Fifth, *conduct regular discussions of individual progress, needs, and expectations*. Some older clients, particularly in the early stages of a group intervention, may be reluctant to voice their needs and concerns. "This is not helping me," a group member may think, "but the doctor knows what is supposed to work, so I'll keep quiet and go along." Open communication is at the heart of good therapy. As already mentioned, older people vary as much as younger people do in their clinical needs. It is up to the group therapist to match interventions and group discussions to individual goals as closely as possible. The therapist can model open communication by honestly expressing his or her feelings about events in the group, offering observations of the group process, and giving reasons for selecting certain interventions. Motivating older group members to voice their concerns and needs also instills in them a sense of ownership and responsibility for the group experience.

Sixth, *use multiple therapeutic tools to maximize individual learning*. Regardless of age, all people have their own optimal ways of learning, and these can vary quite a bit. The use of a range of therapeutic tools (psychoeducational techniques, process-oriented discussion, relaxation exercises, homework tasks) increases the chances that each group member will benefit from the intervention.

Seventh, *be flexible enough to deal with current issues in group members' lives*. Allowing time in each session for group members to catch up with one another and discuss current issues is particularly important with older clients. Recent losses, health problems, medication difficulties, worries about the future, and so forth, can affect how an individual client responds to the group process on a given day. Current issues can be used as examples in coping-related discussion and education aimed at improving individual functioning.

Allowing time to focus on current issues also highlights individual growth as group members observe how others may be changing.

These keys to harnessing group-therapeutic factors grew out of the successes and failures of our day-to-day clinical work with older adults. They are reliable, we feel, in a general sense, but their application may vary significantly according to the specific needs of individual clients. Each diagnostic category poses a unique set of demands on the geriatric group therapist. The following examples highlight these demands in three discrete but often overlapping clinical areas within geropsychological practice: posttraumatic stress disorder (PTSD), bereavement, and dementia.

The Senior Veterans Program: A Structured Group Treatment That Works

Estimates are that World War II and Korean War–era veterans account for more than 50 percent of all males in the United States over the age of sixty. Little attention has been paid to the incidence and treatment of PTSD in this segment of the older adult population. PTSD, a serious Axis I disorder, may be a hidden syndrome in older combat veterans, given possible lack of awareness among clinicians and the tendency of elders to somatize anxiety and minimize psychological symptoms. In our experience, the question "Did you serve?" is critical in assessing men from this cohort. Once uncovered, this disorder can be treated effectively with time-limited group psychotherapy, and a good level of psychosocial functioning can be restored.

The second and third authors of this chapter developed the Senior Veterans Program (SVP) four years ago at the Cleveland Veterans Administration Medical Center, to provide comprehensive treatment for elderly veterans experiencing the long-term effects of war-related PTSD. Our treatment plan arose from our awareness that World War II and Korean War veterans constitute a special population in terms of the course of the disorder and concurrent developmental issues. Consequently, an intervention model integrating findings from geropsychology and PTSD was needed to meet their particular needs.

A burgeoning literature documents how older war veterans, upon repatriation, responded to society's exhortations to put it all behind them. Believing that emotional problems related to war were signs of character weakness, they hid postwar trauma conflicts, maintained secrecy, and suppressed emotional symptoms, often through overwork and substance abuse. For many of them, however, latent symptoms of traumatic stress became manifest with the aging process. It is reasonable to expect, then, that some veterans who suffered war traumas and then demonstrated a seemingly adequate postwar adjustment may now be faced, in late life, with a reactivation of PTSD symptoms. For most of the men we treat, these symptoms arose in response to an increasing array of stressors, as well as from the developmental imperative to reflect on and integrate their personal life histories. Defenses that had allowed many of our men to cope without professional help in the past stopped working well in older age. Therefore, a cornerstone of our work in the Senior Veterans Program is building a more relevant and age-appropriate coping plan for each patient.

How the SVP Works

The SVP is a thirty-two-week outpatient manualized psychoeducational treatment program presented in two sixteen-week modules (see Exhibit 6.1). Eight veterans are seen four times monthly in ninety-minute groups, and once monthly for individual case management, an arrangement that makes it possible for two full-time therapists to facilitate numerous groups. During weeks six through nine, two-hour meetings are scheduled so that each of the veterans can present a one-hour life-review presentation.

Phase I consists of educating them about psychotherapy and PTSD symptoms, having them complete and present life-review assignments, and beginning the skill-building process. Phase II focuses on advanced skill building, trauma processing, and

Exhibit 6.1. Senior Veterans Program Plan for Recovery, Phases I and II.

Phase I

Part I: Education

Week 1. Senior Veterans welcome group
Week 2. Testing session
Week 3. Introductions—What Is Psychotherapy?
Week 4. Individual treatment goals
Week 5. Introduction to life-review assignment; learning about PTSD
Week 6. Learning about PTSD
Week 7. Ageism and recovery from PTSD

Part II: Life Review

Week 8. Life-review presentations
Week 9. Life-review presentations
Week 10. Life-review presentations
Week 11. Life-review presentations

Part III: Stress Management and Healthy Thinking

Week 12. Stress Management I: Introduction
Week 13. Stress Management II: Prevention
Week 14. Stress Management III: Social support
Week 15. Stress Management IV: Healthy thinking
Week 16. Stress Management V: Healthy thinking

Phase II

Part I: Advanced Skill Building

Week 17. Check-in with veterans
Week 18. Testing session
Week 19. Understanding emotions
Week 20. Expressing emotions
Week 21. Recognizing anger
Week 22. Managing anger
Week 23. Trauma processing
Week 24. Trauma processing: sand-tray work
Week 25. Trauma processing: sand-tray work
Week 26. Trauma processing: sand-tray work
Week 27. Trauma processing: sand-tray work
Week 28. Trauma processing: sand-tray work

Part II: Integration

Week 29. Grief and loss
Week 30. Forgiveness
Week 31. Testing session
Week 32. Celebration

integration of new insights about the self. Weekly homework assignments, involving both writing and reading tasks, make efficient use of time and provide multiple exposures to information for seniors who learn best with repetition, and at their own pace.

The program emphasizes personal responsibility and a proactive posture, which places moderate cognitive demands on the participants. Consequently, realistic exclusion criteria are one key to the program's success. Guidelines for acceptance include the client's meeting DSM-IV criteria for PTSD, his lack of manifest psychotic symptoms or signs of a dementing illness, his not abusing drugs or alcohol, and his ability to commit himself to attending the thirty-two weekly outpatient group sessions.

Although the presence of a comorbid affective or anxiety disorder does not preclude treatment, we have found it prudent in these cases to wait until the most profound symptoms are resolved before embarking on group work. For example, a severely depressed client may need to be stabilized on antidepressant medication before the group intervention.

Guiding Principles

Three principles guide the program. First, as a result of developmental changes and life-stage stressors, individuals who seemed to be coping well in the past now need to explore, in an atmosphere of collaboration and personal responsibility, a range of new, age-appropriate strategies. Second, these veterans need to engage in a process of life review, as a means of coming to terms not only with war-related conflict but also with their own important and unique life histories. Third, social support and family involvement are important components of treatment, and they can provide buffers against age-related stressors, as well as against the exacerbation of PTSD symptoms.

Group therapy is the primary treatment modality because almost all research on PTSD points to supportive relationships as a factor in symptom alleviation and as a buffer against symptom exacerbation. Many of these veterans have suffered cumulative social-network losses, especially the loss of a spouse, losses that have significantly reduced their social networks, with the result that there are few opportunities for them to socialize. Others, because of their war trauma, have shunned the support of close friendships in adulthood. Preliminary outcome data from our program suggest that one major benefit of treatment resides in the social-support structure it affords to group members. This base of support is in turn generalized to improved social functioning in other areas of these veterans' lives.

Group therapy also provides a means for the therapist to facilitate and reinforce insights through peer interaction. Many of the veterans use their new insights to develop healthier behaviors, mend relationships, and increase their social-support networks. They learn the importance of working through developmental tasks and the peace of mind this can bring. Retirement, illness, death, grief, and self-value are central issues that are explored. Through a discussion of these themes, they learn how to accept changes and make appropriate accommodations as a sign of healthy aging, without accepting a distorted picture that degrades their strengths and minimizes their considerable potential.

Treatment Techniques

An important aspect of treatment is the intensive use of videotapes, audiotapes, and reading materials made available to the men in the treatment area. Most of the material is carefully chosen to reinforce what has been covered in the group. The topics include aging issues, healthy living, and PTSD and so these materials reflect and expand on the themes presented during the various treatment modules. This is a crucial component of treatment because, as already mentioned, repetition is such an important part of the learning process for older adults.

The veterans are encouraged to take these materials home with them on loan and to share them with family members and supportive friends. Viewing or reading these materials in the comfort of their own homes enhances learning for the veterans, and their family members also take advantage of the treatment materials, reviewing them with the veterans and becoming intimately involved with their recovery. In this way, we promote family education and involvement as an additional intervention to reinforce and support treatment goals. Our outcome data to date show a discernible positive change in the primary support system, as well as enhancement of the quality of life for most of the men in the program. It is notable, from a managed-care perspective, that our veterans report significant increases in their satisfaction with health, altruism, friendship, family relationships, and loving feelings after just sixteen weeks in the program.

The current SVP is the result of a four-year maturation, during which therapists and clients alike had to move beyond our subtle, barely acknowledged assumptions that old psyches are more fragile than young psyches. One manifestation of this bias was our initial reluctance to include trauma processing in the treatment of traumatized World War II and Korean War veterans. The current program recognizes the capacity of elder veterans to process traumatic material, as well as the crucial role this processing plays in recovery.

In addition to traditional techniques, our trauma processing includes an innovative method known as *sand-tray therapy*, adapted from an intervention developed by Lori Daniels of the U.S. Department of Veterans Affairs National Center for Stress Recovery, in Honolulu. It is a helpful tool for promoting emotional awareness, expression, and catharsis. The group room is equipped with a sand table and with shelves containing hundreds of small figures (soldiers, civilians, tanks, houses, trees, and so forth). The veteran relates a traumatic event by setting up the crucial scene in the sandbox. Therapists and group members, who are often the first persons ever to hear the trauma, help the veteran verbalize his experience and emotions by asking supportive questions and bearing witness to his story. Distortions are often corrected in this process ("Being afraid does not mean you were a coward"), and the veterans' statements about themselves are reframed ("I did the best I could under the circumstances"). Veterans who have used the sand-tray technique report relief and consolation, and empathic group members feel empowered by their ability to help. Preliminary data reveal a significant reduction in avoidance symptoms, but reexperiencing and hyperarousal symptoms remain stable.

The receptivity of these men to the program, and particularly to sand-tray work, has been an exciting element of our clinical work with older veterans. Our program is living proof that older clients can benefit from fresh, progressive group treatments. Furthermore, we have found that symptom alleviation and improved life satisfaction are both realistic, attainable goals with elderly clients in the group milieu.

Grief-Related Depression and Anxiety: An Open Market for Group Services

Loss and grief are universal experiences in older age. Losses accumulate as people age, and how effectively older adults adjust to significant losses (for example, the death of a spouse, retirement, changes in physical health) is a critical factor in their quality of life and their future health. For example, older widowers are statistically more likely to commit suicide, or to deteriorate more rapidly from physical illness, than their married counterparts are. Older widows, as a group, are at a heightened risk for clinical depression and symptoms of anxiety in the months following the spouse's death, particularly if social support is limited. Researchers have estimated that as many as 20 percent of older widow(er)s may be at risk for complicated grief reactions (see the definitions in Exhibit 6.2) and may be in need of professional intervention. Numerous informal and lay grief-support structures exist in cities across the United States, but psychologists and other mental health professionals have been slow to respond to the clinical needs of bereaved older adults. This population represents a largely untapped market for professional mental health services.

Exhibit 6.2. Forms of Complicated Grief Expression.

Absent grief	This very rare form involves persistent, almost total, denial or shock for many months or years after a loss from death (see inhibited grief, below).
Chronic/Acute grief	This form involves the expression of high levels of grief-related distress for years after a loss from death. No clear adjustment or resolution process occurs.
Conflicted grief	This form usually occurs after the loss of a very troubled or conflicted relationship, but where there was still a strong sense of attachment. Early grief expression may be somewhat muted by feelings of relief that the conflict is over, but soon acute grief-related distress emerges (which may include strong guilt feelings, anger, and self-reproach) and is likely to last for many months or years. This form is similar to chronic grief but has a distinct relational etiology that distinguishes it.
Delayed grief	In this form, for example, the bereaved individual consciously chooses to delay certain aspects of grief (processing anger toward the deceased) until a later time. When these delayed aspects of grief are finally expressed, either "normal" or complicated reactions may materialize.
Distorted grief	In this form, grief expression is dominated either by extreme anger or by guilt feelings that last for many months or years. Anger or guilt occurs at the expense of other important grief processes and prevents healthy adaptation and/or resolution.
Inhibited grief	This form involves the inhibition of important aspects of the bereavement process and prevents full adaptation or resolution. For example, the bereaved individual may process only the positive memories of the deceased in mourning, ignoring negative memories and emotions.
Clinical disorders	Symptoms of clinical depression and anxiety may occur in response to a significant loss, either as separate syndromes or as part of a known complicated grief response. Such symptoms are most likely to occur during chronic/acute, conflicted, or distorted grief.

Widowed elders (see Chapter One of this volume) most often turn to their primary-care physicians to treat various health complaints, many of which may actually represent somatic responses to grieving. Expensive medical tests and treatments are tried, often when what is really needed is emotional support, education about the grief process, and counseling to foster improved grief-related coping and adjustment. A well-designed group psychotherapeutic intervention can address all these needs while reducing unnecessary and costly medical treatment.

Consulting the Literature

This knowledge is not new to the psychological literature. A number of studies dating back to the late 1970s show the effectiveness of group interventions for promoting positive grief-related adjustment and improved health. To our knowledge, only one treatment protocol for a short-term bereavement group has been published for general use. William Piper and associates at the University of Alberta Medical Center developed an "adaptation to loss" group ten years ago, to serve adults experiencing complicated grief reactions, including the symptoms of clinical depression and anxiety. Their treatment, a combination of psychodynamic and grief-related approaches, consisted of groups of five to eight adults meeting with a trained therapist for twelve weekly ninety-minute sessions. The result was improved emotional adjustment and reduced medical utilization for group participants (as also reported in Chapter One).

Although it is helpful to consider Piper's protocol, it leaves much to be desired in work with bereaved older adults. The average age of the Alberta sample was thirty-six, and the interventions were mostly discussion-based. Many of the keys to therapy that we suggest in this chapter are not included in the Piper model, partly because of the much younger ages of Piper's clients. Professionals interested in providing group therapy services to the bereaved elder market will need to do some homework to develop an age-appropriate group therapy protocol for grief.

Defining such a protocol is beyond the scope of this chapter, but there are a number of basic "truths" in the grief literature that can serve as topical guideposts. For example, the traditional belief that grief occurs in stages, one after another, and ends in complete resolution (that is, detachment from the lost object, and cessation of all symptoms) is no longer accepted. Grief symptoms are almost always intense shortly after a major loss, but they usually fluctuate in their level and presentation for many months, even years, in normal grieving. Anniversaries and holidays often bring an increase in symptoms, as do day-to-day reminders of what's missing. Successful adjustment does not mean an end to the symptoms of grief, but rather a renewed sense of emotional balance and an understanding of what has been lost in the context of continuing life. Grief is not resolved in older age; rather, it is adjusted to as a process that occurs time and again for all older people.

It is not uncommon, and it may actually be the norm, for an older adult to maintain a continuing bond with a deceased loved one (for example, as a fond remembrance or a source of advice: "What would John do in a situation like this?"). A publication by respected grief researchers Dennis Klass and Phyllis Silverman suggests that nurturing such bonds may be one way to support healthy adjustment in bereaved older adults.[3] Another way is to process losses in the larger context of the bereaved person's life story. As suggested earlier, life review is not just a way of building cohesiveness among group members; it is also a meaningful intervention to help older adults understand present concerns in the larger context of their lives. It is in this larger context that important coping resources and character strengths are likely to be found.

The Challenges of Marketing

Structuring a bereavement group to encompass these ideas and meet HCFA reimbursement guidelines should not be difficult for the motivated professional. Getting older clients to participate in a group-therapy intervention, whether the primary focus is grief, depression, anxiety, or memory loss, is another matter altogether.

Gone are the days of long-term hospital stays, when captive inpatients could be readily gathered for group meetings. Now, even adults with significant psychiatric illness are treated on an outpatient basis. Not only must the entrepreneurial therapist get clients into the office, he or she must convince the clients (and often their primary-care physicians and managed-care providers as well) that group treatment is worthwhile.

The marketing picture is further complicated for the therapist who serves older people. Societal awareness of mental health issues has improved consistently over the years, but the current cohort of older adults was brought up at a time when the public perception of psychological treatment was synonymous with "lying on a couch." In our experience, the simplest place for a therapist to find motivated clients for group interventions is from his or her own existing client base. At the Center for Healthy Aging (CHA), we periodically form groups from our existing individual client bases when we see that we have a critical mass of individuals with similar problems. Group therapy is offered to address specific problems (for example, memory-enhancement training for clients diagnosed with early dementia) or as an adjunct to individual therapy, to promote more effective interpersonal functioning and use of support.

Another way to bring older clients in for group interventions is through referral relationships with primary-care physicians, the health professionals most likely to see elders who are experiencing psychological distress. Fostering such referral relationships takes patient communication, a willingness to work cooperatively, and a bit of education. Primary-care physicians are often not as aware of the mind-body connection as one might think, and we frequently instruct physicians on how psychological interventions can improve both physical and mental health. Our facilitated support group for fibromyalgia patients at CHA is a case in point. Fibromyalgia is an illness involving chronic muscle pain, fatigue, sleeplessness, and a whole host of psychological symptoms. Cognitive-behavioral psychotherapeutic treatment has been shown to lessen the impact of the disease process on the individual's functioning and sense of well-being. Many of the referrals to our group came as a result of our educational efforts with primary-care physicians. A referral from their doctors is usually enough to get older adults in the door for treatment, at which time erroneous stereotypes can be challenged. Once older adults come to see a behavioral health intervention as worthwhile, they are very likely to make a commitment to treatment and stick to it.

Another option for building interest in a behavioral health intervention is through strategic use of the mail and the media. At the Center for Stress Recovery, we amassed a great deal of experience in treating PTSD in Vietnam War veterans before we developed the Senior Veterans Program. We were experienced, but that didn't mean that World War II and Korean War vets were knocking down our doors in the beginning. First we had to reach out and educate them about the effects long-term PTSD, offering tangible hope for recovery. We encouraged physicians to be on the lookout for signs of PTSD in their older patients and to make referrals to our program (this type of encouragement is much easier in a closed system like the Veterans Administration). We also reached out for clients through mass mailings to older vets in our catchment area, through public speaking at Veterans of Foreign Wars and POW meetings, and through helpful coverage in the media.

As our first clients went through the program and their functioning improved, they told others of our existence, and the program grew. Now when we start a new group, we invite past clients to come to a special ceremony and welcome the newcomers and their family members. Getting endorsements from existing and past program participants is a sure way to reduce skepticism among potential older clients and motivate their participation.

Group Therapy and Dementia: Opportunities for the Creative Group Therapist

As the older adult population grows in the coming years, increasing numbers of people will be diagnosed with dementia.

Alzheimer's and vascular (stroke-related) dementias are the most common, and together they have been estimated to affect at least 20 percent of people in their eighties. Dementia is almost a daily concern at the Center for Healthy Aging. We provide neuropsychological testing services to diagnose and document the extent of dementia-related deficits, notably memory impairment. For older adults experiencing the early stages of a dementing disorder, the news of an Alzheimer's disease diagnosis can be very upsetting. We frequently provide short-term therapy for clients we've assessed, to help them understand their dementia diagnosis, make necessary adjustments in their daily lives, and begin to make plans for the future. Family members are regularly included for support and educational purposes.

Individuals diagnosed with the early to mild stages of a progressive dementia such as Alzheimer's disease usually retain sufficient cognitive skills and personal insight to participate effectively in psychotherapy, either in an individual or a group setting. Language and memory problems are most common early on in Alzheimer's dementia, and the therapist must be prepared to make appropriate accommodations to maximize comprehension and potential recall. Speaking in a slow, clear voice, using simple language, and presenting ideas in discrete segments are ways we have found helpful to get around mild receptive language problems. We also make it a point to repeat important information, demonstrate it visually when possible, and write it down for clients to refer to later. The more senses that can be involved, the easier it is to maximize memory inputs and promote long-term storage. There is some evidence that emotional memory may continue to function well, even after verbal memory has started to fail. Using reminiscence and life-review techniques to help clients process feelings in therapy and promoting emotional support in clients' care networks are two interventions that remain viable for years in the dementia process.

When older adults reach the middle to later stages of a progressive dementia, their short-term memory skills and personal insight, among other abilities, may not be sufficient for this type of psychotherapeutic work. Apart from retaining a basic familiarity ("I think I've met you before"), moderately demented adults are unlikely to integrate and recall issues discussed from one therapy session to the next. Training in memory-enhancement techniques (such as chunking, rehearsal, visualization, association, and so on) can help to improve recall ability somewhat. Writing down important information can also still be helpful, but their ability to use this information to effect change in their lives may be quite limited. Social skills are usually still intact in the middle stages of dementia, and group interventions can provide such adults with helpful opportunities for interaction and support.

The challenge for the therapist seeking to offer such a group is how to get paid for it. Groups whose primary purpose is social, recreational, or related to memory enhancement do not meet HCFA reimbursement criteria for psychotherapy. An approach that has worked well for us at the Center for Healthy Aging is contracting directly with long-term-care facilities, outside the insurance system, to provide socialization groups for their residents (see Chapter Ten of this volume). We offer three distinct socialization groups at one facility: one for skilled nursing patients, one for high-functioning demented older adults, and one for low-functioning demented elders. Each group meets once a month and involves a specific topic or topics for reminiscence work. Discussing long-past memories (usually the last to deteriorate) in a group setting provides opportunities for social interaction and support. Isolation is an all too common problem for many demented older people, particularly those living in long-term-care facilities. One reason why our socialization groups have been effective and are valued by the facility is their impact on emotional memory. Residents report feeling happier and more alert after a socialization-group session, and these positive responses have a carryover effect and improve functioning in the following days. This type of group intervention has great value, in our view, and warrants consideration as a reimbursable form of therapy under managed care.

The Menorah Park Model: Functional
Interventions for Demented Elders

Cameron Camp,[4] a research psychologist at Menorah Park Center for the Aging, near Cleveland, applies a "rehabilitation approach" to the treatment of dementia. "We're not interested in maintenance," Camp comments, "but in developing interventions to help people with dementia improve." His interventions involve a fascinating mix of traditional neuroscience and geriatric research, Montessori teaching methods, and occupational-therapy adaptation principles. According to Camp, his intent is to "create a level playing field by reducing the cognitive demands of the situation," thereby allowing demented older adults to employ and build on their remaining skills. New learning, and the boost in self-esteem that accompanies it, is possible even for the more severely demented older adult if the environmental conditions are right.

Much of Camp's work these days involves researching these optimal conditions and designing interventions that can be incorporated into existing service-delivery systems (nursing facilities, adult day-care centers, or senior group homes). Camp emphasizes the importance of a structure that "telescopes to practical activity." He uses common, everyday objects and behaviors, and he links people of varying levels of cognitive ability to promote interpersonal learning. All his interventions start on a simple, concrete level and build to become more challenging, following specific, researched steps.

Memory Bingo is a good example of Camp's methods. In this game, a group of demented adults, whose impairment ranges from mild to more severe, are seated at a table, and each person has four (or more) printed cards placed in front of him or her. The cards may bear the names of old products, movie stars, songs, TV shows, and so on, names that the participants are likely to recognize. The adult day-care or nursing staff person reads a jingle or a statement related to one of the cards and demonstrates the task involved in the game by turning over the related card in front of her. The intervention is obvious on its face, so it does not tax the cognitive resources of the participants, and the mildly impaired players are likely to get it right away. These players in turn act as models for the more impaired participants to learn the task over time. The game is won when a player has all of his or her cards turned over.

A number of theoretical and therapeutic factors underlie this "simple" intervention. First, the task relies on remote memories that are usually the last to diminish in a progressive dementia like Alzheimer's disease. The game of Bingo is well known, as is the information contained on the cards. The task is demonstrated visually rather than through extensive verbal instruction, thus maximizing comprehension. Less demented adults model the required behaviors for more impaired adults, thereby promoting interpersonal learning and helpful social interaction. The less demented participants can both enjoy the game and feel good about the assistance they provide to others, while the more impaired players reap the benefits of being engaged in a task with others.

Memory Bingo is a real favorite in the adult day-care center at Menorah Park, according to Camp. Even if demented participants fail to recall playing Memory Bingo from one day to the next, they are still interested in playing, and they tend to pick up the task quickly as a result of prior exposure. This is a function of "procedural or nondeclarative memory," according to Camp. The task is familiar on some level, and it tends to engage the players' attention while also providing them a needed emotional boost. Even severely demented individuals can learn to play Memory Bingo and become more effective players over time. Memory Bingo also seems to have a ripple effect for participants over the subsequent hours, during which time they appear more alert and interested in what's going on around them. These observations are now being tested in outcome research.

Camp and his team are in the process of developing a wide range of interventions that are beyond the scope of this chapter. One of their current projects involves pairing demented older adults with young children and allowing the older adults to function in a teaching or mentoring role for the children. His early results are impressive: regardless of their dementia status, older adults rise to the task and shine when the intervention is implemented correctly. Camp is also designing a portable Montessori cabinet containing dozens of structured activities that demented older adults can readily understand and enjoy in group settings. Camp's interventions do not meet HCFA reimbursement guidelines right now, but they may in the future if his outcome data continue to show the worth of these efforts.

What sets Camp's work apart is its strong theoretical and research basis. Camp and other researchers around the world are demonstrating that older adults with dementia can learn new information and function more effectively in the proper conditions. Whether an intervention is for psychotherapeutic catharsis or functional memory enhancement, the same principle holds true for geropsychological practice: behavioral interventions with older adults, to be successful, must take account of people's specific developmental and psychological needs.

It has been our contention in this chapter that group psychotherapy is an intervention uniquely suited to the behavioral, psychosocial, and developmental needs of older adults. Group interventions provide excellent opportunities for social support and interpersonal learning, opportunities that can be harnessed in the improvement of day-to-day functioning. Although older people do face particular challenges that come with aging, we have come to learn that they are not as different from younger people as ageist stereotypes say. Older people can and do respond to expectations for success in therapy, and they are capable of involved emotional processing and characterological change over time. For such processing and change to occur, the therapeutic factors of group therapy must simply be tailored to fit the group members' individual needs.

A positive outcome in therapy is more than just symptom amelioration, in our view. For the typical older client, some symptoms (such as grief and stressful memories of war) do not disappear as a result of therapy. What often changes is the older client's perspective on these symptoms, his or her sense of coping efficacy, interpersonal connectedness, and general life satisfaction. We believe that these areas need to be assessed in determining whether an intervention is successful or not.

In this age of managed care and limited healthcare dollars, simply saying that a group intervention is appropriate and effective for a certain problem is not enough. Outcome research is sorely needed on the level of the clinical practitioner. Simple pre-and posttesting that uses available psychometric and life-satisfaction instruments can go a long way in this regard (see Chapter Four of this volume). Including intermediate assessments in the group process can add even more information, which can be used not just to demonstrate benefits to managed-care providers but also to demonstrate progress to individual clients. As mentioned earlier, highlighting growth is an important clinical tool in group work with older adults. Responding to our recommendations in this chapter will take some effort for the new geriatric practitioner. We feel that the rewards are great, however, and worth the effort. We hope you do, too.

Postscript

Since the writing of this chapter, we have reevaluated the Senior Veterans Program with the goal of providing more cost-effective care that better meets the individual needs of our clients. The program has been condensed into a sixteen-week psychoeducational format that consists of PTSD education, life review, and skills-building modules. Sand-tray work is offered as a separate time-limited focus group only with clients for whom trauma processing is clinically indicated.

The revised treatment manual emphasizes patient responsibility through more homework assignments (action plans) and an extensive supplementary section that consists of optional readings and therapeutic activities. Placing more responsibility on the shoulders of these clients conveys to them our confidence in their motivation and competence. Preliminary outcome data suggest that the shortened program is just as effective in terms of symptom reduction and improved life satisfaction

Suggested Reading

Camp, C. J., and Foss, J. W. "Designing Ecologically Valid Memory Interventions for Persons with Dementia." In D. G. Payne and F. G. Conrad (eds.), *Intersections in Basic and Applied Memory Research*. Hillsdale, N.J.: Erlbaum, 1997.

Erikson, E. H. *Childhood and Society*. New York: Norton, 1963.

Frisch, M., and others. "Clinical Validation of the Quality of Life Inventory: A Measure of Life Satisfaction for Use in Treatment Planning and Outcome Assessment." *Psychological Assessment*, 1992, 4, 92–101.

Knight, B. *Psychotherapy with Older Adults*. Thousand Oaks, Calif.: Sage. 1986.

Leszcz, M. "Towards an Integrated Model of Group Psychotherapy with the Elderly." *International Journal of Group Psychotherapy*, 1990, 40(4), 379–399.

Meuser, T. M., and Marwit, S. J. *An Integrative Model of Personality, Coping, and Appraisal for the Prediction of Grief Involvement in Adults*. Unpublished manuscript, 1997.

"Psychiatric Services: Revised Policy." *Medicare Newsletter*. Columbus, OH: Nationwide Insurance Enterprise, April 1995.

Rando, T. A. *Treatment of Complicated Mourning*. Champaign, Ill.: Research Press, 1993.

Raphael, B. *The Anatomy of Bereavement*. New York: Basic Books, 1983.

Richardson, L. M., and Austad, C. S. "Realities of Mental Health Practice in Managed-Care Settings." *Professional Psychology: Research & Practice*, 1991, 22, 52–59.

Schaie, K. W., and Willis, S. L. *Adult Development and Aging*. New York: HarperCollins, 1996.

Vance, D., Camp, J., Kabacoff, M., and Greenwalt, L. "Montessori Methods: Innovative Interventions for Adults with Alzheimer's Disease." *Montessori Life*, Winter 1996, pp. 10–11.

Chapter Seven

Bibliotherapy

A Nontraditional Intervention for Depression

Forrest Scogin

Not too long ago there were questions about whether psychosocial interventions for depressed older adults were effective, or as effective as the converging evidence seemed to suggest for general adult populations. We now know that community-dwelling older adults are quite suitable for various psychological approaches to the treatment of depression. My contribution to this area of clinical geropsychology, and the reason I was asked to contribute this chapter, is my research on a nontraditional treatment for depression: namely, bibliotherapy.

In this chapter I will present some ideas about how bibliotherapy might intersect with present healthcare arrangements and offer information on research evaluations of this form of treatment for geriatric depression. I will also address what I anticipate may be some misgivings about the approach, offering the cautions and benefits of using this mode of treatment. This chapter is intended for use by individuals who provide direct care or have administrative responsibility for the provision of services to older adults. My goal is to introduce you to an approach that may be suitable for some older adults and challenge you to creatively employ this modality to the benefit of consumers and providers.

What Is Bibliotherapy?

Bibliotherapy is a type of self-administered treatment in which the treatment is delivered via written material. Our definition of the term *self-administered treatment* is treatment in which the therapist maintains no more than minimal contact with the client. Synonyms are *self-help therapy* (which is sometimes confused with self-help groups like Alcoholics Anonymous), *do-it-yourself therapy*, and *therapist-reduced treatment*. The degree of therapist reduction may be total (with a person buying a book and working independently) or partial (with bibliotherapy as an adjunct to ongoing psychotherapy). What is interesting is that these two extremes on the continuum (ranging from totally self-paced therapy to therapist-directed treatment) are the most frequent but the least researched applications of bibliotherapy. Most investigations of bibliotherapy have been in the context of minimal contact, in which bibliotherapy is self-paced but monitoring is maintained by a therapist. What follows here is a composite case using elements from patients I have seen or patients who have been treated by students I was supervising. Its purpose is to give you a flavor of bibliotherapy's use in the treatment of depressed older adults.

An Application of Bibliotherapy with a Depressed Older Adult

A seventy-two-year-old married woman was referred to me by her physician for the treatment of depression. The intake session with her suggested a diagnosis of minor depression (more than one but fewer than five symptoms of depression, meeting the criteria for depressive disorder, not otherwise specified). The entity managing her care indicated she was authorized for four sessions of treatment.

She was a cognitively intact, fairly bright person who seemed to have no complicating comorbidities. She enjoyed reading and found the prospect of making a weekly trip to my office a bit burdensome, given her arthritic condition. When presented with the possibility of following a largely self-administered program to treat her dysphoria, she was ambivalent. On the one hand, she was fiercely independent, and this approach minimized her fear that she might become dependent on a therapist, or that someone substantially younger than she was might not understand her problems. On the other hand, she was skeptical of the likelihood of getting much help from a book. Using a gently persuasive approach, including liberal citations of the research on self-administered treatment of geriatric depression, I got a commitment from her to read the book *Feeling Good,*[1] an extremely popular self-help presentation of cognitive therapy, to comply with the suggested exercises and homework in the book, and to meet with me in two weeks to discuss her progress. Plans were made for a brief telephone call one week hence, to monitor the situation. She was assigned a mutually agreed-upon portion of reading to do before our next meeting.

At the next session, I discussed in detail the tenets of cognitive therapy that were presented in the book and the issues involved in implementing the treatment recommendations, as well as the impact that working with the book was having on the target complaint, depression. She reported decreased symptoms of depression and seemed to be internalizing the cognitive therapy procedures of identifying and modifying dysfunctional thinking patterns. Further sessions with this client were directed to consolidating gains and working on the prevention of a relapse.

Practice Applications

In the work of most clinicians, including my own work in my private practice, bibliotherapy materials are used as adjuncts to psychotherapy. Surveys[2] suggest that most clinical psychologists prescribe bibliotherapy, most feel this practice to be helpful, and few are concerned about negative effects. In most circumstances of this sort, bibliotherapy is a homework assignment and is not seen as the focus of treatment. I am unaware of any systematic research that would inform us about whether bibliotherapy improves therapeutic efficacy, but it seems unlikely that it would hurt. It seems to me that there may be ways to serve clients cost-effectively by having them use self-administered treatment. For example, in systems where only limited numbers of sessions are authorized, a program in which bibliotherapy is more prominent may be an option for stretching the services. After an intake procedure, a client who was deemed appropriate for less intensive therapy could be assigned a self-administered treatment and then could be seen every other week or once a month as he worked his way through a book or a workbook. This arrangement probably will not be a moneymaker if reimbursement is forthcoming only for face-to-face sessions, but if what you want to do is maximize the therapeutic effect of treatment, this may be a way to do that.

The use of a self-administered treatment program probably lends itself even more clearly in a capitation model of service delivery. It is clear to me that a substantial number of persons in need of psychosocial treatment can benefit from a well-conceived, self-administered approach. Agreement about the ways in which persons would be selected for self-administered treatment is essential. A protocol for making treatment assignments would also be a necessity and might include such factors as diagnosis, severity of symptoms, reading ability, and, probably most important, the person's willingness to engage in a self-administered program of treatment.

Problems in Implementation

In our work with self-administration of cognitive bibliotherapy (use of the book *Feeling Good*) with older adults, a few problems in implementation consistently emerge. One is that differentiation of thoughts and feelings is difficult. Clients buy the premise that how they think influences how they feel, but then they stumble through such homework as the triple-column exercise in which they are asked to record an event, the thought that was associated with the event, and the feeling that emerged. A related and consistent problem reported by clients using self-administered treatment has to do with following through on the many exercises and assignments suggested in the reading. These two problems are not unique to self-administered treatment, but they may be compounded by the absence of the direct attention that could be offered in traditional psychotherapy.

Although most of the participants in our studies respond positively, there are a number who experience either little or no gain, or who drop out. The most straightforward approach with these clients is to then enter them into a course of traditional psychotherapy or pharmacotherapy, as finances permit. In our current comparative study of cognitive bibliotherapy and individual cognitive therapy, we have provided individual therapy to the bibliotherapy nonresponders. Unfortunately, however, it seems that those who were nonresponders to bibliotherapy are also nonresponders to individual therapy.

Client Characteristics

It has long been the goal of psychotherapy researchers to maximize treatment efficacy by matching certain treatments to certain patients. This process has often been referred to as the *specificity question.* It certainly seems logical to think that a client who has a particular set of characteristics would do better in some types of treatment than another client would. What are some of the factors that might be used to select good candidates for self-administered programs? In this section, I will present an overview of our efforts to identify those participant characteristics that are involved in a positive response to self-administered treatment.

Let me begin by saying that our research to date has not been particularly successful in identifying client characteristics predictive of better outcomes in self-administered treatment for depression. One exception was our investigation with depressed middle-aged adults. Here we found that those who scored high on the Self-Control Schedule, or SCS[3] had a better response to cognitive bibliotherapy. The SCS purports to measure tendencies toward internalized versus externalized coping strategies. For example, someone who indicates that she relies on others to help her with her problems would be evidencing a more externalizing style. We found that those clients who had a more internalized orientation did better in terms of depression reduction, and this finding was consistent with our prediction. A similar finding was reported by Beutler and others,[4] where persons with an internalizing coping style tended to do better in self-directed treatment than in individual psychotherapy. These investigators also found that patients higher in resistance and defensiveness tended to do better in self-directed treatment (they defined resistance as the tendency to respond negatively to the therapist's directives and to authority more generally). Keep in mind that we are not talking about pathological levels of these characteristics, but instead about the normal distribution of these personal styles. What these converging results suggest is that a self-administered approach to depression might be most appropriate for those who are more internally focused and more resistant. Whether these findings on internality and defensiveness would hold true with depressed older adults is not known, although we are currently collecting data on these questions.

Some treatments seem to lead to more negative outcomes or deterioration among clients. Is self-administered treatment for depression one of these modalities? I now turn my attention to this issue.

Negative Outcomes

One of the main objections raised by professionals to the use of self-administered treatments is the possibility of negative outcomes or the client's deterioration while in minimal-contact treatment. This is a legitimate concern for all forms of psychosocial treatment but especially for self-administered treatment. A clear pronouncement on this issue was made by Mohr, who wrote, "There is some indication that minimal interventions with severely distressed patients may result in deterioration."[5] This assertion was based on data from an earlier study, in which 19 percent (three out of sixteen) of the patients in a self-administered treatment program for depression evidenced a negative outcome. For the purpose of his study, Mohr defined a negative outcome as a 1-point increase on a depression inventory after treatment.

On the basis of my experience across several studies of self-administered treatment for depression, Mohr's rate of 19 percent struck me as a bit high. Some colleagues and I looked over data from 188 participants across the life span and found a negative outcome rate of 9 percent. For purposes of comparison, we used the same criterion as Mohr did, and we calculated the negative-outcome rates from the Cognitive Therapy condition of the Treatment of Depression Collaborative Research Program. Here, negative outcomes were 6 percent. Therefore, negative-outcome rates do not seem substantially different in therapist-administered and self-administered treatments, although this impression comes from clinical-trial research data.

Why was the rate higher in Mohr's experience? Our speculation on that matter may have implications for the use of bibliotherapy programs in nonresearch venues. It appears that patients in Mohr's study were expecting more active and intensive treatment than the self-directed program they received. Participants in our studies are initially recruited with the full understanding that they will receive a self-administered program. Therefore, in nonresearch healthcare service settings it may be a bit of an obstacle to mix traditional psychosocial interventions with nontraditional services, such as those outlined in this chapter. However, service provided outside a research setting does not have the constraint of random assignment to treatment, and so treatment decisions can be more of a collaboration between provider and consumer, rather than a function of the luck of the draw. The point is that preparation of the client is important in all forms of treatment but may be especially important in self-administered programs.

Bibliotherapy in Primary Care?

One of the more unexplored avenues for providing services to depressed older adults is to offer them in conjunction with the services provided by primary-care physicians. We all know that, for better or for worse, this is already how most contemporary mental health services are provided, and we know that pharmacotherapy forms the bulk of treatment for depression. It might be possible to arrange for physicians to supplement pharmacotherapy with a minimal-contact bibliotherapy program. I think this would be attractive for several reasons, one being that it is less stigmatizing to be assigned a book to read than to have an appointment scheduled with a psychotherapist. Further, it is my guess that physicians using this arrangement would feel as if they were giving up less control of their patients. For example, the program could be run largely through the physician's office. I honestly believe that the persons who are now taking antidepressants with no psychosocial treatment augmentation would achieve better short-term and long-term outcomes if their medical treatment were coupled with a well-run self-administered treatment program.

Bibliotherapy's Role in Prevention

The self-administered programs described in this chapter have been so far oriented to the treatment of existing, diagnosable depressive disorders. In my opinion, however, their greatest potential application exists in the realm of prevention. My guess would be that most people who purchase a self-help book are applying the treatment in a preventive manner—that is, they are not yet experiencing a clinical level of depression. How much more effective would prevention be if the book were chosen by a knowledgeable professional, and if some minimal level of guidance were then provided?

We are currently testing the utility of such a preventive approach with older patients in a rehabilitation hospital. These patients are primarily experiencing minor depression, and we are interested in how offering them cognitive bibliotherapy with minimal-contact therapy will affect their depression and, more important, their rehabilitation and daily functioning.

I can think of several other possible applications. This sort of minimal-contact program might be well suited to a situation in which you were asked to provide an outreach program for an agency serving older adults. Another application might involve retired employees for whom you had contracted to provide a wellness program. Still another possible application would be to use this treatment modality as a facet of an ongoing support group, such as a group for the bereaved, or a group for people who are providing care to a family member.

Ethical Considerations

What are the ethical contours of implementing a self-administered approach to depression treatment? Let me confess to you that I ask myself that question a lot. I am pretty well convinced that a lot of people can get a lot of benefit from these programs, but I can never fully escape the concern that someone is going to deteriorate during self-administered treatment, and that I will be left to wonder if we did this person a disservice by not getting him or her into more intensive treatment. I am thankful that I have not had to confront a suicide during this series of studies, although we have had to withdraw a few people over the years and refer them elsewhere. I believe that at least minimal contact between therapist and client is clinically, ethically, and legally the proper course of action. Had we not had a weekly telephone check-in procedure in place with our clients, we might have missed the worsening cases, and I know I would not then have felt that an ethical course of treatment had been undertaken. What I am trying to say is that self-administered treatment should not be a vehicle for abandoning clients. A therapist-client relationship still exists, but it is of a different nature.

Finances also raise an interesting question. We have never had to confront this issue, because our programs are free of charge (mostly because we ask participants to devote a fair amount of time to completing assessments that are for research purposes only). But what about a traditional outpatient, private practice service arrangement? I suppose it would be appropriate to bill only for the face-to-face (or voice-to-voice) minimal contact. I have the uneasy feeling that this shortchanges the therapist, but I do not have a ready solution.

Does Bibliotherapy Work?

My research has been on the topic of bibliotherapy with depressed elders. Others have investigated the utility of bibliotherapy with an almost unbelievable variety of ailments, from the mainstream (generalized anxiety disorder) to the highly specialized (nail-biting). In fact, there have been enough empirical studies done on bibliotherapy to support the use of a procedure known as meta-analysis. To put this briefly, meta-analysis is the aggregation of data across studies to provide an overall quantitative summary of a topic. Meta-analysis has become an exceptionally important tool in the social sciences generally, and in the field of mental health services more specifically. Several meta-analytic reviews have indicated impressive overall efficacy for bibliotherapy.[6] The study by Scogin, Bynum, Stephens, and Calhoon found that 82 percent of the average bibliotherapy participants improved more than the average no-treatment control participants did. More to the point, a recent meta-analysis of six studies on bibliotherapy for depression concluded that bibliotherapy for depression is an effective treatment and, further, that bibliotherapy is as effective as individual or group psychotherapy.[7] I am not prepared to make this declaration, but the effect sizes obtained in these reviews (.96 for the Scogin, Bynum, Stephens, and Calhoon study, .76 for the Gould and Clum study, and .82 for the Cuijpers study) are quite comparable to those evidenced in meta-analytic studies of psychotherapy.

But what about the studies that comprise these meta-analyses, you might ask? I would like to review two of these studies in some detail, to give you an idea of the implementation of these programs.

Scogin, Jamison, and Gochneaur examined the efficacy of two forms of self-administered treatment for depressed older adults.[8] One consisted of reading *Feeling Good*, and the other involved reading *Control Your Depression*,[9] a self-help presentation of behavioral therapy for depression. Approximately seventy persons over the age of sixty, who were evidencing at least mild depression, were recruited through media announcements. They were assessed on a variety of measures and randomly assigned either to one of the self-administered treatment conditions or to a delayed-treatment control group. They were given four weeks to read their books and were contacted once a week by a research assistant so that they could report on their levels of depression, answer questions about their reading, and receive encouragement to complete their reading. Counseling was prohibited (this level of contact falls into the minimal-contact category alluded to earlier in the chapter). After the four-week treatment period, they were reassessed on the measures for evaluating the effects of the programs. The results indicated both a statistically and clinically significant reduction in the symptoms of depression. On average, participants changed about 10 points on the Hamilton Rating Scale for Depression, an interview-based assessment of the severity of depression symptoms that is used in virtually all depression-related clinical trials. To put this result more clinically, a 10-point change means reduction on five or so of the cardinal symptoms of depression, and to put it still more concretely, this means a real decrease in suffering. About two-thirds of the participants moved into the nondepressed range.

Some of the things we learned from this study may be of interest. First, it really did not seem to make much difference if a participant read all of the book that was assigned so long as he or she got the gist of the approach (for example, that the way you think influences how you feel, in the cognitive bibliotherapy condition). Second, we learned that education makes a difference. Even within our relatively well educated sample, those with less education were more likely to drop out. In general, my feeling from having done this and several other studies of this sort is that the type of person likely to respond well to bibliotherapy is the same type of person likely to respond well to psychotherapy, or at least to psychotherapy of the briefer, more focused variety.

Follow-up Findings

Do the effects of self-administered treatment for depressed elders last? Apparently so, if the results of a two-year follow-up of thirty depressed older adults are valid. There were no significant changes in depression level two years after the study was completed, compared with immediate posttreatment status. In fact, overall, there was a slight decrease in depression scores. What was most interesting to us is that over half of participants had reread parts of the assigned book during the follow-up interval. We had not instructed or encouraged them to do so, and so this was a self-administered booster of a self-administered treatment.

A second study, currently nearing completion, is a comparison of individual cognitive therapy with cognitive bibliotherapy for depressed elders. For a number of years I had wanted to directly compare treatments in this way, and I convinced Mark Floyd, a graduate student in our clinical psychology program, to take this comparison on as a dissertation project. Individual cognitive therapy follows the Beck, Rush, Shaw, and Emery manual,[10] with modifications and considerations consistent with suggestions from various sources on conducting individual work with older adults. What our data seem to suggest with about 75 percent of the participants recruited is that individual therapy is a bit more effective than cognitive bibliotherapy, but probably not to a statistically or clinically significant degree. This finding is consistent with the results of the aforementioned meta-analyses, in which effects from bibliotherapy and therapist-administered programs were comparable. Dropouts from the two conditions have been interesting in that the situation is much more clear-cut when a person discontinues psychotherapy than if he or she simply does not show up for sessions. Dropout from bibliotherapy is usually more subtle and not entirely palpable until end-of-treatment assessments are failed. Tracking compliance in self-administered treatment has been devilish, and this issue could have ramifications for the use of self-administered treatment in fee-for-service arrangements. For example, can you count a service as rendered when you have no tangible evidence that the participant has engaged with it? Keep in mind that we have not been able to find a reliable connection between degree of compliance (pages read, exercises completed) and success in treatment.

You might reasonably wonder whether we have a program or a process that seems to work without our having much understanding of what accounts for the changes observed. I would answer that this perception is correct, for the most part. What I believe and submit to you is that self-administered treatment capitalizes on the most important variable in treatment outcomes: the client. In attempting to parcel out the relative influences on treatment outcomes—namely, therapist effects, client effects, technical or theoretical factors, and the interminable interactions of these variables—almost everyone agrees that the lion's share of influence must go to the client variables. As I have been known to say, "Give me a good client, and I will look like the second coming of Carl Rogers." This is not to say that such factors as the therapist's skill are unimportant, but it is to say that the amount of difference that variation in such factors can make is small by comparison with the amount of difference attributable to the client.

Alternative Media for Self-Administered Treatments

If you accept my premise—that self-administered treatment for depression in elders has some utility—then allow me some speculation about other potential avenues for this approach. We have relied on low-tech media for our treatment programs—that is, we have used printed material. At the time we began this research, in the early 1980s, this was far and away the most viable means, and in fact that may still be the case. Nevertheless, the potential for providing self-administered programs via video, computerized disks, television, and the Internet seems limitless. For example, Pim Cuijpers, a psychologist in the Netherlands, implemented a television broadcast of a *Control Your Depression* course. A multiepisode presentation was developed that followed the lesson plan presented in the group renditions of this behavioral approach. Prevention of depression is the intent of these broadcasts, and Cuijpers and his colleagues are researching whether this modality is being used, and whether it has had an effect. It clearly has the potential to reach large numbers of people.

A second approach is the computerized presentation of treatment procedures. Selmi and others, through either computer-guided sessions or therapist-administered means, presented cognitive-behavioral therapy for depression to middle-aged patients experiencing major and minor depression.[11] After six sessions, results indicated that both treatments were effective by comparison with the results for a control condition, and that the two treatments were nondifferentially efficacious. This group of researchers has also developed a computerized treatment program for obsessive-compulsive disorder. It has nine clinical steps, twelve computer-controlled interactive voice-response telephone calls, and over a thousand digitized voice files that are responsive to patients' reports during calls. These approaches are certainly a step forward in terms of technology, but they still require patients to come into a central treatment facility, thereby imposing one of the constraints that bibliotherapy programs minimize. Until personal computers become fixtures in homes, this will remain a stumbling block to the use of computerized treatment programs.

Another frontier for self-administered treatments is the Internet. We did a nonexhaustive search of the resources available via the World Wide Web and did not turn up anything that would fit our description of a self-administered program for the treatment of depression—that is, there were no sites that presented a programmatic treatment approach following one of the empirically validated therapies. What we did turn up were a number of depression-specific support groups, as well as several sites with information about depression. For example, at the site http://www.cyberpsych.com, information is provided on depression and cognitive therapy techniques, but sales of books by the site's doctor seem to be the main intent. This, of course, brings the high technology of the Internet back down to the level of the written material with which we have practiced for a number of years. What is probably more realistic is the use of compact disks to present a program of self-administered treatment for depression. *Feeling Good* and *Control Your Depression* would both lend themselves nicely to an interactive presentation on a personal computer. This surely must have been done, but I am not aware of the availability of any such products or of any efforts to examine how well they might work.

I am sometimes asked, by friends who know of my research, "Are you continuing your assault on therapists?" This is said mostly in jest, but there is an underlying concern that is shared by many who are new to the concept of self-administered treatment. My intent has never been to cut people out of anything, but instead to make what we know works available to as many people as possible. But lately my thinking has begun to change a bit. Increasingly, psychosocial treatments for depression are being offered by less trained practitioners—essentially, the lowest-cost providers who can be found—which leads me to the following rhetorical question: If you were depressed, which would you choose: to read a self-help book that could skillfully lead you through a course of treatment with a strong grounding in research, or to meet face-to-face with a therapist, probably not of your choosing, who has not been trained to understand the research on treatment and is a practitioner of the therapy that was presented last weekend in a workshop at the Buckaroo Inn? Put directly, I'll take a book based on sound treatment principles over a poorly trained psychotherapist any day, and I think a lot of other people would, too, if they knew the score.

The use of self-administered treatment by people in distress is a reality. This chapter is an effort to think about some applications of this approach with depressed older adults in today's healthcare market. Two trends suggest that we will need all the resources we can muster to meet the needs of depressed older adults in the years to come. One is the well-known aging of the baby-boomer cohort.

The second and less frequently mentioned phenomenon is the extraordinary increase in depressive disorders in the post–World War II birth cohorts. Put these two together, and the potential for (unfortunately) very high rates of depressed older adults is evident. Pharmacotherapy and psychotherapy will continue as mainstays in the treatment of depression, but it is my belief that well-organized and validated self-administered programs may also play a role in meeting the needs of depressed persons across the life span.

Suggested Reading

Scogin, F., and others. "Negative Outcomes: What Is the Evidence on Self-Administered Treatments?" *Journal of Consulting and Clinical Psychology*, 1996, 64, 1086–1089.

Chapter Eight

The Mental Health Professional in Long-Term Care

Gael Gabrielle Smookler Jarrett, Stephen Jarrett Smookler, James J. Riemenschneider, Thomas A. Riemenschneider

In light of the constantly evolving practice environment, we wrote this chapter to help mental health professionals identify the many opportunities now available in elder care. These opportunities exist in the diverse settings where elder care is provided: primary-care settings, community service and home healthcare organizations, and facilities where residential care (including assisted living and skilled nursing) is offered. Transforming these opportunities into career sources for mental health professionals requires a focus on three core factors in the practice environment.

The first factor is the larger system in which the elderly live. This system includes residential settings, long-term-care facilities, personal homes within a matrix of interfacing organizations (such as hospitals), doctors' offices, churches and temples, and numerous community organizations in which the elderly participate. It is in the system's environment that the behavioral healthcare practitioner will explore options for career expansion and service provision. Today, in many cases, services must be provided outside the traditional office setting. When the place of service changes, the service must also change. It is essential for the practitioner to think of his or her self in a new role, as consultant in addition to therapist. The age-old maxim of social work is useful at this juncture: meet clients where they are. The "where" now alludes to external, nontraditional therapeutic environments as well as to the inter-personal therapeutic level.

The second factor is the elderly individuals who are being affected by changes in managed care. What are the needs of elderly people? What is their experience? What can a mental health pro-fessional really do to contribute to the harmony and well-being of their lives? How can a therapist as a consultant effect changes in their environment, while also effecting changes in them as indi-viduals?

The third factor is personal transformation as a clinician in a changing role. Mental health professionals now mediate among political realities, medical needs, familial needs, and the individual older person, who is often the most disempowered entity in the long-term-care milieu. A clinician must make the transformation from individual appraisal to systems-level appraisal, while staying open to the organic process of interpersonal changes in the shifting healthcare environment. New roles may encompass or transcend the roles of practitioner as therapist and consultant.

In the changing environment of long-term care, mental health professionals have several options. One is to react with fear and anxiety to situations that invoke powerlessness and little if any influence. Another is to deny the existence of the "elephant in the living room" and continue practicing as if nothing had changed. A more optimistic response is to expect even more change, adopt an attitude of curiosity, and create short-term responses to the new and ever-changing patterns. Obviously, an anxiety-based reaction is not useful, nor will a pragmatist find denial helpful to survival, but curiosity and creativity are always productive and useful options requiring personal growth.

A Model for Chronic Care

Our consulting group, Stephen Thomas Associates, has developed a unique model for serving the elderly in a managed-care system. It was conceptualized in the late 1980s in the design of an education-oriented retirement community that we developed as a "living village." The care-management framework that was developed is now in the early phases of implementation, as part of a collaborative effort among an alliance of seventeen not-for-profit nursing homes, continuing-care retirement communities, and community-based service organizations in central Ohio.

This organizational effort resulted in a not-for-profit legal entity, called the Central Ohio Non-Profit Integrated Network (CONPIN), which comprises a consortium of chronic-care organizations and provides a continuum of elder care to the greater Columbus area. The allied organizations offer homemaker services, home healthcare services, support for independent living and assisted living, skilled nursing care at various levels, adult day care, and other associated supportive services. The current services will be organized into a service package marketed by CONPIN to managed-care organizations. The organizations have banded together to approach managed-care organizations as a group, ultimately to provide subcapitated chronic-care services to elderly clients on the organizations' own campuses and in the general community.

The model discussed in this chapter offers opportunities for mental health professionals to play a significant role in the clinical assessment and care management of elderly people. We describe the model here for two reasons. First, it is an example of an organizational response to the rapid and dynamic changes occurring in the healthcare field. Second, we urge the inclusion of mental health professionals in the development of ideal and appropriate critical-care pathways because we believe that psychosocial assessment of the elderly will improve the outcomes of behavioral healthcare for this group. It is in the best interests of the political and financial systems to reduce costs, which means that mental and emotional healthcare is itself a valuable resource in a system of resource allocation.

A unique feature of our approach will be a model of care management that allows assessment of each elderly subscriber in the consortium's managed-care system, that is, CONPIN, and determines the kind and level of service required (for example, home healthcare, skilled nursing, or psychological support). The assessment, which is to include substantial psychosocial assessment by a care-management nurse coordinator, will help link the elderly subscriber with the appropriate level of service as early as possible and as often as necessary. The goal is to ensure high-quality service in the least expensive setting, and in support of the subscriber's highest level of psychological and physical independence.

In the managed-care model as it will be used in nursing homes and other chronic-care settings, it is proposed that a nurse practitioner will assess each elderly person entering the consortium-based system. A significant assessment will be made of the individual's emotional and mental needs, as well as of his or her medical and financial requirements. Representatives from the fields of psychology and social work will have a major influence on the development of the tool for assessing the individual's emotional and cognitive well-being. She or he will be assessed for emotional balance and mental health, not just for indications of conditions defined by the categories listed in the fourth edition of the *Diagnostic and Statistical Manual of Mental Disorders*.[1] The short-term goal of the assessment will be to discover areas for intervention; the long-term goal will be to maximize the individual's functioning and personal development.

Another opportunity for assessing the individual's emotional needs will occur during the initial visit with a primary-care physician, who will have been educated about the need to ask the most effective questions in the most genuinely caring and gentle manner. Obviously, caring is a personality-dependent requirement, but it is a prerequisite if elderly clients are to feel safe enough to share emotionally charged concerns.

Expanding Opportunities for Mental Health Professionals

If mental health professionals are to sustain their involvement in elder care, it will be vital for them to network with primary-care physicians and other professionals. Links with primary-care physicians will be of value both to the physicians and to the mental health professionals. The physicians will become more knowledgeable about the skills and professional focus of the mental health professionals, and the mental health professionals will gain the opportunity to market their own services to a valuable source of referrals.

Along with the roles mental health professionals traditionally have played in assessment processes, additional networking techniques will have to be developed to gain access to the expanded opportunities in this area. As a provider of consulting services, the mental health professional will need to market as a consultant, and charge accordingly. Physicians are generally open to networking with therapists and counselors in their geographic service areas. Relationships with primary-care physicians in your service area are not just strategic; they are appreciated by physicians. When a physician identifies counseling needs for a patient, she or he can refer the patient by supplying your name or card, which is a more effective referral than simply recommending that elderly patients find their own counselor. After your introduction to a primary-care physician who works with the elderly, a brief follow-up call or note is another step you can take in consolidating and nurturing a mutually beneficial relationship.

Nursing Homes

Another way for mental health professionals to position themselves is to visit nursing homes and meet with the administrators. During these visits, explore the programs that already exist for assessing the emotional and social needs of residents. Then offer to organize and run groups for residents. You can offer short training sessions for the staff, to teach them how to identify residents' needs and make referrals to appropriate groups or to individual assessment and counseling. You can also take on innovative roles, beyond the traditional fee-for-service activities reimbursable under Medicare, that enhance the living environment, quality of life, and satisfaction of residents. Creative administrators will increasingly develop such opportunities for mental health professionals. In this situation the mental health professional acts as a consultant and, again, charges accordingly.

Death is inevitable for all humans, but experience with and thoughts about death are understandably much more common among the elderly. Mental health professionals working in nursing homes can play a substantial role in leading bereavement groups after the deaths of family members or other residents, or after other kinds of losses. Promoting a program that serves as a model to acknowledge, comfort, and support the dying resident is necessary, as preparation for death often requires an extended period of reflection on the part of the mentally intact elderly person.

One model for intervention does include such a program. It helps prepares residents of nursing homes for their own and their friends' deaths. This preparation is most effectively achieved in a group that has developed an atmosphere of safety, which can foster open sharing of the human fears and beliefs surrounding the process of dying. A life-review process is a major component of the group's interaction. The healing of old wounds is an essential part of dying in peace, and group members often share hitherto unrevealed events of long ago. The practices of these groups can be highly creative. For example, one group leader invited a local harpist to come in and play for a dying resident, to facilitate a peaceful death. Other residents then entered the dying resident's room, to offer their support and befriend the resident's family. In situations like this one, death becomes a peaceful passage and an opportunity to give and receive comfort.

Quality Assurance, Utilization Review, and Credentialing

We believe that changes in the service-delivery system itself will also create key new opportunities for mental health professionals, which are distinct from and in addition to those created for clinical work in nursing homes and other institutional settings. These opportunities will involve the need of managed-care organizations to ensure that the highest quality of care is being provided. How will they ensure, on a continuing basis, that their subscribers are receiving the quality of care they demand? It is our belief that the development of standards and practices for quality assurance, utilization review, and credentialing will afford mental health professionals the opportunity to play a larger role in the delivery of services to the elderly in a managed-care framework.

Quality Assurance

Managed-care entities will rely more and more on quality-assurance programs to produce outcome indicators that describe how subscribers have benefited from the services they have received. We believe that if mental health professionals become involved in the process of defining outcome indicators that include psychological and social parameters of care, the result will be not just more effective treatment but also more cost-effective programs. The following example illustrates the involvement of one behavioral healthcare professional in such a role:

> Jennifer is currently employed as a social worker in a nursing home with which we consult. One of her specific responsibilities is to improve the quality of services to patients by participating in the facility's quality-assurance program.
>
> The nursing home has a quality-assurance committee whose goal is to track and improve patients' progress on the basis of outcome measures and critical pathways of care. Jennifer is in charge of analyzing and assessing patients' psychosocial status and documenting mental health interventions. After she has completed this process, she and the committee evaluate the efficacy of treatment and review its outcome in terms of days of care in the nursing home, the cost of care, and final disposition. On the basis of this assessment, the committee determines whether a patient was managed effectively according to the criteria that have been developed for the management of his or her condition. Jennifer, for example, has developed the "ideal" management

of a depressed patient; she uses this protocol as an aid in evaluating how actual patients with depression were treated. In this way, Jennifer offers valuable expertise to the nursing home in its efforts to control costs and provide appropriate and timely care to its patients.

Utilization Review

It is well known (as is evident throughout this volume) that the psychological state of the elderly has a marked impact on their consumption of medical resources, and that attention to the psychological state of the elderly can reduce their resource consumption. Therefore, another area for the participation and involvement of mental health professionals, an area closely linked to quality assurance, is utilization review. To ensure that emotional issues are adequately addressed, chronic- and long-term-care organizations need to include a psychosocial dimension and psychosocial services in their care plans for clients.

Credentialing

The credentialing process is yet another area in which managed-care organizations can create opportunities for mental health professionals. Increasingly, the long-term-care and chronic-care facilities contracting with managed-care organizations will be required to receive certification from nationally recognized organizations like the Joint Commission on Accreditation of Health Care Organizations or the National Commission on Quality Assurance. Certification will reassure consumers that the managed-care organizations are signing up providers who meet at least minimal standards of care. It is our belief that as standards become more stringent over time, the participation of mental health professionals will increasingly be required in chronic-care delivery. Mental health professionals should approach local facilities and define the roles in which they can be involved, either as consultants or as staff.

Mental health professionals can also approach chains or consortia of chronic-care facilities to provide services on a group or collaborative basis. In their efforts to save money, managed-care organizations encourage collaboration, and innovative chronic-care organizations can enjoy a price advantage if they as a group can employ a mental health professional to address quality assurance and utilization review, among many other issues. The cost of employing the mental health professional could be shared by several community agencies. As an added advantage, their methodologies would be uniform and consistent, and outcome measures would be uniformly applied among them.

Networking in the Community

Taking advantage of new and creative opportunities includes networking not just with medical professionals and nursing homes but also in the community. Mental health professionals need to conduct an ongoing dialogue with the facilities and services that target the older population in their community. You can link to these organizations in almost unlimited ways. For example, you can offer short-term sessions (eight to twelve weeks) in the continuing-care community or in the community at large. Art therapy, creative-writing groups, journal-writing circles, nutritional education, movement therapies, and spiritual-growth groups have all been well received and can be effective in enhancing the well-being of the elderly.

David Schell, as executive director of Breckenridge Village, oversees one of the most effective continuing-care retirement communities in northern Ohio and has discussed many innovative programs with us. For example, the staff at Breckenridge Village has organized a program in which residents tutor students from local junior highs and middle schools. Sometimes the students come to the facility, and sometimes their tutors meet them at their schools. In another program, residents support the child-care center developed for the Breckenridge Village staff by participating during the day, as they are able, in nurturing and entertaining the children. The mental health professional can organize such programs in other facilities.

Consultation

In addition to working directly with residents or community networks, as a mental health professional you have the opportunity to consult with the staffs of continuing-care communities. For example, staff in nursing homes and continuing-care facilities often feel that they have no voice in programming or policy development even though they are usually closest to the residents. We have found a two-dimensional approach of grievance hearing and educating to be highly effective in troubled situations. In many instances it is possible to perform an organizational assessment that involves interviewing departmental directors individually and staff members in small groups, an assessment that can lead to the identification of opportunities for enhancing the care and the activities of residents.

Staff members in these facilities are often untapped sources of information, and this information should be used to develop programs and offerings that meet the psychosocial and emotional needs of residents. For example, housekeeping and dietary staff members or nursing aides may be able to offer reliable assessments of a resident's emotional status because they have almost continuous contact with the resident. They know the resident's needs, and they know the attitudes of the family members who visit. Again, this kind of knowledge can be augmented by the involvement of a behavioral healthcare professional, as the following example shows:

In addition to her quality-assurance responsibilities in the nursing home where she works, Jennifer, the previously mentioned social worker, is responsible for providing in-service education to the nursing and housekeeping staff, helping them learn ways to identify patients' psychological problems and teaching them principles that they can use to help the patients as they come into daily contact with them. The in-service training has proven invaluable to the staff, who are now able to identify patients who are at risk for psychological problems. The training also gives staff an opportunity to learn about nonmedical problems and issues that patients commonly face, as well as about the patients' behavioral patterns.

An ombudsman associate, Penn Sockman, says that the staffs she has observed need education for developing sensitivity to the relocation stress experienced by residents of nursing homes, especially in room-to-room relocation, not to mention in initial placement in a facility (which is probably one of residents' biggest life changes). Staff members also need to be included in death-and-dying issues, she says. Moreover, when mental health is a treatment goal, aging persons' sensitivity to the stigma attached to mental illness must also be recognized. There is also a need for sensitivity with respect to living wills, according to Sockman. As a mental health professional, you are in an excellent position to educate staff members and bring about solutions to common problems, and you need to explore these opportunities.

In all of the options just described, one thing remains clear. Positioning yourself within the changing healthcare environment requires dedication and a comfort level commensurate with taking initiatives, dealing with opportunities in a creative vein, and exploring possibilities while remaining flexible and enthusiastic. Moreover, central to positioning in the outer world are the ability and the openness to position internally.

The Mental Health Professional as a Self System

An essential aspect of positioning yourself to take advantage of opportunities is a periodic review not just of your external environment but also of your internal milieu: your values, conflicts, energy level, and sense of well-being. You are not going to be successful in the outer world of the elderly unless you have at least acknowledged (if not resolved) some very salient concerns of your inner world. Do you really value elderly people? Do you grow and learn from their wisdom, their handicaps, their joys, and their sorrows? Do you enter their lives with loving kindness as well as with professional objectivity and assistance? Have you resolved your own conflicts with your parents and family members? Have you healed your own wounds?

What is your past experience with death? How do you really view dying? What is your spiritual philosophy regarding death? What is your response to helplessness, defeat, and sorrow among the elderly? What is your response to their unhealed wounds? How do you receive their fear and honor their willingness to speak of fear?

How do you nurture yourself and replenish the energy given to your clients and their lives? Do you find joy in your work? Do you have peace in your life? Do you have a sense of success in your efforts? Do you create a sense of well-being, purpose, and harmony in your own life?

Jaeger, a mental health professional who is one of our clients, offers a glimpse into the transformation he consciously chose in response to being burned out in his role as "talking therapist" for the past ten years:

> I found myself reading the "help wanted" ads every Sunday. I could not picture myself in an agency, teaching, or selling insurance, even though I knew I had those skills. Sadly, I could not picture myself continuing in my private practice, either. The insurance maze, the reduced and delayed payments, and the expectation that I would heal thirty-five years of pain and suffering in six sessions caused my anger, helplessness, and sleeplessness to match my clients'! I had to do some of the things I was telling my clients to do—write in a journal, meditate, read, join a health club, walk, and look inside as to where I was out of balance.
>
> I had two consulting meetings and realized I could also use my skills as a consultant. I took no new clients who were insured with companies that prevented treatment. I began to review my community, to see where else my skills could be profitable, and I took a marketing course at our local community college.
>
> There was an initial gap in income when I refused to work with insurance carriers that prevented mental health rather than mental illness. But today my new "clients" are directors of nursing homes: I could see the elderly population as our next large marketing area. I have learned to create and facilitate groups in nursing homes. By contrast with the patriarchal work ethic, I now work fewer hours and make more money. Mainly, though, I welcome each day. The transition was difficult and will continue to present challenges, but the outcome is joy.

Chapter Nine

Practitioner Liability Issues in Behavioral Healthcare

David A. Weil II

I wrote this chapter to help behavioral healthcare practitioners who provide services to senior clients maneuver through the liability issues that arise from Medicare's increased use of managed-care concepts in the financing and provision of healthcare services. My primary objective is to provide you with practical insights that you can use in considering and minimizing your potential liability in the managed-care setting, whether payment is based on discounted fees for service, capitation, or some other method.

Medicare Managed Care: Threat or Opportunity?

Some practitioners view Medicare's trend toward managed care as a threat; others see it as an opportunity. Regardless, the magnitude of the trend cannot be overlooked. Managed-care enrollment of Medicare beneficiaries since the passage of the Tax Equity and Fiscal Responsibility Act of 1982 (TEFRA) has been minuscule by comparison with commercial enrollment in the 1980s and early 1990s. More recently, however, there has been a tremendous influx of Medicare beneficiaries into managed-care plans, as a result of managed care's cost-saving potential for beneficiaries and government programs alike. For example, more than 2.3 million beneficiaries were enrolled in managed-care plans during 1995—double

The information presented in this chapter is not to be considered or construed as legal advice or counsel nor as policy of Columbia/HCA Healthcare Corporation or any of its affiliates.

the number of Medicare managed-care beneficiaries in 1993. As efforts are pursued to control Medicare costs, this growth in enrollment is likely to continue.

In their financial aspect, Medicare managed-care plans are attractive to beneficiaries primarily because they offer reduced copayments and deductibles. Beneficiaries do face restrictions, however, on the providers from whom they can seek services and on the services actually covered (many services that were covered under the traditional fee-for-service–based Medicare program are not covered under the new Medicare managed-care plans). The impact of these changes will continue to be felt and hotly debated in the behavioral healthcare arena.

One result is that you as a behavioral healthcare practitioner will need to adopt a marketing perspective as you evaluate the plans for which you need or want to become a provider, as well as the panels on which you need or want to serve: What plans are now enrolling, or likely to enroll, your current and potential clients? You will also need to evaluate the services that the managed-care plans offer, and to determine whether these plans cover the services that you now offer or can be qualified to offer.

Denial of Claims

Managed care's concentration on cost control can often result in improper denial of claims. For example, a Medicare Part B carrier may deny payment for psychotherapy services, especially when the client is a resident of a nursing home, even though it is your professional opinion that the services were clinically necessary (in view, say, of the client's severe depression). I personally have seen some practitioners denied 50 percent of such claims.

This is a liability because it constitutes lack or loss of compensation for reasonable and necessary services actually provided. You should keep in mind that, as a result of an extensive set of federal laws and regulations, you are not without recourse if a claim is denied. Not only for the sake of getting paid but also for the sake of protecting your credibility, you should assert and enforce your due process rights and support your claims with documentation that demonstrates the clinical necessity of the services rendered. An attorney, especially one who practices in the area of Medicare and Medicaid reimbursement, can prove to be a valuable resource in determining what recourse you have and how you can take appropriate action.

Plan-specific, administrative, and judicial review are available to beneficiaries through a clearly established federal appeals procedure, and some states also regulate the provision of managed-care benefit plans (note, however, that state remedies are often preempted by the Employee Retirement Income Security Act of 1974, known as ERISA, in which case federal laws and regulations apply). In reality, though, and for several reasons, those due process protections that are available are rarely invoked:

- Many beneficiaries and their advocates are unaware of the appeal rights and procedures that are available to them.
- Denial of a claim usually occurs when the beneficiary is ill and unlikely to be in a position to challenge the system.
- The beneficiary may not be able to produce the proof required to establish that the services provided met the medical and other criteria of reasonableness and necessity.
- The beneficiary may decide to leave the plan rather than challenge the system (federal law traditionally has allowed beneficiaries to disenroll from Medicare managed-care plans on short notice).
- The beneficiary may be disinclined to appeal or disenroll from his plan because he fears jeopardizing an established practitioner-client relationship of long standing.

If a claim is denied, you as a practitioner are in an excellent position to determine your client's reason for not pursuing recourse and to help your client take appropriate action. As a first step, you can produce diligent documentation establishing that the services you provided were clinically reasonable and necessary, and you can submit a brief letter to the plan. In this letter you should explain why the services were reasonable and necessary, and you should ask the plan to reconsider the denied claim. In one case of which I am aware, a plan began to scrutinize a psychologist, denied a number of the claims she submitted, and threatened to drop her from its panel. Because she was confident of her professional judgment, kept excellent records, and understood the rules of the game, she was able to demonstrate clinical necessity, maintain her position, and keep her patients. The lesson is that practitioners can work together with plans and clients to evaluate and improve relationships, minimize disenrollment, and keep all parties satisfied with services and payment.

Economic Credentialing

As cost control plays a more dominant role in the provision of healthcare services, factors based on the use of services (rather than on the quality of the services) become more important in determining which practitioners, as panelists, will be given access to managed-care plan members. The practice of basing these decisions on use of services is known as *economic credentialing*.

Economic credentialing ensures that the practitioner's aggregate use of healthcare resources (for example, the ordering of tests or other procedures) falls within the parameters deemed acceptable by the managed-care plan or provider. On the one hand, the plan or provider may evaluate the practitioner on the basis of explicit cost parameters. On the other hand, the practitioner may be evaluated on the basis of individual resource-use data. The determination of what constitutes acceptable resource use is often problematic, as is the determination of outcomes for psychotherapy and other types of mental health interventions. Although economic credentialing has generated considerable controversy, it does effectively minimize the prospect of conflict in individual cases between a practitioner and a plan or provider. Ideally, cost para-meters or resource-use data will be a single if significant component of the overall equation, and economic credentialing will be used in combination with quality-based data (for example, client satisfac-tion and clinical outcomes) in selecting practitioners to serve on the panels of managed-care plans. As a behavioral health practi-tioner, you can make appropriate inquiries and help ensure that the plans are applying appropriate standards of practice and using acceptable guidelines.

Cost Control and the Role of Practitioners

As already mentioned, the primary focus of managed care is on control over costs. Some practitioners, arguing that this focus imposes or intrudes on the traditional practitioner-client relation-ship, object to the consideration of cost as an explicit factor in deci-sion making. You as a practitioner, however, need to recognize the conflicts that arise between fiduciary obligations to clients and lim-itations on payment for appropriate services. You have a fiduciary responsibility to play the role of the client's advocate. Therefore, whether or not the requested services are approved by the man-aged-care plan, you have not only the right but also the ethical and legal obligation to provide the services. If a request for authoriza-tion of individual psychotherapy, for example, is denied by the managed-care plan's reviewers, you will have to consider how you can appropriately make your objections known to the plan and any available opportunities for pursuing an appeal. You may also want to advise your client of your objections to the denial, and to care-fully document your objections. It is important for you to be mind-ful that your primary loyalty is owed to the client, regardless of any intrusions into the client-practitioner relationship.

Unfortunately, however, in view of the economic realities brought on by the imposition of managed-care principles, your fidu-ciary duty to clients entails conflicts that may be exacerbated in the behavioral healthcare setting, especially where the care of senior clients is concerned. There are several reasons why this is true, and practitioners who provide services to seniors will want to take the following issues into consideration as managed care becomes a more predominant component of the Medicare program.

First, there is little apparent consensus on what constitutes a standard course of treatment for many mental illnesses. Given the lack of consensus, behavior and mental health practitioners are at a relative disadvantage in arguments about what constitutes "medical necessity." As a result, managed-care and third-party payers have assumed broad latitude in defining not only the parameters for practice but also guidelines for outcomes.

Second, the availability of coercion (particularly through the use of civil commitment), in combination with the potential risks incurred by third parties, as well as the liability that may be created for practitioners, raises issues that are distinguishable from those encountered in other healthcare settings.

Third, the chronic nature of many mental illnesses, in combination with continuing discontinuity and fragmentation in the delivery of mental health services, increases opportunities for shifting costs in the managed-care setting and adds financial challenges that will need to be addressed by many behavioral healthcare practitioners.

Informed Consent

As a practitioner, you should be aware of your ethical and legal requirement to obtain your clients' informed consent to treatment. Even in the managed-care setting, the client should be fully informed, before services are provided, about the options that are available, the cost of each option, and the risks anticipated with each option. The more specific and explicit the client's consent, the greater your ability to defend yourself in any actions that arise as a result of the provision (or the withholding) of services.

When treating elderly clients, practitioners are often dealing with issues of competence, which is a matter addressed by state law.

In general, unless and until informed consent is provided by a surrogate decision maker, you should not provide care and treatment to a client who is not legally competent. The surrogate may be a court-appointed guardian, a person vested with durable power of attorney for healthcare, or a proxy decision maker. You need to stay attuned to each client's level of competence and coordinate or facilitate efforts to ensure that plans for a surrogate decision maker are made before the time when the surrogate is needed. If no such plan has been made, and if the client is not competent, then you should consult or retain an attorney who is familiar with your state's laws regarding competence and informed consent.

Common Potential Tort Liabilities

In managed care, as in any other healthcare setting, the most common potential tort liability is for malpractice, or the failure to provide services in accordance with applicable standards of care. In the managed-care setting it is especially important to remember that malpractice allegations can result from the withholding of services, as well as from their actual provision. The withholding may have occurred as an oversight on the part of the practitioner, or it may have been the practitioner's decision, based on the denial of a requested authorization for the services.

Healthcare professionals are generally held responsible and liable for their own malpractice. In malpractice cases involving practitioners who provide services to members of managed-care plans, however, there are increasing efforts to include other parties as codefendants—the managed-care plans themselves, for example, or independently contracted utilization-review or management companies—on the basis of theories of vicarious liability, corporate negligence, or negligent credentialing. (ERISA, as will be described in the section titled "Trends in ERISA Law," is often used to limit the potential malpractice liability of these other parties.)

An organization may be vicariously liable for the acts or omissions of a practitioner whom it employs or includes on its panel, or with whom it has a contractual arrangement, when there has been created, from the client's perspective, the appearance of an agency relationship between the organization and that practitioner, and when the client has reasonably relied, to his or her detriment, on this apparent relationship in obtaining services from that practitioner. Because of this potential liability, it is usually the organization that wants to avoid or minimize the appearance of an agency relationship, but the appearance of an agency relationship could have implications for the practitioner as well.

In general, an organization is vicariously liable for the negligence of its own employees when those employees are acting within the scope of their employment. But an organization is also potentially liable for corporate negligence and, therefore, for the malpractice of an independent contractor when that contractor is effectively under the organization's control, and when the services rendered by the contractor fall within the regular business of the organization.

Liability for negligence may also arise when the organization fails to exercise due care in investigating, screening, and selecting competent practitioners, or when it fails to monitor the quality of the services provided by those practitioners who have been selected. It is well established that a hospital has an independent duty to properly select and monitor the practitioners who have been appointed to its medical staff and who have been granted clinical privileges. It has also been determined that managed-care plans have corporate responsibility for the proper selection of practitioners. Therefore, a managed-care plan may be held liable for the negligent selection of contracting practitioners.

A health maintenance organization (HMO) may be immune to liability under an HMO-authorizing statute. Nevertheless, it may still have a duty to conduct a reasonable investigation of each practitioner's credentials and reputation in those communities where the practitioner provides services. An independent practice association, or IPA-model HMO, may be found to have a duty, which cannot be delegated, to select and retain only competent primary-care practitioners. It is particularly important that practitioners be appropriately credentialed, selected, and supervised in a capitation arrangement where the contracting organization accepts the risk of providing services that it is not itself licensed to provide. Therefore, if you as a practitioner are involved in credentialing, selecting, and supervising other practitioners, you should keep in mind that you have a clearly established duty to exercise due care in carrying out these functions.

Trends in ERISA Law

The Employee Retirement Income Security Act (ERISA), which governs employee-welfare benefit plans, has a clause that provides that state laws that *relate to* employee benefit plans are preempted by ERISA. This law is applied to cases where malpractice allegations have been brought against a managed-care plan (for example, a staff-model HMO). If *all* the conduct connected with a managed-care plan is considered to be related to an employee benefit plan, then the malpractice claim against a plan's practitioner, or against the entity itself, must be brought under ERISA. If only the *administrative* aspects of the plan are related to the employee benefit plan, then the malpractice action is ordinarily pursued in state court, where the potential liability is far greater.

Trends in ERISA law have demonstrated that employers who have self-insured health plans in addition to fully licensed managed-care plans may be exposed to malpractice exposure in state courts and may not be able to remove these suits to federal court. (Historically, HMOs have sought and been allowed to remove state malpractice actions to federal court, where damages are limited, no punitive damages are allowed, and trials are more often held before a judge than before a jury.) From the client's perspective, as a result, it often appears that the only remedy available in an action brought under ERISA is limited to the difference between the services that actually should have been provided and the services that were not provided.

If the alleged negligence of a practitioner employed by an HMO is the cause of harm for which relief is being sought, and if the claim against the HMO is based only on the HMO's role as the practitioner's employer, the courts have tended to decide that ERISA does not preempt the claim. It remains to be fully determined whether ERISA preemption, which is favorable to licensed managed-care plans and to employers with self-insured health plans, will be limited in its application in cases where the issue can be framed in terms of quality of care. If ERISA preemption is narrowed, and if malpractice is considered to be an issue far removed from a benefit plan's administration, then employers who are involved in forming provider panels, or who take an active role in the actual delivery of healthcare services, may be liable for the malpractice of the practitioners involved.

In light of developments in the area of organizations' potential tort liability, and given the recognition of and advances in the fields of geropsychology and geropsychiatry, it is odd that managed-care organizations do not request documentation of practitioners' experience or expertise in treating older adults. My experience has been that managed-care organizations do not ask much in the way of background and seem not to care. Here, I suggest, is an opportunity for education.

Potential Liabilities from Contract-Related Activities

A number of capitation-based (or risk-based), contract-related activities may expose an organization to malpractice liability under theories of vicarious liability and corporate negligence. These activities include those that involve responsibility for deciding whether, and precisely what, services are to be provided to managed-care plan members. Practitioners in general, but behavioral healthcare and mental health practitioners in particular, given the lack of consensus on what constitutes standard treatment for many mental illnesses, need to exercise due care in participating in such activities. For example, let's say that neuropsychology services are determined to be clinically necessary on the basis of a primary-care physician's opinion that a patient is demented and needs to be in an Alzheimer's unit, but that these services are not allowed by the patient's managed-care plan. At that juncture, the patient's family takes the patient in for neuropsychological testing and pays for it out of pocket. The neuropsychologist concludes that the patient is severely depressed, not demented, and needs treatment for that condition, not a prescription for Aricept or placement in an Alzheimer's unit. Do you think the denial of treatment for Alzheimer's dementia should be the basis of a liability claim against the managed-care plan or the third-party payer?

Another risk-based, contract-related activity that exposes a managed-care plan or participating organization to potential malpractice liability is the plan's or organization's involvement in compensation and other financial relationships that have the potential of adversely or inappropriately influencing the professional judgment of those responsible for the organization or its contracted or employed practitioners. This may arise, for example, in a situation where a medical review officer is compensated with a bonus based in part on the money saved by the plan as a result of claims denied or requests for treatments or tests not authorized or not certified.

Risk and the Gatekeeper Role

There is potential exposure to liability for practitioners responsible for making decisions about authorizing the services of other practitioners, as well as for the organizations on whose behalf they perform this function. Incentives for these practitioners, especially incentives related to meeting the utilization-review objectives of a managed-care plan or organization, may be used as evidence that a denial of authorization was based on economic rather than clinical factors. This allegation may arise, for example, in an action based on bad-faith denial and breach of contract.

If you are a practitioner who conducts utilization review, or who acts as a gatekeeper or care coordinator for a managed-care organization or plan, you should have your contracts carefully reviewed by an attorney and negotiate for contractual provisions that limit your exposure to liability. Such a provision may indemnify you and hold you harmless when you are required, as a utilization reviewer, plan gatekeeper, or administrator, to make clinical or other decisions that have clinical consequences for managed-care plan members.

When a patient who is enrolled in a managed-care plan goes to a hospital's emergency room and the plan's designated practitioner is consulted, the practitioner-patient relationship is established, and the practitioner owes that patient a duty of care. For example, a psychiatrist on the panel of a Medicare managed-care plan may be consulted by the physician on duty in the emergency room to diagnose an enrolled beneficiary's mental condition and provide appropriate intervention and follow-up. If you are designated as the practitioner acting for the managed-care plan at the time when a plan member requires services, you may be exposed to liability for negligence under the practitioner-patient relationship established by the contractual provisions of the plan.

Liability and Utilization Review

With the proliferation of managed care among Medicare beneficiaries, practitioners are increasingly asked to perform utilization-review activities, and there have been several cases of liability arising from it. Managed-care plans and other third-party payers may be held liable for clinically inappropriate decisions resulting from defects in the design or implementation of utilization-review or cost-control mechanisms (for example, if an appeal is made on a patient's behalf for clinical or hospital care, and if the appeal is arbitrarily ignored or unreasonably disregarded or overridden). This is one of the reasons why it is important for you as a practitioner to object if services that you believe to be necessary are denied, and to document your objection. It will also be helpful for you to keep in mind that, under the traditional test for joint liability, you can be held liable for conduct that is a substantial factor in bringing about harm. For example, if the outcome of your utilization-review activity is a decision not to approve services or treatment for a patient, and if that decision is a substantial factor in bringing about harm to that patient, the managed-care company may be held liable for that harm, and you may also be held liable under the test of joint liability.

If you are a practitioner involved in utilization review, making decisions about whether care will be rendered, the level of care, and payment for care, you have a duty to conduct a complete investigation before making these determinations. A plan administrator's failure to make a treatment decision on the basis of a complete clinical record (a record that includes correspondence from the treating practitioner that explains the reasons for hospitalization and tests and requests authorization of services), as well as the failure to follow proper procedures in reaching that determination, constitutes conduct that may give rise to liability, as may the failure to conduct an independent review of the need for services requested by the treating practitioner before denying authorization. The method you have used in reviewing a claim may be subject to intense scrutiny by a court and may be found to fall short of conduct considered legally acceptable.

Communication and Risk Management

Under managed care, proper communication with clients is the most critical component of a practitioner's plan for preventing loss and managing risk, but it is also a component that is frequently overlooked. If you are a practitioner employed by or working as an independent contractor for a managed-care plan, you should consider the relationships that you have with your clients and, as appropriate, tell them why a request for authorization of services or payment for services has been denied, tell them who actually reviewed the claim, and inform them of their right to appeal the denial.

Responsibilities of Third-Party Payers

A number of actions on the part of a managed-care plan or third-party payers can leave the plan or payer open to liability for breach of good faith and fair dealing:

- Failure to inform plan members or beneficiaries of their right to contest a denial of benefits
- Failure to advise a plan member or beneficiary of his or her contractual right to impartial review and arbitration when a claim for benefits has been denied
- Failure to inform a plan member or beneficiary of the reason for a denial of benefits, especially in hospital inpatient admission

Denial of a claim is usually based on a finding that the requested level of service is not clinically necessary. In general, the reason for the denial of benefits must be properly communicated to the beneficiary, and the clinical criteria of the utilization review must be properly coordinated with the language of the benefit contract or policy. Therefore, when you are objecting to a denial of services, you may want to evaluate how the denial was communicated, and whether it was consistent with contractual or policy language. You may have an opportunity to point out the duty owed to the plan member or beneficiary, and to work with the managed-care plan or third-party payer toward minimizing its potential liability.

Another opportunity for you as a practitioner is presented in situations where the utilization-review personnel of a managed-care plan or third-party payer fail to honestly inform a beneficiary that a claim has been reviewed only by the administrative staff, and not by the clinical department. This failure may render the plan or third-party payer liable for violation of its duty of good faith. What you can do in this situation is communicate with the utilization-review personnel, determine who is involved in reviewing claims, and use appropriate means to ensure that those individuals have enough knowledge and experience to understand what services have been requested or provided, and why. This may be particularly important in the area of behavioral healthcare and mental health services if the clinical department does not involve psychiatrists and psychologists in the review process. You should also keep in mind that you are entitled to proper and complete communication about any denial of payment on claims for services that you have provided.

The Need for Prior Approval

A managed-care plan or third-party payer is responsible to the practitioner for identifying the records on which a denial is based, and if it fails to do so, it may be liable for acting in bad faith. As a practitioner, you should know what records have been reviewed by the managed-care plan or third-party payer so that these can be appropriately supplemented, as necessary.

Inappropriate language in the denial of a claim—language, for example, in a letter from a reviewer alleging that a number of claims were unnecessary and that the practitioner has overcharged, and threatening to report the practitioner to the applicable state professional organization—may constitute grounds for a claim of defamation.

A professional reviewer's failure to apply a standard of care in accordance with that of the appropriate professional community (a standard of care in accord with that of a state psychiatric association, for example, in a claim for psychiatric services) may expose the managed-care plan or third-party payer on whose behalf the review is conducted to liability. As a practitioner, you should make sure that appropriate standards of care are being applied, and may want to challenge reviewers and plans if the standards being applied are inappropriate. A managed-care plan or third-party payer that fails to have claims reviewed by the practitioner (and, arguably, by practitioners in the appropriate fields or specialty areas) may also be subject to liability for bad-faith denial of claims.

As a practical matter, you should have at least a general idea or working knowledge of which services require precertification or prior approval. A managed-care plan or third-party payer may not be liable for payment if plan members or beneficiaries could have complied with utilization-review requirements but failed to do so. For example, a plan member who knows that certification is required before hospitalization but fails to obtain it, even though doing so would have been possible, may incur a financial penalty. In the area of mental health services, it may be necessary for the plan member to obtain prior approval of individual psychotherapy services. The request for this approval often presents an opportunity for you to educate the gatekeeper, care coordinator, or other staff members involved in the prior-approval process.

A managed-care plan may be held liable only for services that its contracted practitioner has determined in advance will significantly improve the client's condition. If you provide additional services without obtaining authorization for them, the plan member or beneficiary who received them will be held liable for payment. The plan member or beneficiary must adhere to the limits and conditions established under the plan's contract; courts are reluctant to redefine contractual obligations as creating coverage for benefits where no coverage is actually due. Therefore, it will be helpful for you to remember that any services you propose to provide may require prior approval, and that obtaining approval may, as a matter of law, be necessary in order for you to obtain payment.

Confidentiality and Indemnification

Another area of potential exposure to liability under a risk-based contract is the unauthorized or otherwise impermissible disclosure of confidential client records or information, the improper direct release of such records or information, or the inappropriate inclusion of client-specific information in data reports provided to the managed-care plan. I cannot emphasize enough how important it is to maintain the confidentiality of information about clients. Clinicians should avoid disclosing information about clients to others, including adult children of clients, without the specific written consent of their clients to do so. Unless a judge has determined that a client is incompetent, the sharing of confidential information exposes clinicians to the risk of liability.

Contractual indemnification ("hold harmless") provisions are another fertile field of potential exposure to liability for practitioners. Indemnification provisions hold the practitioner responsible for, and protect the managed-care plan from, any and all liability that may arise as a result of unfavorable patient outcomes, regardless of the culpability of the managed-care plan. Some theories favor an approach that would exclude indemnification of the managed-care plan and subject malpractice to applicable laws. These theories include the argument that the practitioner has more to lose from the obligation to hold a managed-care plan harmless for malpractice than he or she has to gain from any agreement of reciprocal indemnification that has been reached with the managed-care plan. Those who argue for this approach explain that applicable law may require the indemnification of the managed-care plan anyway, but at least the managed-care plan would have to sue the practitioner in order to get indemnification.

As a practitioner, you should try to have indemnification clauses removed from your contracts, or to limit their application. You may also want to negotiate mutual indemnification with the managed-care plan, to make it clear that you will not be held liable for acts of the managed-care plan that give rise to liability.

Other Types of Potential Liability

As a practitioner, you should keep in mind that there are several other types of potential liability. Federal fraud and abuse law, for example, prohibits payment or the exchange of something of economic value to induce the referral of clients for services covered by Medicare or Medicaid or other federal or state healthcare plans. Some state laws prohibit such referrals regardless of the third-party payer. Certain types of conduct may be subject to regulatory exceptions to federal fraud and abuse law. These are known as "safe harbor" regulations. Several safe harbor regulations address issues arising in the managed-care setting. These include, for example, discounts, increased coverage, reduced cost-sharing amounts or reduced premium amounts offered by health plans, and price reductions offered to health plans. In order to afford the protection of an applicable safe harbor, certain enumerated standards must be satisfied. The federal government has also published interpretative documents known as "Fraud Alerts" on various issues. These include, for example, financial arrangements between hospitals and hospital-based physicians, psychological testing, and multiple billing for psychotherapy sessions. Fraud and abuse issues and the application of the safe harbors must be analyzed in arrangements or transactions involving Medicare or Medicaid.

Physicians and those who have financial relationships with physicians need to be cognizant of federal law that prohibits physicians from referring clients to entities with whom they have financial relationships for designated health services covered by Medicare or Medicaid unless an exception to what constitutes an investment interest or compensation arrangement applies. This law is often referred to as the "Stark law" or "Stark II." Designated health services include eleven categories of services, among them inclient and outclient hospital services. Again, many states have similar laws, some of which apply to referrals for services that are covered by third-party payers other than Medicare and Medicaid. Certain types of investment interests and compensation arrangements need to be analyzed to minimize potential liability under the Stark law and any applicable state bans against physician self-referral.

Some state laws prohibit physicians from splitting their professional fees with other physicians or nonphysicians. Some states have laws that prohibit physicians (and certain other types of healthcare professionals) from working as employees for entities that are not professional corporations incorporated specifically for the purpose of practicing medicine (or the applicable profession). These laws are often referred to as "corporate-practice-of-medicine laws." The preceding are some of the potential liabilities that arise in the healthcare setting in general that need to be evaluated in the Medicare managed-care setting as well.

Clinicians may try to make financial arrangements with Medicare clients who want services that are not deemed medically necessary and, therefore, are not paid by Medicare. I think this is a bad idea. If clinicians do it, though, they should document in writing, by issuing a notice of noncoverage to the client, that the client fully understands that Medicare will not cover the services provided. If the clinician charges the client, these charges should be consistent with the Medicare-allowable rate. A client may, for example, want weekly therapy for personal self-development although there are no symptoms of depression or anxiety that warrant weekly sessions. The clinician should have the client sign the agreement and notice of noncoverage.

Preventing Loss and Managing Risk

This discussion is by no means exhaustive, but it should give you some practical guidance to the types of liability that you may incur as a result of your participation in managed-care arrangements. It is advisable for you to develop and implement a plan for preventing loss and managing risk under managed care. Your plan may include the concepts discussed here, and it should be readily adaptable to the provision of behavioral healthcare or mental health services to senior clients under Medicare managed-care arrangements.

The implementation of managed-care principles means that you as a practitioner will be required to assume more financial risk and clinical responsibility. The risks and responsibilities that you take on must be carefully assessed in light of the clients served and the services to be provided. You will have to weigh the services that you have traditionally provided in your practices against the services that managed-care plans determine to be reasonable, necessary, and cost-effective. This is important because economic credentialing plays an increasingly significant role in the placement of practitioners on the panels of managed-care plans.

It is advisable for you to be cognizant of the legal issues arising in the realm of managed care. You need to remember that you owe a fiduciary duty to the client, and that conflicts will arise as a result of the incentives you encounter under managed-care arrangements. Therefore, you should focus on your role as the client's advocate. You should fully inform your clients, or their guardians or surrogate decision makers, about appropriate treatment options and take steps to ensure that your clients receive those services for which appropriate authorization has been given.

The need for you to communicate with your clients or with their surrogate decision makers cannot be emphasized enough. A unique problem in working with older patients, especially those in retirement communities or nursing homes, is that they may be technically competent, but their family members make their financial decisions. Family members with power of attorney may refuse to pay for psychological examinations or treatment, even when a competent client specifically requests the examination or treatment and the clinician can prove clinical necessity and demonstrative favorable outcomes. Unfortunately, there is no simple way to reconcile the clinician's legal and ethical responsibilities to the client, on the one hand, and the practical issue of being paid, on the other. Ideally, you will be able to sort this issue out through open and honest communication with your client and the family member who has power of attorney.

Your services should be adequate, in accordance with applicable standards of care, and provided only when they are clinically necessary. If authorization or payment for treatment is denied, you should communicate the reasons, document your objections, and attempt to appeal a denial of authorization when the services that were requested are warranted. You may also want to take care to release confidential information only when your clients have given their written consent for you to do so.

If you are involved in the credentialing, selection, and supervision of other practitioners, you should exercise due care. Moreover, if you are conducting utilization review or acting as a gatekeeper or care coordinator for a managed-care plan, you should negotiate contractual provisions that limit your exposure to liability and that presume a duty of care owed to each patient enrolled in the plan on whose behalf you are acting. You should also make decisions only with reliance on complete records and in accordance with proper procedures. You should identify and request any information that you need, use only appropriate language, and apply the appropriate standard of care. You should educate clients about utilization-review requirements, which may include certification or approval before services can be provided.

You should also review, understand, and negotiate contractual provisions, especially those that shift liability from a managed-care plan to you. It is important that you take steps to limit your potential liability under these contractual arrangements. You should weigh and understand the obligations and the risks that you assume, and it is crucial to acknowledge that these arise not only as a contractual matter but also as a function of the various relationships that are established. Finally, if you are a practitioner in a managed-care arrangement, you should develop a relationship with an attorney who has expertise in the areas of Medicare and Medicaid reimbursement and managed care.

Suggested Reading

Boyle, P. "Managed Care in Mental Health: A Cure, or a Cure Worse Than the Disease?" *Saint Louis University Law Journal,* Spring 1996, *40,* 437–456.

Edson, G. D. "Annotated Bibliography: Medicare and Managed Care." *The University of Kansas Law Review,* July 1996, *44,* 793–805.

Jimenez, C. S. "Medicare Overview." In *Planning for Aging or Incapacity 1994: Legal and Financial Issues.* PLI Tax Law and Estate Planning Course Handbook Series, no. 231. Philadelphia: Practice Law Institute, 1994.

Petrila, J. "Ethics, Money, and the Problem of Coercion in Managed Behavioral Health Care." *Saint Louis University Law Journal,* 1996, 40, 359–405.

Rodwin, M. A. "Managed Care and Consumer Protection: What Are the Issues?" *Seton Hall Law Review,* 1996, 26, 1007–1054.

Stayn, S. J. "Note: Securing Access to Care in Health Maintenance Organizations: Toward a Uniform Model of Grievance and Appeal Procedures." *Columbia Law Review,* 1994, 94, 1700–1701.

Wilson, S. H. "Medicare Health Maintenance Organizations: Bright Promise, Troubling Reality." *Bifocal,* Summer 1995, p. 3.

Chapter Ten

Marketing Strategies for Geriatric Behavioral Healthcare

Paula E. Hartman-Stein, Marina Ergun

This chapter is about marketing behavioral services for older adults in the context of the changing healthcare arena. As lead author of this chapter and editor of this volume, my ideas are largely a result of my experiences as a geropsychologist in private practice and as founder of the Center for Healthy Aging, a multidisciplinary behavioral group practice. My coauthor, who has a master's degree in psychology, is a self-employed writer with experience in fundraising and in consulting in media relations. Her role at the Center for Healthy Aging is in business planning and public relations. Our perspectives therefore reflect our experiences in the healthcare and business worlds.

The marketing ideas in this chapter will help if you work in a small or large private practice or as an independent consultant. We address issues specific to geriatric behavioral healthcare professionals who devote a substantial amount of time to marketing and who enjoy a large degree of professional autonomy. We assume our readers are familiar with general marketing principles and skills; therefore, we have focused on marketing issues particular to the field of geriatric behavioral healthcare, and as they are related to our five commandments: *know thy market, know thy customer, know thy business, know thy finances,* and *know thy outcomes.*

Know Thy Market

Trying to use general marketing tips in marketing behavioral healthcare for older adults is like trying to shoot a hummingbird with a bazooka. Knowing your market is a critical factor because you are offering such a highly specialized niche service. The only way to know your market is to research, research, and research. Successful research will be an ongoing task, akin to trying to hit those hummingbirds in a carnival game. Only if you have up-to-date research information will you have a chance of marketing successfully and surviving in today's competitive behavioral healthcare environment. Here are some of the areas in which to ask research questions.

Geographic Factors

What is your geographic area? This is the first question to address. As Medicare becomes increasingly "managed," this question will become more important. You will be in an optimal position if you are in an area devoid of other behavioral healthcare practitioners and populated exclusively by older adults! Practicing next to retirement meccas like Sun Valley, Arizona, or St. Petersburg, Florida, will be quite different from practicing in Brisbane, North Dakota, or in the Rust Belt of the Midwest, where many older adults become "snowbirds" and flee to warmer climates shortly after retirement. In the areas more lightly populated with older adults, marketing efforts need to be more intensive. If you live in an area that has a high percentage of older adults who speak another language, then offering bilingual services will put you at a definite advantage.

What is the percentage of older adults in your area, as compared with the national average? How many behavioral healthcare practitioners are in your area, as compared with the general population? Increasingly in geriatric behavioral healthcare, there are numerous practices that provide services in nursing homes and retirement communities. More uncommon are behavioral healthcare practices that offer a range of services, such as counseling individuals and groups and providing intergenerational family therapy, neuropsychological testing, and geriatric care management, as well as consultation to and therapy in nursing homes.

Medical Climate

Behavioral healthcare for older adults is more closely tied to the medical profession than are behavioral healthcare services for young and middle-aged adults. Our analysis of referral sources for geriatric behavioral healthcare clients shows that the majority of referrals come from community-based physicians and from such hospital programs as geriatric assessment centers. That's why an important component of market research is to follow and track the medical field in your area.

Healthcare players who one day are closely aligned may become competitors the next. In the market in which we live and work, we are consistently amazed by the bitter rivals who cheerfully merge and by the competent, well-entrenched entities that fail. It's a combination of the Wild West of the last century and the free love of the Woodstock generation. At least the unexpected liaisons and failures make for never a dull moment!

Another medical area to track is the long-term-care industry in your area. Who owns the nursing facilities and retirement communities? Do they have special dementia units? What is their range of services, and what is their client profile? (Later in this chapter we discuss the special marketing opportunities in the environment of long-term care; see also Chapter Eight of this volume.)

We advise you, as you research the medical climate, to avoid publications specific to your profession. Instead, focus on sources like business publications with a healthcare beat, as well as on periodicals specific to the healthcare and long-term-care industries. Our local business publication publishes a list of the largest managed-care companies in the area—the kind of list you want to track. The Internet is also a source of news about managed-care mergers and acquisitions.

We have found that the behavioral healthcare practitioners who are the most successful businesspeople spend less time with organizations associated with their particular professions and affiliate themselves instead with the healthcare and managed-care industries. For example, the American Association of Health

Plans, an organization of insurance executives, holds national conferences that address the future of Medicare-based managed care. In a recent seminar, I was the only psychologist on the roster of participants, yet the issues will have a direct impact on the future of geropsychology.

Relationships with Physicians

Because many older adults won't even consider consulting a behavioral healthcare practitioner unless referred by a physician, it is essential to have collegial relationships with physicians who treat older adults. Older adults frequently present behavioral healthcare problems as somatic complaints, or they have coexisting physical conditions. Therefore, we advise you not only to find out who the primary-care doctors are with large caseloads of geriatric patients but also to find out the networks and hospital systems with which they are affiliated. The days of the solo medical practitioner who makes his or her own referrals are dwindling because increasing numbers of physicians are joining group practices, but in some markets autonomous physicians still exist. In small towns or close-knit neighborhoods, personnel in senior centers will know the primary-care doctors who have large caseloads of elderly patients.

Family practitioners and internists with added qualifications in geriatrics often consult to nursing homes. You can call nursing homes in your area and ask who the medical director is, and you should certainly find out who the geriatric practitioners in your area are by calling the local state physicians' organization or branch office of the American Medical Association and asking for a listing of physicians by specialty. Neurologists, ophthalmologists, optometrists, and podiatrists may also be a source of geriatric referrals.

Medicare

The primary and largest third-party payer for geriatric behavioral healthcare is Medicare. In most areas of the country the majority of people sixty-five and older have traditional fee-for-service Medicare. Therefore, it makes sense to be intimately acquainted with Medicare rules and regulations. Your core service offerings should be designed with this in mind.

For example, it is foolhardy to market neuropsychological assessments of depression and dementia that involve ten-hour testing batteries and require four hours for you to score and write up. (See Chapter Five of this volume for information on brief assessment batteries.) Find out what your Medicare insurance carrier views as acceptable with respect to time limits for testing services and limits on the frequency and duration of therapy. These limits are not always openly shared by the carrier, but our experience shows that pressure from professional groups can sometimes open up the secrets of Medicare coverage. Cultivating a personal relationship with the head of the provider relations department of the Medicare insurance carrier for your region can be invaluable in interpreting changes in Medicare regulations. Although Medicare is a federal program, many such interpretations are left to the discretion of the regional insurance carrier.

The days of assuming that because you are a professional no client needs to worry or even ask about the cost of your services are over. It is your duty to be up front and clear about the time and cost involved in your services and to keep them within the boundaries of the allowed rates set by the largest managed-care entity for older adults: Medicare. One of the most dangerous things a practitioner of geriatric behavioral healthcare can do is to behave in a sloppy or cavalier manner toward Medicare. Medicare officials will catch you and make you pay money back (with interest) if you have not followed their regulations! Your claims may be scrutinized more closely, and the officials may request that treatment plans be submitted before claims are paid. If violations are regarded as severe, your status as a Medicare provider may be revoked. Operation Restore Trust, an antifraud initiative of the Department of Health and Human Services, recently published its findings that about one-third of psychological services provided in nursing homes were medically unnecessary in the charts reviewed.[1] As a result of these and related findings, Medicare intermediaries across the country have been limiting the frequency and types of psychological services for which they will pay in nursing homes.

Therefore, part of your necessary research is to seek out the rule changes made by the Medicare carrier in your region. An in-depth understanding of the Byzantine maze of Medicare can be attained with careful review of the written regulations. Monthly Medicare newsletters are invaluable. You will receive them automatically if you have a Medicare provider number. I used to file them after a cursory and quick perusal; now both my billing administrator and I read them as soon as we receive them, and we highlight sections related to psychiatry and psychology.

The Medicare rules change with remarkable frequency. The most knowledgeable people are entirely self-taught and have cultivated pleasant relations with local and regional Medicare administrators. Don't place all that knowledge and power in the hands of a competent administrative assistant or director of billing services: people can and do leave their jobs. As a marketing practitioner and/or lead professional, you need to concern yourself with this information.

Medicare regulations are increasingly being tightened for providers. Follow what is happening at the state and federal levels. Good sources of this information are local community and healthcare planning organizations that monitor these initiatives, professional lobbying groups for organizations like the American Association for Retired Persons, the nursing home industry, and other medical and behavioral healthcare organizations. There are subscription newsletters providing the most up-to-date information, such as the *Medicare Report*, published by the Bureau of National Affairs, Inc. out of Washington, D.C. The independent newspaper *The National Psychologist* routinely covers changes in Medicare regulations that affect psychologists.

Medicare-associated, risk-based HMOs are increasing in popularity. In 1996 about 4.5 million Medicare beneficiaries were enrolled in Medicare managed-care programs, with a 2.5 percent increase per month in expected enrollment (see Chapter Nine of this volume). Although these programs must provide the same level of benefits as in the fee-for-service Medicare system, managed-care companies require precertification of services (such as the type of assessment instruments used in a neuropsychological evaluation) or preauthorization of therapy sessions. Behavioral healthcare providers must learn these new rules for managed care, which vary from one program to another.

Services Specific to Seniors

Our experience is that most older adults will value a referral from a physician above all other referrals to behavioral healthcare professionals, but it is still useful to be aware of the services specific to senior citizens in your area. You may be able to pick up occasional referrals from senior centers, support groups like those for widows and widowers, or advocacy groups like the American Association of Retired Persons.

Know Thy Customer

The current cohort of older adults does not readily seek behavioral healthcare services. They will, however, use them when encouraged by their physician and family members. When you are working with older adults, at the beginning of treatment expect skepticism, lack of knowledge about what to expect from therapy, occasional hostility, and misunderstandings about what the behavioral healthcare professional can offer. The beginning of most assessment and therapy sessions must involve educating the older adult and involved family members about just what you can do. The older client is probably accustomed to the medical model in which the physician gives advice, prescriptions, and directives. The idea of negotiating goals for treatment and working in a partnership capacity, a hallmark characteristic of therapy in managed-care plans, may be foreign to the older client. Part of marketing your services is providing education from the time of initial contact.

On rare occasions I have had potential older clients call as a result of my ad in the phone book, or because of a column I wrote in a local newspaper. I always take the time to answer such inquiries personally. The typical result is that the timid or hesitant first-time client actually makes an appointment. If your market is the older adult population, you must take the time to answer phone questions from potential clients personally. Because the elderly client typically does not know what psychological or other behavioral services are all about, relegating this role to a secretary or answering service personnel will often result in lost opportunities.

The Role of Adult Children

The adult child of the elderly client, especially the adult daughter, is a powerful and important referral source. The cohort of middle-aged adult children tends to be somewhat more familiar and comfortable with the concept of behavioral healthcare services. In addition, the adult children find themselves in decision-making roles for frail elderly parents. They are accustomed to paying for professional services, and they are usually more than willing to make Medicare copayments or out-of-pocket payments for services not covered by Medicare.

Referrals from adult children often involve and result from certain common questions: Can my mother safely live alone? Are my dad's decline in grooming and his withdrawal from activities due to depression? Does my parent have early Alzheimer's dementia? How can I improve the quality of my parent's life? Even when the older parent objects to behavioral services and to any payment for them, the persuasive adult child is often the initiator of the referral for behavioral healthcare services. Therefore, marketing your presence and services to groups like professional women's networks, the Junior League, and church or other service organizations can prove fruitful for referrals.

Using Referrals and Client Profiles

It is essential to know who your customers are and what or who is their referral source. What is the age range of your clients? What is their average age? What is their median age? How is their health in general? If you want to build your outpatient caseload, you will probably see the younger age group of seniors (clients between sixty-five and the middle seventies). Retirement and nursing homes typically supply clients who are in their eighties or well into their nineties, and possibly a few centenarians as well.

Keep track of referrals by developing an intake form that is entered directly into your database. Sample referral codings may include *physician* (include the physician's name, hospital affiliation, and specialty), *adult child, spouse, word of mouth, other professional, geriatric assessment program, long-term-care facility, inpatient consult,* and *community senior center.* Such data will prove valuable to your marketing plan. For example, if most of your referrals come from only one or two sources, it is wise to spend energy diversifying your referral sources. When I began my private geropsychology practice, the majority of referrals came from a hospital-based geriatric assessment center. A short time later, a new geriatrician became the director, and the number of new referrals took a nosedive.

What zip code areas do your clients reside in? Data that show how far people are driving, or whether they use public transportation to see you, may prove impressive to a skeptical provider-review panel down the road, when you are trying to get on board. If you decide to do mass mailings for any new programs, knowing what zip codes to target helps you decide what commercially available mailing lists to buy.

What are the reasons why clients first come to your practice? Are they seeking help because of memory concerns, health-related problems, or depression and other behavioral problems? For example, if many of your referred clients have memory complaints, offering a course on memory enhancement may prove fruitful. If you have a high number of clients with impaired vision, offering a

"Coping with Vision Loss" therapy group makes good clinical and financial sense.

What services are your customers using? Again, develop a coding system for your services. Are you primarily doing diagnostics? brief psychotherapy? Are you referring clients that you can't or don't wish to treat to other providers? For example, if you specialize in grief work and don't wish to diagnose clients for depression and dementia but find that 60 percent of your referrals need that type of assessment, you may want to consider affiliating with a professional who can offer it.

Managed-Care Companies as Customers

As more Medicare beneficiaries join HMOs and other, similar plans, the managed-care organization, rather than the individual client, will become the behavioral healthcare practitioner's customer. Most managed-care companies and HMOs do not require specialized or additional credentials in geriatric behavioral healthcare for their panel of providers who care for older adults. However, if you have such additional qualifications you may have a chance to gain membership on an officially closed panel. Having practitioners with geriatric credentials enhances the managed-care company's marketing efforts in attracting new senior clients.

One aggressive tactic is to call the provider relations staff of the managed-care companies in your area and attempt to get on their preferred-provider panels, regardless of whether they offer special programs for seniors. In many markets, most provider panels are closed, but don't give up: changes are so rapid in managed care that it really does pay to keep on trying and to hedge your bets by keeping in regular, personal contact. Remind provider relations staff of your specialty in geriatric health, and give them outcome data and case studies for the kinds of specialized services you offer. Why? Because Medicare will become increasingly managed, and you don't know which managed-care companies in your market will get a piece of the pie. It is your responsibility as a specialist in geriatric behavioral healthcare to educate the staff at managed-care companies about what you can offer clients and their families.

You are attractive to managed-care companies and HMOs if you are willing to see clients in their homes or in long-term-care facilities. One local HMO that uses the traditional staff model for its mental health services sought out my group on a consulting basis for patients in nursing homes. The reason? We are willing to travel to a nursing home to do assessment and therapy for that HMO's clients, whereas the HMO's in-house staff of psychologists and social workers saw clients only in the HMO's suburban office. Developing a good relationship with the case manager who makes such referrals is essential.

Know Thy Business

Experts in geriatric behavioral healthcare can apply their unique knowledge in settings and in ways that go beyond "medically necessary" services for older adults and their families. Exploring business opportunities that meet the needs of older adults in nontraditional ways can open up a variety of exciting professional avenues.

Consulting and Training

As the population ages, all kinds of businesses that serve older people are in need of training for their staff with respect to good customer service. For example, I approached several banks a few years ago, and one progressive company hired me to put on a series of seminars for its trust department and management staff. The purpose was to educate the trust officers about dementia so that they could recognize it in their clients. We also discussed how to make the bank's environment user-friendly to older adults. For example, we evaluated the lobby lighting, the availability of chairs, the size of the print on the bank's brochures, the staff's style of approaching hearing-impaired customers, and other issues. In the seminars, I demonstrated appropriate styles of communication with hearing-impaired and possibly confused customers. In essence, I used my general knowledge of gerontology to help the bank's management increase the staff's sensitivity to the unique needs of older customers.

An agency that serves developmentally disabled people by providing case management to keep individuals in home settings has hired my group to train its staff about aging issues. Why? Because the agency's clients are living longer, and the agency wants to branch out into the senior market. The same resources and skills that the agency offers to younger, disabled clients can be used with older adults who want to remain independent and at home as long as possible. We also serve a utilization-review function for the agency's treatment-planning team.

Other settings that use behavioral healthcare consultants include continuing-care retirement communities, home-healthcare agencies, adult day-care centers, and adult protective agencies, to name a few. For example, some retirement communities hire behavioral experts to evaluate causes of job dissatisfaction among staff and to screen potential employees. Serving as the leader of a support group for staff is yet another behavioral consulting role related to the constant problems of employee recruitment and retention in the long-term-care industry. Constructive meetings in which gripes are aired in a confidential setting, followed by opportunities for problem-solving discussions, can be a very powerful vehicle for increasing staff morale. This is an excellent selling point to administrators.

Advising the top administrator of an organization devoted to serving older adults is yet another role for a behavioral healthcare consultant. Industrial and organizational psychologists have long known how isolated the leaders of corporate organizations can be, and how they benefit from professional support and feedback. The behavioral consultant versed in gerontology can interpret research findings pertinent to long-term care. For example, the consultant can suggest environmental and programmatic changes that will enhance the independence and improve the functioning of demented residents.

We have one contract with a long-term-care facility that offers two levels of care (skilled nursing and assisted living). We conduct psychological screenings for all new admissions to the facility. This is obviously a direct-care service, but it is not a billable service under Medicare regulations. As the system now stands, only medically necessary services can be billed to Medicare, not "fishing expeditions" (as screenings are referred to in the long-term-care business). However, this retirement community values our fishing expeditions because we identify mood disorders, memory loss, and other psychological conditions early, thus helping staff devise treatment plans and appropriate placement and services from the outset.

The facility pays us a monthly retainer, for which we perform the screening evaluations and conduct socialization groups for residents. Group programs are not psychotherapy in the strict sense (see Chapter Six of this volume), and therefore they are not covered by Medicare. The residents of the facility and their family members value the groups because the participants feel less lonely and isolated, and new residents appear to adjust more easily to having moved to the facility.

Some facilities will not pay retainer fees for staff training, behavioral consultation with staff, or activities like admission screening and socialization groups. They may propose contracts in which a certain percentage of referrals is guaranteed through standing orders for treatment. Because of the tightening of Medicare rules for nursing homes, mentioned earlier in this chapter, you should be wary of contractual arrangements like these.

Forensic Services

Geriatric mental health professionals may receive requests from attorneys and family members to perform mental competency evaluations of older adults for the purpose of deciding the need for a

legal guardianship with respect to personal care or financial decisions. If there is no frank medical necessity, these professional services are to be paid for by private funds. Assessments of
testamentary capacity are yet another private-pay service that is
performed by geriatric mental health experts. For example, I was
hired by a family member of a former client to render an opinion of
my former client's ability to make a valid will. When I evaluated
her, five years before she died, she was in the moderate stages of
Alzheimer's dementia and could barely identify her children. We
had a two-hour-long phone deposition, during which I was grilled
on my knowledge of dementia, psychometric testing, and my former client's attitudes toward her family. If you are willing to learn
how to operate in the often aggressive arena of courts, depositions,
and attorneys, this is a fascinating niche-service area.

Adult protective agencies sometimes also hire psychologists
and social workers as consultants to evaluate indigent clients whose
decision-making ability is called into question because of odd
behavior involving issues of safety or self-neglect. These evaluations can be paid for by state funds used at the discretion of the hiring agency. The work requires not only knowledge of the
parameters of legal and mental competency but also the willingness
to venture into sometimes filthy and unsavory living conditions.
These home visits are always an adventure, to say the least.

Public Education and Support

Community agencies and advocacy groups invariably call on geriatric behavioral experts to conduct support groups and educational
seminars and to give public lectures. These endeavors typically pay
small honoraria (when they pay anything at all), but we believe it
is wise for you to agree occasionally to conduct such activities. You
will succeed in creating a positive image of yourself with respect to
public service, and you will gain name recognition that is helpful
in obtaining direct referrals. Unless you become famous through
other notable accomplishments, however, you will not be able to
make a living by your wonderful skills in public speaking.

Know Thy Finances

You need to know your income intimately, and on several different levels. A preliminary analysis may include referrals, payment sources, and profit margins, broken down by service categories. Other variables to examine are monthly performance and practitioner productivity, as well as productivity and services broken down by location. By developing or purchasing standardized forms and a computer database that can encompass these variables and others, you will be able to see where you are making money and where your efforts are nonproductive.

Allow yourself at least nine to twelve months of analysis before making any judgments: geriatric behavioral healthcare is a seasonal business, just like Christmas retailing! For example, we have found that the winter months, particularly January, are slower for new clients who want outpatient therapy services; the cold temperatures and snowy roads are the most likely reason for this slowdown. Opportunities for new business in retirement communities and nursing homes are more constant because you are bringing your services to the clients. Examining the trends in your location is an important part of marketing. You will find that the results are often counterintuitive and fascinating.

Look carefully at how much time you actually spend performing each service (in both its billable and nonbillable aspects), and use this information to determine which services are your most profitable ones. Also look carefully at your accounts receivable. Medicare may take longer to pay than some private insurers do, but that is part of the cost of doing business with older adults. However, we have found that using electronic billing for Medicare significantly reduces the waiting time for payment. Examine your Medicare accounts carefully: we have found occasionally that payment for one or two service dates per month may be delayed by the carrier and may require repeat billing.

Don't be surprised if your analysis reveals the 80/20 adage: that 80 percent of your money is made from 20 percent of your customers, jobs, and referral sources. What this means, unfortunately, is that you are vulnerable at all times to losing 80 percent of your income. Even in the best of times, you need to be constantly on the lookout for new sources of income and referrals. In fact, we promise you that as geriatric health becomes increasingly "managed," you will see great shifts in your client base. But if you know your finances, customers, business, and market, you have a fighting chance of survival.

Know Thy Outcomes

The new mantra is *outcome*. If we learn anything from these wacky and often crunchy times, it is that we have to provide outcomes to survive in the managed-care environment.

An in-depth, longitudinal study is obviously beyond the reach of many of us, but it is essential that you keep track of some simple facts and use them in your marketing efforts. How long do you work with people? When they finish with you, are they less depressed or anxious and more functional than they were when they began? (See Chapter Four of this volume.) How long are your sessions? If you provide neuropsychological assessments, how long do they take? Have you saved clients and their families needless problems by your services and diagnoses? Have you saved hospitals or nursing homes from potential disasters because of your intervention as part of a team? Are your treatment plans in line with the expectations of Medicare and third-party Medicare insurers? What areas of expertise do you have available? How many locations? Communicating outcomes in a cost-effective, timely manner to managed-care companies will show them that you are a serious practitioner and will give you a competitive edge.

Methods and Materials

So now you have dutifully conducted your research, and you know your market, customer, business, finances, and outcomes. Earlier we promised not to discuss general marketing, but the simplest way to describe the general process of marketing is to look at those personality characteristics of successful salespeople that emerge from analysis of their psychological tests. According to James Schuerger, professor of psychology at Cleveland State University, the most salient characteristic of successful salespeople is discipline: they work at selling every day, and they never give up.[2] That's what marketing is all about.

The professional who spends a fortune on a beautiful brochure, stationery, and business cards and then fails to use them properly is like the person who spends a fortune on exercise equipment and lets it gather dust. Marketing tools are helpful only in conjunction with the discipline and enthusiasm of the person who uses them.

Targeted and Tailored Materials

Do you need materials in order to market your business properly? Absolutely. But use materials that are flexible and tailored to the audience. With today's technology, there's no reason to use the same outdated brochure or listing of services for different audiences. You should be able to modify and print targeted and tailored materials at a moment's notice. The savvy professional will have different materials for clients and their families, managed-care companies, and physicians. Just as job seekers are advised to use tailored résumés for each potential job, behavioral healthcare professionals should use different marketing materials for different audiences.

For example, managed-care companies need to hear about such factors as your location and the geographic areas you serve, your areas of subspecialty, your average treatment plans, the cost of your services, the quickness of your response to referrals, and your affiliation with hospitals and networks in your area. They will also be interested in how treatment by a qualified professional specializing in behavioral healthcare for older adults will ultimately contribute to their clients' general health and well-being and thus lessen healthcare costs.

Clients and families need to know how you can help them as individuals. Clearly written, lively case studies about older people who have been able to maintain their independence and to experience improvement in their behavioral health are of special interest to potential clients. They need to know that they are not "crazy" and that issues of behavioral health are common in the older population. Clients and their families benefit from hearing a message of hopefulness and knowing that many behavioral health problems, such as depression, are treatable and that the treatment generally has a positive outcome. It is advisable to use a larger type size for printed materials meant for older adults.

Physicians respond well to data and case studies illustrating the connection between behavioral and physical health. For example, many physicians have patients whose anxiety- or depression-related complaints place an inappropriate burden on physician and staff resources. Furthermore, because older adults frequently go first to a physician to present complaints, they may work with a behavioral healthcare professional only on referral by the physician. It can be very useful simply to bring some of these facts to the attention of physicians in a simple business letter. Another useful approach to physicians is to circulate reprints of relevant research. Physicians will also be interested in the professional training of a behavioral healthcare practitioner and in his or her affiliations with hospitals, managed-care companies, and physician groups.

Personalizing Yourself

Another principle of effectively marketing behavioral healthcare services for older adults is to personalize yourself, especially true in communications targeted to clients and families. A faceless generic brochure that merely lists services, in terminology that a potential client has never heard, will be thrown in the trash. Keep in mind that it may require a tremendous leap of faith and trust for a client or the client's family to pick up the phone and schedule an initial appointment. That's why your photo and your personal statement of your beliefs about aging and behavioral healthcare will be remarkably effective.

Photos and belief statements will not do you much good with decision makers at managed-care companies, but personal contact will. We recommend the book *Marketing for Therapists: A Handbook for Success in Managed Care*[3] as a source of information on successfully marketing to managed-care companies.

Another general bit of advice is to follow up any letter or mailing with a phone call to an individual (for example, the executive director of a long-term-care facility or of an agency where there may be consulting opportunities). Find out the person's name, and make a note of it. You don't have to turn yourself into a used-car salesman or a telephone solicitor in order to achieve personal contact; you do have to tell the person who you are, why you are calling, and what you hope you can accomplish together.

Achieving personal contact with physicians can be more difficult because of schedules, and because of the office managers who serve as gatekeepers. Nevertheless, a simple phone message is still effective as the follow-up to a letter. Office managers can be very helpful, and you should tell them exactly why you are calling, and that you hope to encourage a referring relationship. I receive many direct referrals from secretaries, receptionists, and physician's assistants. The physician needs to know who I am, but support staff often make the actual referrals and provide my phone number.

If you are affiliated with a hospital, attending grand rounds is an excellent way to speak with physicians and introduce yourself. Once a physician does refer a client to you, make sure that you communicate with the physician promptly. Tell the physician how his or her patient is faring under your care.

The Challenge of Marketing

Marketing efforts can be daunting for the geriatric behavioral specialist who is first and foremost a clinician. Just remember that you may have excellent products to offer—your expert diagnostic, therapy, and consulting services, for example—but unless potential referral sources get to know you and your expertise, no one will knock down your door for your help.

In the first three years of our group practice at the Center for Healthy Aging, we had many discouraging results from our marketing efforts. For every ten or so ideas implemented, about one paid off. We have sunk money and time into endeavors like postmenopausal support groups, book clubs around healthy-aging topics, and groups for those recently diagnosed with early Alzheimer's dementia, to name a few of our offerings. We write articles for a local senior newspaper, and we have spoken at churches, seniors groups, bookstores, and various support groups in the area. We have been on the radio and have been featured in several local newspaper articles about senior-related topics. We have even produced an educational video about psychotherapy with a ninety-five-year-old woman. Not one of these efforts resulted in any immediate financial return. In fact, we have not even recouped much of the direct costs.

The benefits, if any, appear to be long-term benefits involving our professional reputation. Once in a great while, however, an unusual and unexpected benefit comes along. For example, we had organized a travel seminar for older adults and invited representatives from several travel agencies and some of my well-traveled clients to speak. Someone in the audience liked the seminar and asked that we coordinate it again for a long-term-care facility. We did so, and the executive director of the agency attended. We met after the program, and he offered us the chance to provide services to the facility. That one travel seminar turned into a two-year contract! The moral is that you cannot reliably predict the outcome or the value of your marketing efforts, and once in a while the benefits are outstanding.

If you want professional autonomy, you must be ready and eager to sell yourself. In a small practice, you must set aside time each week solely for the purpose of marketing. This may mean some phone calls, a business lunch, or just time to think. In a larger practice, specific individuals can take over this role. One option is to affiliate yourself with a large, established behavioral practice so that you are well positioned with managed-care companies as they enroll a larger percentage of Medicare beneficiaries. As a geriatric behavioral specialist, you could manage a specific division of older-adult services for a large, general behavioral practice. The ideal would be to earn your income from a mix of consulting contracts, professional training seminars or similar activities, and Medicare dollars for direct care; watching *Meet the Press* a few times will convince you not to depend solely on Medicare for your family's income.

In a practice devoted to the behavioral healthcare of older adults, your income and referral sources will be many and varied. Geriatric behavioral services are truly at the final frontier of independent practice. Space travel on *Star Trek* has its share of hazards and threats, and so does this work, in addition to the exciting challenges and opportunities available in any pioneering effort. Your only limit is your capacity for creativity, courage, and determination.

Suggested Reading

Hartman-Stein, P. E. (1995). "Organizational Development Consultation in Long-Term Care." *Psychologists in Long Term Care Newsletter*, 1995, *9*, 3–5.

Lichtenberg, P. A., and Hartman-Stein, P. E. "Effective Geropsychology Practice in Nursing Homes." In L. VandeCreek, S. Knapp, and T. L. Jackson (eds.), *Innovations in Clinical Practice: A Source Book*. Vol. 15. Sarasota, Fla: Professional Resource Press, 1997.

Epilogue

Hope Amidst the
Behavioral Healthcare Crisis

Paula E. Hartman-Stein

Every crisis produces challenge, conflict, change, and, ultimately, growth. Behavioral healthcare is in the midst of such a crisis. For at least ten years the industrialization of healthcare, and the subsequent ushering in of managed care, have been shaping the delivery of medical and behavioral services in the employer-driven insurance industry. More recently, managed-care principles and methods have been applied to Medicaid in some states. As a result of such measures, costs have been reduced in the delivery of mental health services, but not without controversy about the impact on quality of care.

As managed-care systems mature, positive trends emerge. Emphasis is shifting to client satisfaction, treatment outcome measures, and the medical-cost offset of behavioral interventions. Systems that integrate physical and behavioral healthcare are starting to replace managed-care programs that "carve out" mental health services, with the result that more attention is being paid to how psychological interventions reduce medical service utilization. Experts predict that carve-out models have limited tenure in the scheme of healthcare systems.

Still, Medicare regulations are slow to change, partly if not primarily because there are potential negative political ramifications for legislators. No Medicare beneficiary wants his or her benefits reduced or insurance premiums increased; therefore, older voters have significant influence on legislators' willingness to lobby for major revamping of the Medicare system. As Medicare nears insolvency, however, pressures mount to reduce costs.

Clinical service providers feel the tightening first. Mental health practitioners experienced the impact in 1996 through limits on reimbursement by Medicare "carriers" or insurance administrators appointed by the Health Care Financing Administration (HCFA). As an example, for several months the carrier for Ohio and West Virginia, Nationwide, limited payment for psychological treatment to one or two sessions per month for all patients in nursing homes. This change in the rules, when applied to severely depressed or suicidal patients, made no clinical sense.

Arbitrary changes like this one are not grounded in scientific principles of effective care. They are measures of cost control. Providers can appeal, but because reviews can take several months, there can be a negative effect on cash flow. Significant delays in payment of legitimate claims can reduce services for some needy clients and cause layoffs among competent professionals associated with mental health groups operating in nursing homes.

A general market-oriented solution to Medicare cost cutting is the government's granting of more health maintenance organization (HMO) applications. Although beneficiaries are promised the same level of benefits as in fee-for-service Medicare, HMO rules can limit procedures by requiring preauthorization of services. For example, psychotherapy is usually authorized in terms of a specified number of treatment sessions, with the focus on stabilization and crisis management. Neuropsychological evaluation may be reimbursed, but only in relatively rare circumstances, and only specific tests may be authorized. (See Chapter Nine for a discussion of these rules and their ramifications for providers.) As increasing numbers of Medicare beneficiaries enroll in HMOs, behavioral health practitioners will experience limitations in their access to older adults. Well-trained geropsychologists or geriatric social workers who have not already been admitted to membership on insurance panels associated with local Medicare HMOs may find themselves unable to make a living by practicing with older adults.

Geriatric behavioral specialists, as well as the faculty in prestigious academic institutions who have trained them, must be modest in any expectation that insurance executives care about or even know of any differences in levels of training and competence among clinicians. We must take a proactive stance and have dialogues and conferences with the business executives who make the decisions about managed care. Academic arrogance has no place in managed behavioral healthcare; graduate training programs must include practical coursework that realistically addresses the exigencies of today's healthcare environment.

The Big Picture

My frightened and cynical psychologist friends fear that behavioral services will eventually be eliminated altogether as Medicare-reimbursable procedures, but that scenario is unlikely. In Medicare, as in the private insurance sector, there are fewer unnecessary costs associated with psychological treatment than with medical and surgical procedures that appropriate psychological treatment could have prevented. Thirty years of research document the high frequency of the so-called functional complaints that account for overuse of medical and surgical services. A review of this vast literature is beyond the scope of this chapter, but legislators and other governmental decision makers need to be aware of how much money can be saved through the use of appropriate behavioral services. Chapter One presents data that illustrate this point, and Chapter Two describes a demonstration program that has a chance of becoming a permanent part of Medicare and Medicaid services. As physical and mental healthcare become more integrated, the cost-saving benefits of behavioral interventions will become even more obvious.

Although more research is needed on the savings that result from providing behavioral services to frail elders in long-term-care facilities, cost reduction should not be the only rationale for these services. In geriatric healthcare the goal is often not to "cure" but to balance the preservation of life while enabling a greater quality of life, a goal similar to the goals of the hospice movement. We are in the very early stages of knowing exactly how to quantify improvement in the quality of life for our frail, chronically ill elders. Outcome measures that only capture symptoms or functional status are of limited usefulness to individuals who suffer from chronic, incurable diseases, and whose functional status predictably declines over time. A promising example of an instrument that measures domains of life satisfaction is the Missoula-Vitas Quality of Life Index by Ira Byock,[1] which was developed for use with terminally ill patients. I recommend that those who design the behavioral health components of Medicare-associated, risk-based HMOs, and particularly HMOs that enroll beneficiaries in long-term-care settings, incorporate these more sensitive outcome measures.

Another hopeful sign of potential improvement in the quality of care delivered to older adults is the trend toward a capitation model or prospective payment systems. These systems encourage preventive programs, such as those geared to lifestyle changes (smoking cessation, relaxation and stress reduction), caregiver support, bereavement groups, memory-enhancement seminars, and other healthy-aging programs. In a capitation model, socialization groups for older adults in assisted-living settings and nursing homes would be encouraged, as would cognitive-stimulation programs for moderately demented older adults, by contrast with the situation in fee-for-service Medicare (see Chapter Six).

Qualifications of Providers and Standards of Care

I strongly recommend that those responsible for the quality-assurance aspect of Medicare risk-based HMOs require the preferred or prime providers on their panels to have appropriate qualifications and experience in the geriatric field. (See Chapter Nine for a discussion of the liability incurred by HMOs that do not insist on competent providers.) Besides requiring basic competence of their direct-care providers who work with older adults, HMOs should consider hiring experts in geropsychology to consult with quality-assurance programs and contribute to the design of behavioral benefit packages for Medicare beneficiaries.

The American Psychological Association has developed requirements for the qualifications, training, and supervision of practicing psychologists who seek recognition of proficiency in geropsychology. The national group Psychologists in Long Term Care has also formulated standards for psychologists working in the long-term-care field. I have been personally involved with both of these efforts to recognize basic standards of practice and training qualifications for professionals in the field of aging. Both groups sought input from many sources, and, in my opinion, the documents that were produced are fair and reasonable with respect to standards and qualifications. Other professional groups, however, are establishing excessively restrictive qualifications because of the fear of being cut out of the marketplace altogether. For example, some organizations argue that only board-certified neuropsychologists should administer diagnostic evaluations of older adults for dementia (see Chapter Five for a review of the different training routes that psychologists can take to become competent diagnosticians and therapists with older adults). Moreover, other professional organizations, such as those in social work and psychiatry, either have developed or are involved in creating indicators of added qualifications in their respective fields.

Services Covered Under Managed Behavioral Care

The decision of what behavioral services to cover for older adults, and for what duration of treatment, is a most difficult one. Most employer-driven managed-care programs allow about twenty sessions of outpatient therapy per episode of illness, or per calendar year. These service limits are efforts to control costs; they are not based on empirically validated research to improve the quality of patient care. We need more studies to develop psychotherapy treatment protocols, a goal that has been resisted by organized psychology. According to Cummings, treatment protocols fit about a third of the persons suffering from the psychological conditions being addressed.[2] Nevertheless, the development and use of treatment protocols appropriate for older adults, both as outpatients and in long-term-care settings, are important steps toward increasing the effectiveness and efficiency of care.

With empirically derived treatment protocols still being researched, what can managed-care executives do in the meantime? They can require clinicians to write out treatment plans, to estimate the duration of treatment, and to use appropriate outcome measures covering the areas of cognition, mood, behavior, and quality of life (see Chapter Four). The guidelines for treatment plans and records recently adopted by the National Committee for Quality Assurance[3] can easily be adapted to older adults, including those in nursing homes.

Managed mental healthcare systems sometimes exclude payment for psychotherapy with patients whose diagnosis is dementia. A body of research exists, however, that demonstrates the efficacy of psychotherapy with patients suffering from Alzheimer's dementia who also meet the criteria for depression. Teri and Uomoto[4] and Teri and Wagner[5] have demonstrated that these patients have excess disability (a greater degree of functional impairment than is accounted for by their cognitive declines) and more functional and behavioral problems. Preliminary results of behavioral interventions with demented-depressed patients are promising. Future research in this area is needed on the savings that could be realized from psychological treatment that prevents both premature institutionalization of patients and health problems for their caregivers.

Neuropsychological evaluation is often not a covered procedure, especially in the "carve out" models of managed care. I strongly recommend that Medicare-affiliated managed-care systems allow brief, timely neuropsychological evaluation of older adults for diagnostic and treatment-planning purposes (see Chapter Five for a discussion of why and how to implement this recommendation). One cost-effective, reasonable strategy is to cap the reimbursable amount of time spent on this kind of evaluation, an approach that would allow a qualified provider to choose specific test instruments rather than precertify tests one at a time. The following case example illustrates this point:

A psychiatrist and a primary-care physician referred Ben, a seventy-three-year-old man, for the purpose of determining whether his reports of memory loss indicated early signs of dementia, depression, or both conditions. Although Ben showed signs of clinical depression, the psychiatrist was reluctant to start antidepressant therapy before seeing the results of a neuropsychological evaluation. Similarly, Ben's primary-care physician did not want to try one of the newer cognitive-enhancement medications used for Alzheimer's patients.

Ben was covered by a Medicare HMO that allowed cognitive evaluation as a reimbursable service so long as prior authorizations were given for specific testing procedures. After completing an initial interview with Ben and his wife, I called the quality-assurance nurse for authorization of the test instruments. I described the patient's history and listed several standardized psychometric tests, all with older-adult norms, that sample areas of cognitive functioning that can be impaired due to dementia. The proposed assessment procedure is relatively brief: usually two hours of direct testing time, with one to two additional hours for test interpretation and write-up of the results. (For a more detailed description of such tests, see Chapter Five.) After listening politely, the nurse responded that the only test she could certify among those I had listed was a five-minute measure of visual-motor tracking and the ability to shift mental sets (Trail Making, Part A and B). I expressed my incredulity at this severe degree of restriction in the evaluation of dementia and decided that a phone consultation with the plan's medical director was the next step.

The subsequent phone contact with the medical director was frustrating, to say the least. Although the tone of the conversation was civil and professional, the medical director informed me that fifty psychological tests were approved by the insurance plan, but none of the memory tests or dementia-screening instruments I had mentioned was among them. The company specifically disallowed any of the Wechsler tests[6] because of their association with intelligence testing, which was strictly forbidden. I explained that my purpose was not IQ testing, and that I planned to administer a few sections from both the memory instrument and the cognitive instrument, but my arguments failed to convince the medical director. I then proposed that she send me the list of authorized instruments so that I could choose from those familiar to me. She answered that this solution would not work either, because the list was proprietary information. I suggested another approach: cap the time allowed for testing, but permit the use of instruments with which I have experience and training. My arguments did not prevail: "We're not about to reinvent the wheel!" she replied. The conversation ended with the medical director's suggestion that Ben's family doctor just go ahead and try the cognitive-enhancement medication, with no testing. The implication was that a neuropsychological evaluation, even a brief one, is a waste of time and money.

In order to deliver what I considered to be an appropriate clinical evaluation, I proceeded to administer my usual brief battery of tests, without reimbursement, and absorbed the financial loss. Ben demonstrated relatively mild memory loss, with no evidence of additional cognitive deficit. He did not meet the criteria for dementia, and I recommended treatment of his depression.

Practitioner Recommendations for the Present

To survive in the current climate of increasingly managed Medicare, behavioral clinicians must begin to change their treatment strategies. The practice standards developed by Psychologists in Long Term Care provide basic guidelines and a solid foundation.[7] Clinicians, when documenting progress, must begin to use treatment-outcome measures that include several dimensions, rather than relying only on such measures as the Global Assessment of Functioning or the Geriatric Depression Scale (see Chapter Four).

Even before treatment limits are in place, therapists can begin to contract with clients for treatment sessions in specific blocks of time—four to eight sessions, for example, at the end of which progress is evaluated and summarized. The client, the therapist, and sometimes family members (in the case of institutionalized older adults) can then decide together whether therapy should continue (see Chapter Nine for a discussion of informed consent). I have found that many older adults respond favorably to time-limited treatment, both because they are concerned about the cost of treatment and because short-term therapy often fits with their view of themselves as self-sufficient individuals who do not need much help from psychologists.

Whenever such arrangements are feasible, I encourage clinicians to either supplement or substitute individual therapy sessions with group therapy around similar themes or clinical conditions (see Chapter Six for suggestions). Another recommendation that stems from experience with the managed-care movement is to use all the community resources available (such as layperson-led support groups) to supplement outpatient therapy. Similarly, in continuing-care retirement communities and freestanding nursing homes, therapists can incorporate other services available in the facility into individual treatment plans. For example, cultivating a relationship with the activities director is useful in seeing what types of recreational and social-skills programming are offered that could enhance the clients' care.

Another recommendation, which applies to traditional fee-for-service Medicare, may be a particularly bitter pill to swallow: terminate formal therapy when you determine that treatment is no longer necessary for specific behavioral issues. This recommendation sounds both simple and obvious, but the therapist in an institutional setting can easily become the main source of social support for the client. When this happens, it is difficult to sever the ties of the therapeutic relationship, not only because of the financial consequences for the therapist but also because of the emotional repercussions for the patient. If possible, arrange for a friendly visitor to take your place, and limit your contacts with the client to brief social calls when you are in the facility. Similarly, a therapist may begin working with a mildly demented older adult, but as the dementia progresses, the client may not be able to benefit from psychotherapy. It may be more appropriate for such a client to participate in a cognitive-stimulation group than to attend individual therapy sessions. Clinicians may wrestle with the ethical problems of abandoning demented clients; under the rules for both traditional Medicare and managed care, however, other opportunities for social support should be arranged for them.

An unanswered and often debated question is how to reimburse psychologists and social workers for working with institutional staff to design behavioral interventions for demented or psychotic patients. There is no currently allowable code for this service under Part B of Medicare. This service is not psychotherapy, and only physicians are permitted to use the procedure codes for evaluation and management; nevertheless, governmental rules covering nursing homes do require efforts to use behavioral interventions before resorting to chemical or physical restraints. Some nursing facilities will reimburse psychologists for their work with staff, but this appears to be the case only in a fairly small percentage of institutions. In my opinion, the regulations should be changed so that therapists can be reimbursed for this important service. In the meantime, psychologists may need to give some pro bono services or work out other arrangements. These can be made with the facility, or they can be made with family members who may be willing to pay for a well-designed treatment plan that staff can follow. For example, I have worked with an individual who had the money to continue treatment for personal self-development (at the age of ninety-two!) and opted to pay for the sessions out of pocket. An arrangement like this one is perfectly legitimate so long as the therapist charges the Medicare-allowed rate. Or, again, family members may ask a therapist to continue individual sessions with a moderately demented parent because of their own belief in the value of therapy, and possibly because of their denial of their loved one's degree of cognitive deficit. In such a case, the therapist can request that treatment costs be out-of-pocket expenses, given the current Medicare regulations, and the occasional family will gladly pay for such services. (Chapters Eight and Ten offer more suggestions for therapists' roles in nursing homes.)

The Future: A Need for Paradigm Shifts

Nick Cummings, a successful visionary and controversial futurist in the field of behavioral healthcare, writes that several paradigm shifts are essential for the practitioner who will ultimately survive and thrive in this new era of managed care.[8] Some of his ideas fit well with the field of geriatric behavioral health. For example, in the traditional model of psychotherapy the practitioner sees few clients, and therapy is conducted individually over a long time. In the new or "catalyst" model, as Cummings calls it, the therapist sees many clients, and brief treatment is conducted in nontraditional modes. In the future more group therapy will be conducted with older adults, and different modes of treatment (such as bibliotherapy and computer-based psychoeducational treatment; see Chapter Seven) will be available.

Cummings[9] and others[10] have promoted the idea that psychologists can and should take the role of primary-care providers. A well-trained clinical health psychologist could be the first or second (rather than last) clinician to see the patient in the process of diagnosis and treatment. In my own experience, the long-term-care setting is particularly ripe for increased collaboration with physicians, and such liaisons can be especially productive in the treatment of older adults. I predict that the behavioral clinicians who survive managed care under Medicare will have joined forces with their medical colleagues, not only for financial survival but also because such models of practice can result in higher quality of care for older adults.

Psychotherapeutic treatment in the traditional model is continuous, often weekly. In the catalyst model,[11] treatment is time-limited, but it is also available intermittently throughout the life cycle. I predict that older adults will be seen intermittently throughout their older years as they seek treatment for very different reasons across the spectrum of advanced age. The problems and issues of a depressed older adult in his or her early sixties are usually very different from those of the typical frail individual in his or her mid-nineties. For example, as a therapist practicing in the same community for many years, I have sometimes treated an individual in his or her early seventies for depression due to the loss of a spouse, or to a decline in health. Ten years later this client's adult children have brought the client back to me for a cognitive evaluation because of memory deficits, and two years later I have become the therapist again because of the client's anxiety over the recent move to an assisted-living facility (see Chapter Ten for a discussion of these issues as they pertain to marketing practices).

The traditional model, both in the United States and in Canada, is a fee-for-service model. The probable model for the future will be a capitation model, which can free geriatric behavioral specialists to provide whatever psychological services are needed. In addition to covering preventive outpatient programs, a prospective payment arrangement will make both consultation with staff and the design of behavioral programs for demented older adults standard in long-term-care facilities. In the capitation model the emphasis is on providing essential services only, preventing health and behavioral problems, and conducting treatment in innovative ways. I see the move to the capitation model as requiring the most challenging paradigm shift.

New Roles for Geropsychologists

In the future, mental health professionals who specialize in the care of older adults not only will provide direct patient care but also will have a number of new roles available to them. Chapters Eight and Ten describe some of these creative opportunities; here are a few more predictions:

Doctorally trained clinicians who specialize in treating the elderly will become supervisors of master's degree–prepared clinicians and psychologists who are seeking added qualifications in geropsychology.

Treatment protocols will be increasingly available in the future, but, as noted by Cummings, two-thirds of clients will not fit into these protocols and will require the skill and supervision of a doctorally trained clinician.

Geropsychologists and geriatric social workers will be instrumental in quality assurance in Medicare risk-based HMOs.

As increasing numbers of agencies develop home-healthcare services, behavioral specialists will find more opportunities to become staff trainers and to play a role in quality assurance for home-based geriatric care management.

Geropsychologists will be instrumental in designing and executing outcome research in long-term care involving medical-cost offset.

Geriatric mental health experts will be involved in the design of service delivery in capitation models for the care of older adult patients.

The era of the Renaissance of the Knowledgeable Provider is upon us. As managed care evolves, the rules become increasingly influenced by the clinical roots of former successful treatment so that high-quality service can be ensured. Clients' voices and demands for quality are being heard in the employer-driven world of managed care. In our country the strongest political voices are those of Medicare beneficiaries. Therefore, I predict that the cry for quality will become even more powerful and vociferous in managed care under Medicare. The provider who not only can predict and control costs but also can practice in the most quality-conscious manner will survive the behavioral healthcare crisis and, even more, successfully contribute to future innovations.

Clinicians, legislators, and insurance executives probably all share one major common goal: the desire to have a healthcare system that can serve the medical and behavioral needs of our children when they reach retirement, as well as the needs of many generations to come. Now is the time to design and implement innovative methods that can ensure not only the survival of programs for this nation's older adults but also the meaningful future growth of those programs.

This volume is a starting point, a beginning guidebook for these changing times. It speaks to the present and the future of behavioral healthcare for older adults, suggesting guidelines for cost-conscious clinical practice. The contributors have presented model programs, pragmatic suggestions for clinicians and managed-care executives alike, and a vision of future roles that have yet to materialize. The book has posed questions that need to be studied, as well as ideas open to debate in the legislative arena. Most important, this book has offered the beginnings of a forum for communication among various parties who rarely sit at the same table. I invite beneficiaries as well to join in on the deliberations that the contributors and I hope this book will inspire.

Suggested Reading

Hartman-Stein, P. E. "What Constitutes Quality Clinical Geropsychology Service?" *Advances in Medical Psychotherapy*, 1997–98, 9, 169–180.

La Rue, A. *Aging and Neuropsychological Assessment*. New York: Plenum, 1992.

Notes

Foreword

1. *Public Papers of the Presidents of the United States: John F. Kennedy*. Washington, D.C.: U. S. Government Printing Office, 1963, p. 189.

Preface

1. Department of Health and Human Services. "Mental Health Services in Nursing Facilities in the Operation Restore Trust States." OEI-02-91-00861. New York: Office of Inspector General, May 1996.

Chapter One

1. Bandura, A., Adams, N. E., and Beyer, J. "Cognitive Processes Mediating Behavioral Change." *Journal of Personality and Social Psychology*, 1977, *35*, 125–139.
2. Seligman, M.E.P. *Helplessness: On Depression, Development, and Death*. San Francisco: Freeman, 1975.
3. Antonovsky, A. *Unraveling the Mystery of Health: How People Manage Stress and Stay Well*. San Francisco: Jossey-Bass, 1987.

Chapter Two

1. Pfeiffer, E. "A Short Portable Mental Status Questionnaire for the Assessment of Organic Brain Deficit in Elderly Patients." *Journal of the American Geriatrics Society*, Oct. 1975, *23*.

Chapter Three

1. Personal communication with Dr. Paul E. Brooke, healthcare consultant and Regional Dean of Allied Health, Texas Tech University Health Sciences Center in Odessa, Texas, 1996. Dr. Brooke is also a Fellow in the American College of Health Care Executives.

2. World Health Organization. *International Statistical Classification of Diseases and Related Health Problems*. Editions I–X. Geneva, Switzerland: WHO. First edition published in 1893, tenth edition in 1992.

3. George, L. K. "Depressive Disorders and Symptoms in Later Life." *Generations*, Winter/Spring 1993, pp. 35–38.

4. American Psychiatric Association. *Diagnostic and Statistical Manual of Mental Disorders*. Editions I–IV. Washington, D.C.: American Psychiatric Association, 1952–1994.

5. See, for example, the following:
Anthony, J. C., and Aboraya, A. "The Epidemiology of Selected Mental Disorders in Later Life." In J. E. Birren, R. B. Sloane, and G. D. Cohen (eds.), *Handbook of Mental Health and Aging*. (2nd ed.), San Diego, Calif.: Academic Press, 1992.
Blazer, D. G., and Williams, C. D. "Epidemiology of Dsyhoria and Depression in an Elderly Population." *American Journal of Epidemiology*, 1980, *124*(2), 372–388.
Blazer, D. G., Hughes, D. C., and George, L. K. "The Epidemiology of Depression in an Elderly Community Population." *Gerontologist*, 1987, *27*(2), 281–287.

6. George, L. K., and others. "Psychiatric Disorders and Mental Health Service Use in Later Life: Evidence from the Epidemiological Catchment Area Program." In J. Brody and G. L. Maddox (eds.), *Epidemiology and Aging*. New York: Springer, 1988.

7. Conn, D. K., Lee, V. L., Steingart, A., and Silberfield, M. "Psychiatric Services: A Survey of Nursing Homes and Homes for the Aged in Ontario." *The Canadian Journal of Psychiatry*, 1992, *37*(8), 525–530.

8. Burns, B. J., and others. "Mental Disorders Among Nursing

Home Patients: Preliminary Findings from the National Nursing Home Survey Pretest." *International Journal of Geriatric Psychiatry*, 1983, *140*(80), 1003–1005.

Rovner, B. W., and others. "Prevalence of Mental Illness in a Community Nursing Home." *American Journal of Psychiatry*, 1986, *143*, 1446–1449.

Teeter, R. B., and others. "Psychiatric Disturbances of Aged Patients in Skilled Nursing Homes." *American Journal of Psychiatry*, 1976, 143, 1430–1434.

9. National Center for Health Statistics. "The National Nursing Home Survey: 1977 Summary for the United States." *Vital and Health Statistics*, Serial 13, Number 43. Washington D.C.: U. S. Government Printing Office, 1979.

10. Study conducted by the Rand Corporation, cited in Schreter, R. K., Sharfstein, S. S., and Schreter, C. A. (eds.). *Allies and Adversaries: The Impact of Managed Care on Mental Health Services.* Washington, D.C.: American Psychiatric Press, 1994, p. 4.

11. Gurland, B. J., and others. "The Epidemiology of Depression and Dementia in the Elderly: The Use of Multiple Indicators of These Conditions." In J. O. Cole and J. E. Barrett (eds.), *Psychopathology of the Aged.* New York: Raven Press, 1980.
Blazer and Williams, 1980.
George and others, 1988.

12. American Psychiatric Association, 1994, p. 326.

13. American Psychiatric Association, 1994, p. 124.

14. Lipowski, Z. J. "The Need to Integrate Liaison Psychiatry and Neuropsychiatry." *American Journal of Psychiatry*, 1983, *140*(80), 1003–1005.

15. American Psychiatric Association, 1994, p. 126.

16. Christenson, R., and Blazer, D. G. "Epidemiology of Persecutory Ideation in an Elderly Population in the Community." *American Journal of Psychiatry*, 1984, *141*, 1088–1091.

17. Shulman, K. I. "Regionalization of Psychiatric Services for the Elderly." *Canadian Journal of Psychiatry*, 1991, 36(1).

18. Gurian, B., and Goisman, R. "Anxiety Disorders in the Elderly." *Generations*, Winter/Spring 1993.

19. Rochefort, D. A. "More Lessons of a Different Kind: Canadian Mental Health Policy in Comparative Perspective." *Hospital and Community Psychiatry*, Nov. 1992, 43(1).

20. Pollack, R. "Eleven Lessons from Canada's Health Care System." In A. Bennett and O. Adams (eds.), *Looking North for Health*. San Francisco: Jossey-Bass, 1993.

21. Rochefort, 1992.

22. Foote, D. K. *Boom, Bust and Echo*. Toronto, Canada: McFarlane, Walter and Ross, 1996.

23. Foote, 1996, p. 163.

24. Koop, C. E., and Johnson, T. J. *Let's Talk*. Grand Rapids, Mich.: Zondervan, 1992.

25. Quoted in Beatty, P. "A Comparison of Our Two Systems." In A. Bennett and O. Adams, *Looking North for Health*, San Francisco: Jossey-Bass, 1993, p. 28.

26. Bachrach, L. L. "Overview: Model Programs for Chronic Mental Patients." *American Journal of Psychiatry*, 1981, *137*(9), 102–103.

27. Personal communication with Dr. Paul E. Brooke, 1996.

28. Bachrach, L. L. "Spotlight on Canada." *Hospital and Community Psychiatry*, 1993, 44(10), p. 931.

29. Bigelow, D., and McFarland, B. "Comparative Costs and Impacts of Canadian and American Payment Systems for Mental Health Services." *Hospital and Community Psychiatry*, 1989, 40(8), 805–808.

30. Ruddman, W., citing current projections by the Congressional Budget Office and the Office of Management and Budget. Speech at Trinity University, San Antonio, Texas. January 18, 1997. Cited in the *San Antonio Express News*, January 19, 1997, p. 5G.

31. Gramm, P. "Medicare: Pay Now or Pay Later." Speech. Summarized by the *Wall Street Journal*, February 4, 1997.

Chapter Four

1. For lists and reviews of available instruments, see the following: Costa, P. T., Jr., Williams, T. G., and Somerfield, M. *Recognition*

and Initial Assessment of Alzheimer's Disease and Related Dementias. Clinical Practice Guideline no. 19. Rockville, Md.: Agency for Health Care Policy and Research, Public Health Service, U.S. Department of Health and Human Services, 1996.

Lawton, M. P., and Teresi, J. A. (eds.). *Annual Review of Gerontology and Geriatrics. Vol 14: Focus on Assessment Techniques.* New York: Springer, 1994.

National Center for Cost Containment. *Geropsychology Assessment Resource Guide.* Washington, D.C.: U.S. Department of Veterans Affairs, 1996.

National Center for Cost Containment. "Assessment of Competency and Capacity of the Older Adult: A Practice Guideline for Psychologists." Washington, D.C.: U.S. Department of Veterans Affairs, 1997.

Stewart, A. L., and Ware, J. E. (eds.). *Measuring Functioning and Well-Being: The Medical Outcomes Study Approach.* Durham, N.C.: Duke University Press, 1992.

2. Costa, Williams, and Somerfield, 1996.
3. National Center for Cost Containment, 1996 and 1997.
4. Costa, Williams, and Somerfield, 1996.
5. American Psychiatric Association. *Diagnostic and Statistical Manual of Mental Disorders.* (4th ed.) Washington, D.C.: American Psychiatric Association, 1994.
6. Costa, Williams, and Somerfield, 1996.
7. Numerous other functional measures are reviewed in Costa, Williams, and Somerfield (1996), Lawton and Teresi (1994), the National Center for Cost Containment (1996, 1997), and Stewart and Ware (1992).
8. Stewart and Ware, 1992.

Chapter Five

1. Albert, M. "Geriatric Neuropsychology." *Journal of Consulting and Clinical Psychology,* 1981, *49*, 835–850.
2. Gurley, R. J., Lum, N., Sande, M., Lo, B., and Katz, M. H. "Persons Found in Their Homes Helpless or Dead." *The New Eng-*

land *Journal of Medicine*, 1996, *334*, 1710–1716. N = 387 home visits by ER personnel over a twelve-week period.

3. Storandt, M., Botwinick, J., and Danzinger, W. L. "Longitudinal Changes: Patients with Mild SDAT and Matched Healthy Controls." In L. W. Poon (ed.), *Clinical Memory Assessment of Older Adults*. Washington, D.C.: American Psychological Association, 1986.

4. Eslinger, P. J., Damasio, A. R., Benton, A. L., and Van Allen, M. "Neuropsychological Detection of Abnormal Mental Decline in Older Persons." *Journal of the American Medical Association*, 1985, *253*, 670–674.

5. Morris, J. C., and others. "Consortium to Establish a Registry for Alzheimer's Disease (CERAD)." *Neurology*, 1989, *39*, 1159–1165.

6. Lichtenberg, P. A., Manning, C. A., Vangel, S. J., and Ross, T. P. "Normative and Ecological Validity Data in Older Urban Medical Patients: A Program of Neuropsychological Research." *Advances in Medical Psychotherapy*, 1995, *8*, 121–136.

7. Benton, A. L., Hamsher, K., Varney, N. R., and Spreen, O. *Contributions to Neuropsychological Assessment*. New York: Oxford University Press, 1983.

Chapter Six

1. Yalom, I. R. *The Theory and Practice of Group Psychotherapy*. New York: Basic Books, 1995.

2. Yalom, 1995.

3. Klass, D., Silverman, P. R., and Nickman, S. L. (eds.). *Continuing Bonds: New Understandings of Grief*. Washington, D.C.: Taylor and Francis, 1996.

4. Camp, C. Personal communication, February 7, 1997.

Chapter Seven

1. Burns, D. *Feeling Good*. New York: NAL/Dutton, 1980.

2. For example, Starker, S. "Do-It-Yourself Therapy: The Prescription of Self-Help Books by Psychologists." *Psychotherapy*,

1988, *25*, 142–146.

3. Rosenbaum, M. "A Schedule for Assessing Self-Control Behaviors: Preliminary Findings." *Behavior Therapy*, 1980, *11*, 109–121.

4. Beutler, L., and others. "Predictors of Differential Response to Cognitive, Experiential, and Self-Directed Psychotherapeutic Procedures." *Journal of Consulting and Clinical Psychology*, 1991, *59*, 333–340.

5. Mohr, D. C. "Negative Outcomes in Psychotherapy: A Critical Review." *Clinical Psychology: Science and Practice*, 1995, *2*, 23.

6. See, for example, Scogin, F., Bynum, J., Stephens, G., and Calhoon, S. "Efficacy of Self-Administered Treatment Programs: Meta-Analytic Review." *Professional Psychology*, 1990, *21*, 42–47, and Gould, R. A., and Clum, G. A. "A Meta-Analysis of Self-Help Treatment Approaches." *Clinical Psychology Review*, 1993, *13*, 169–186.

7. Cuijpers, P. "Bibliotherapy bij Unipolaire Depressies: Een Meta-Analyse." *Gedragstherapie*, 1995, *28*, 279–295. Translation unpublished.

8. Scogin, F., Jamison, C., and Gochneaur, K. "Comparative Efficacy of Cognitive and Behavioral Bibliotherapy for Mildly and Moderately Depressed Older Adults." *Journal of Consulting and Clinical Psychology*, 1989, *57*, 403–407.

9. Lewinsohn, P. M., Muñoz, R. F., Youngren, M. A., and Zeiss, A. M. *Control Your Depression.* Englewood Cliffs, N.J.: Prentice Hall, 1986.

10. Beck, A. T., Rush, J., Shaw, B., and Emery, G. *Cognitive Therapy of Depression.* New York: Guilford Press, 1979.

11. Selmi, P. M., and others. "Computer-Administered Cognitive-Behavioral Therapy for Depression." *American Journal of Psychiatry*, 1990, *147*, 51–56.

Chapter Eight

1. American Psychiatric Association. *Diagnostic and Statistical Manual of Mental Disorders.* (4th ed.) Washington, D.C.: American Psychiatric Association, 1994.

Chapter Ten

2. Schuerger, J. Personal communication, 1985.
3. Davis, J. (ed.). *Marketing for Therapists: A Handbook for Success in Managed Care.* San Francisco: Jossey-Bass, 1996.

Epilogue

1. Byock, I., Kinzbrunner, B., and Pratt, M. (1994) "Assessing Quality of Life in the Terminally Ill: A Developmental Approach" (abstract). *Journal of Palliative Care,* 1994, *10,* 127.
2. Cummings, N. A. "The Impact of Managed Care on Employment and Professional Training: A Primer for Survival." In N. A. Cummings, M. S. Pallak, and J. L. Cummings (eds.), *Surviving the Demise of Solo Practice: Mental Health Practitioners Prospering in the Era of Managed Care.* Madison, Conn.: Psychosocial Press, 1996b.
3. National Committee for Quality Assurance. *Standards for Accreditation of Managed Behavioral Healthcare Organizations.* Washington, D.C.: National Committee for Quality Assurance, 1997.
4. Teri, L., and Uomoto, J. "Reducing Excess Disability in Dementia Patients: Training Caregivers to Manage Patient Depression." *Clinical Gerontologist,* 1991, *10,* 49–63.
5. Teri, L., and Wagner, A. (1992). "Alzheimer's Disease and Depression." *Journal of Consulting and Clinical Psychology,* 1992, *60,* 379–391.
6. Wechsler, D. *Wechsler Adult Intelligence Scale: Revised Manual.* New York: Psychological Corporation, 1981.
   Wechsler, D. *Wechsler Memory Scale: Revised Manual.* New York: Psychological Corporation, 1987.
7. "Standards for Psychological Services in Long Term Care Facilities." *Psychologists in Long Term Care Newsletter,* 1997, *11,* 1.
8. Cummings, N. A. "Behavioral Health After Managed Care: The Next Golden Opportunity for Mental Health Practitioners." In N. A. Cummings, M. S. Pallak, and J. L. Cummings

(eds.), *Surviving the Demise of Solo Practice: Mental Health Practitioners Prospering in the Era of Managed Care*. Madison, Conn.: Psychosocial Press, 1996a.

Cummings, 1996b.

9. Cummings, 1996a, 1996b.

10. Hartman-Stein, P. E., and Reuter, J. M. "Proactive Health Care Reform: Integrating Physical and Psychological Care." *The Independent Practitioner*, 1994, *14*, 29–33.

11. Cummings, 1996b.

About the Authors

PAULA E. HARTMAN-STEIN is a clinical psychologist with over fifteen years' experience, focusing on health psychology and geropsychology. She is president and founder of the Center for Healthy Aging, a multidisciplinary practice in Akron, Ohio. Active in clinical work, she provides diagnostic and therapy services in the outpatient setting as well as in several retirement communities and nursing homes. Currently she is a senior fellow at the Institute for Life-Span Development and Gerontology, University of Akron. Hartman-Stein is a graduate of the University of Pittsburgh and received her master's degree from West Virginia University and her doctorate in clinical psychology from Kent State University. She received additional training through the Interdisciplinary Geriatric Clinician Development program at Case Western Reserve University.

In 1992–93 she served as a member of the Technical Consulting Group for clinical psychology at the Harvard School of Public Health for the Resource-Based Relative Value Scale study. She has been a steering committee member of Psychologists in Long Term Care and currently serves on the American Psychological Association's task force on qualifications for practice in clinical and applied geropsychology. In 1997 she was elected president of her local association of professional psychologists. She has written many articles and conducted numerous seminars about clinical geropsychology practice, consultation in long-term care, and proactive healthcare reform. She is a consulting editor for *Professional Psychology: Research and Practice*.

TOM SAWYER is a sixth-term member of the U.S. House of Representatives and is a member of the House Committee on Commerce. He also serves on the subcommittees for Telecommunications; Trade and Consumer Protection; Finance and Hazardous Materials; and Oversight and Investigation. For six years, he served as the chairman of the House subcommittee that oversaw national policies on the Census, demographic issues, and the federal statistical system. He has served on the Congressional committees for Education and Labor; Transportation and Infrastructure; International Relations; Government Operations; and the Post Office and Civil Service. Sawyer has also been a member of the House Ethics Committee. Before serving in Congress, he was a public school teacher, a member of the Ohio State Legislature, and mayor of Akron, where he lives with his wife, Joyce, and their daughter, Amanda.

❖

MARTHA W. CLOWER is a supervising psychologist at the Veterans Administration Medical Center, Cleveland. She earned her B.A. in English at St. Mary-of-the-Woods College, Terre Haute, Indiana, and both her M.A. and Ph.D. in clinical psychology at Case Western Reserve University. Clower is coordinator of the Senior Veterans PTSD Program at the Center for Stress Recovery, which is a psychiatric treatment unit for veterans with military-related posttraumatic stress disorder. She has published articles as well as a treatment manual for group psychotherapy with elderly persons. She has also been an instructor of psychology at Case Western Reserve University and at John Carroll University. Her research activities have focused on adult development and group psychotherapy for older adults.

NICHOLAS A. CUMMINGS, former president of the American Psychological Association, is a clinical psychologist known for his innovations. In his several careers, spanning more than forty years, Cummings has had far-reaching effects on the field of behavioral health. He recently retired as CEO of American Biodyne, which he founded (and which is now MedCo Behavior Care Corporation, a wholly owned subsidiary of Merck), to become president of the Foundation for Behavioral Health and to chair the board of directors of the Nicholas and Dorothy Cummings Foundation. Cummings's other current roles include president of U.K. Behavioral Health Ltd., London, England, and distinguished professor at the University of Nevada, Las Vegas. Cummings served as an adviser to Presidents Kennedy and Carter, and during the 1950s he and his colleagues were responsible for designing and developing the first comprehensive mental health policy in the United States and, later, for founding the twenty-nine Kaiser Permanente psychotherapy centers that implemented this policy. Cummings also acted as chief psychologist of the Kaiser Permanente Health Plan. In addition, he founded the four-campus California School of Professional Psychology and served as its president from 1969 to 1976.

MARINA ERGUN is an independent consultant working in the areas of writing, marketing, and fundraising for nonprofit and for-profit organizations. She earned her B.A. in communication and her M.A. in clinical psychology at Cleveland State University. As a psychology assistant, she has worked in a rehabilitation center for people with brain injuries, in an Alzheimer's research unit associated with a teaching hospital, and in several private practices, one of them devoted to geriatric behavioral healthcare. She also has experience in marketing professional services (including behavioral healthcare) as a member of a media relations and marketing group and as an independent consultant, and she has been director of development for a nonprofit agency. Ergun serves on the board of the Federation for Community Planning, a Cleveland-area community organization, and is a member of the North American Association of Masters in Psychology, a group working for the independent licensing of master's-level psychologists.

DEBORAH W. FRAZER is currently director of behavioral health at Genesis Eldercare, Kennett Square, Pennsylvania, where she is responsible for designing and implementing a behavioral health program across the continuum of care throughout the Genesis network. For eleven years she served as director of clinical psychology at the Philadelphia Geriatric Center (PGC), where she was also director of training for the center's postdoctoral fellowship program in clinical geropsychology. Before her service at PGC she was chief geropsychologist at Norristown State Hospital and director of geriatric programs for Northeast Community Mental Health Center. Frazer has served as a reviewer for the National Institute of Mental Health, the Agency for Health Care Policy and Research, *Clinical Psychology Review, The Gerontologist,* and *Contemporary Gerontology.* She currently serves on the Veterans Administration Technical Advisory Group at the National Center for Cost Containment to develop practice guidelines for geropsychologists. She has also chaired a work group associated with Psychologists in Long Term Care to develop practice guidelines for geropsychologists. Frazer is the author of numerous book chapters and articles and is a frequent presenter at conferences. She is a graduate of Swarthmore College and received her doctorate in clinical psychology from Temple University. She has been married to Jack Malinowski for twenty years, and they have one son, Nicholas, who is ten years old.

JAMES M. GEORGOULAKIS earned a B.S. degree in science and an M.S.W. degree at the University of Alabama, a degree in counseling from Western Kentucky University, and a Ph.D. in counseling psychology from Kansas State University. He is currently earning an M.B.A. degree at Our Lady of the Lake University in San Antonio, with a concentration in healthcare management. Georgoulakis is a graduate of the U.S. Army's Command and General Staff College and served in a variety of clinical and research positions with the Army's medical department. His military decorations include the Legion of Merit with Oak Leaf Cluster and the Order of Military Medical Merit. He has published more than forty articles and book chapters and has lectured nationally and internationally. He is currently associate professor of psychology at Our Lady of the Lake University, in San Antonio, Texas, and has served as adjunct professor at a number of universities in departments of psychology and healthcare administration. In addition to his academic positions, he has served as a mental health consultant to the Health Care Financing Administration, the Canadian Institute of Health Information, the American Psychological Association, and a number of state and private mental health organizations.

GAEL GABRIELLE SMOOKLER JARRETT is in private practice in the Cleveland area. Her diverse background includes executive positions with the Cleveland Regional Perinatal Network, the American Heart Association, and Coyle and Associates Advertising and Consulting, Inc. Jarrett earned a master's degree in social administration and a Ph.D. in psychology and women's studies at the Union Institute in Cincinnati, Ohio. She has published a booklet for grieving parents and has worked with many organizations.

PETER A. LICHTENBERG is currently associate professor of physical medicine and rehabilitation at Wayne State University School of Medicine and associate director of rehabilitation psychology and neuropsychology at the Rehabilitation Institute of Michigan. Lichtenberg received his Ph.D. in clinical psychology from Purdue University, where he also minored in issues related to aging. He completed specialty internship training in clinical geropsychology at the Veterans Administration Medical Center in Gainesville, Florida, and postdoctoral training in geriatric neuropsychology at the University of Virginia Medical School, where he also served on the faculty from 1987 to 1990. He recently wrote *A Guide to Psychological Practice in Long Term Care* and is chief editor for the book series *Advances in Medical Psychotherapy*. His book in progress deals with mental health treatment in geriatric healthcare settings. Lichtenberg has also written more than fifty scientific papers in the areas of clinical geropsychology and geriatric neuropsychology.

ELIZABETH MAUSER is an economist with the Office of Research and Demonstrations at the Health Care Financing Administration

(HCFA). She is project officer for the study evaluating the Program of All-Inclusive Care for the Elderly (PACE), as well as for a project to develop a quality-assurance and performance-improvement system for PACE. In her work at HCFA she also focuses on developing a prospective payment system and a quality-assurance and performance-improvement system for Medicare home healthcare, and she conducts research related to long-term and postacute care users. She has a Ph.D. in economics from the University of Wisconsin–Madison.

THOMAS M. MEUSER is a clinical psychologist and former associate administrator at the Center for Healthy Aging, a multidisciplinary behavioral health practice in Akron, Ohio. He earned his B.A. degree in psychology at the College of the Holy Cross, Worcester, Massachusetts, and both his M.A. and Ph.D. degrees in clinical psychology at the University of Missouri–St. Louis. As part of his training, Meuser completed a one-year psychology internship at the Cleveland Veterans Administration Medical Center, with specialized training in geropsychology, group psychotherapy, and posttraumatic stress treatment. He also worked for a number of years as a neuropsychological examiner with the Division of Behavioral Medicine at the St. Louis University Health Sciences Center. Before pursuing graduate education, Meuser served as assistant director of a nonprofit agency, Bread for the City, in Washington, D.C. His principal research has focused on the bereavement process, and notably on those factors (coping style, personality traits) that affect grief outcome for good or ill. He has published on spousal bereavement among older adults in OMEGA: *The Journal of Death and Dying* and has done numerous presentations on successful grieving.

NANCY A. MILLER is director, Division of Aging and Disability, of the Office of Research and Demonstrations at the Health Care Financing Administration, where she directs research, demonstrations, and evaluation related to service delivery and financing of acute- and long-term-care services for persons with disabilities. Her major projects include the Program of All-Inclusive Care for the Elderly; the Social Health Maintenance Organization; the Community Nursing Organization; EverCare; Home Health Prospective Payment; D.C. Health Services for Children with Special Needs, Inc.; and Minnesota Senior Health Options demonstrations. She has also developed several initiatives with state-level Medicaid agencies. Her research activities focus on trends in the characteristics, systems, and financing of services for individuals with disabilities. Miller also teaches courses in healthcare financing and healthcare organizational behavior in the Policy Sciences Graduate Program at the University of Maryland, Baltimore County. She has an M.A. and a Ph.D. from the Graduate School of Public Policy at the University of Chicago.

STEFAN N. MILLER has spent almost thirty years in the healthcare field and is currently a project officer with the Office of Research and Demonstration at the Health Care Financing Administration (HCFA). In addition to his responsibilities with the Program of All-Inclusive Care for the Elderly, he manages other demonstrations designed to provide services to frail seniors by altering traditional delivery and payment systems. Besides having held various management and administrative positions at HCFA, he has collaborated with the Maryland State Department of Health and Mental Hygiene in planning the provision of community health services, and he has directed a hospital-based entity for the design and manufacture of durable medical equipment. From 1967 to 1969 he was a lieutenant in the U.S. Army, stationed at Walter Reed General Hospital, Washington, D.C., where he provided physical therapy services, primarily to Vietnam returnees. He earned his bachelor's degree in physical therapy at the University of Maryland and his master's degree in counseling at Springfield College (Massachusetts).

KATE O'MALLEY is director of On Lok Senior Health Services and oversees the day-to-day operation of On Lok's comprehensive long-term-care program. She has been with On Lok since 1980, holding the positions of clinic nurse, home-care supervisor, and geriatric nurse practitioner. She also joined On Lok's national replication, known as the Program of All-Inclusive Care for the Elderly (PACE). As PACE's site liaison, and later as service-development manager, she has provided technical assistance and program development for ten PACE sites. Before joining On Lok, O'Malley worked as a staff nurse and nursing instructor in a long-term-care facility and taught in a nursing school in Kenya, East Africa, as a Peace Corps volunteer. She received her B.S. in nursing from the University of Rhode Island and her training as a geriatric nurse practitioner at the University of California, San Francisco. She earned her M.S. in health education at San Francisco State University.

EDGARDO PADIN-RIVERA is a clinical psychologist and deputy director of the Center for Stress Recovery at the Veterans Administration Medical Center, Cleveland. He earned his B.A. degree at George Mason University and his Ph.D. in clinical psychology at Vanderbilt University. He was formerly an instructor of psychology at Vanderbilt University. Padin-Rivera has conducted ethnographic research on the emotional lives of mentally retarded and nondisabled persons in work environments and has examined how family systems adjust to the presence of a disabled child. His current interests are in the area of posttraumatic stress disorder (PTSD). He has been coauthor of several articles on PTSD risk factors and treatment and is currently engaged in research on PTSD and health risks, psychohistorical and phenomenological differences in PTSD manifestations, and treatment outcomes. He is a member of the International Society for Traumatic Stress Studies, and at the organization's annual meetings he has offered presentations on treatment considerations with elderly veterans.

JAMES J. RIEMENSCHNEIDER is a partner of Stephen Thomas Associates, a healthcare management consulting firm that focuses on services for the aging population, where he has served full-time for the past three years. He recently earned his M.B.A. in health care, with a focus on long-term care, at Cleveland State University, and he has developed expertise in hospital operations, employee relations, and ambulatory-care clinics and networks. In 1993, as an administrative fellow of Genessee Memorial Hospital, in Batavia, New York, he led a hospitalwide planning effort to renovate the areas of ambulatory care, emergency care, and admitting.

THOMAS A. RIEMENSCHNEIDER is president of Stephen Thomas Associates, a healthcare management consulting firm that focuses on services for the aging population. He is board-certified in medical management, pediatrics, and pediatric cardiology. After spending sixteen years as a pediatric cardiologist, medical educator, and researcher, Riemenschneider moved into full-time medical administration in 1988, serving as associate dean at the medical schools of Case Western Reserve University and the State University of New York, Buffalo. From 1993 to 1996 he was vice provost for health sciences and hospitals for the State University of New York system. He is currently director of graduate business management at Baldwin-Wallace College, Berea, Ohio. Riemenschneider and his partners have been working with long-term-care facilities for the past six years, using the experience and knowledge they have gained in the acute-care field to prepare organizations for the environment of managed care.

FORREST SCOGIN is currently professor of psychology and director of graduate studies at the University of Alabama, Tuscaloosa. He received his undergraduate degree from the University of Tennessee, Knoxville, and his Ph.D. in clinical psychology from Washington University, St. Louis. Scogin's research has been primarily in the areas of psychotherapy, depression, and clinical geropsychology, and he has written or been coauthor of more than sixty articles, book chapters, and books on these topics. He is a fellow of the American Psychological Association's Division 12, which is involved with clinical issues, and Division 20, which concerns adult development and aging. Scogin is also cochair of Division 12's task force on empirically validated treatment for older adults. In addition, he directs the Geropsychology Services Clinic for the Department of Psychology's training clinic. He maintains a part-time private practice in clinical geropsychology and sports psychology.

STEPHEN JARRETT SMOOKLER is vice president of Stephen Thomas Associates, a healthcare management consulting firm that focuses on services for the aging population, where he has served for eight years. He has more than twenty years' experience in healthcare planning and administration. As associate dean and executive director of the Office of Community Health at Case Western Reserve University School of Medicine, he developed and administered the medical school's outreach and regional program activities. He was formerly with the Cleveland Health Systems Agency, assisting in the development and review of health service programs.

DAVID A. WEIL II is an attorney who practices in the area of health law as operations counsel in the legal department of Columbia/HCA Healthcare Corporation. He was previously with the health law department of Buckingham, Doolittle & Burroughs, served an internship in the legal department of Aultman Hospital, and served as a law clerk at the Northeastern Ohio Universities College of Medicine. He has been a member of the faculty of Medical Management Development Associates and has spoken across the country on issues arising in the Medicare/Medicaid and managed-care settings. He has also written or been coauthor of several publications addressing issues of importance to healthcare professionals. Weil earned an M.B.A. in management and a J.D. degree at the University of Akron, where he worked as a graduate research and faculty assistant. He has served as a guest lecturer at the University of Akron's School of Law and its College of Business Administration.

Index